FARSCAPE™

Strange Detractors

ROSS RICHIE
chief executive officer

ANDREW COSBY
chief creative officer

MARK WAID
editor-in-chief

ADAM FORTIER
vice president,
publishing

CHIP MOSHER
marketing director

MATT GAGNON
managing editor

Farscape: Strange Detractors — published by BOOM! Studios. Farscape is © 2009 The Jim Henson Company. © Hallmark Entertainment. JIM HENSON mark & logo, FARSCAPE mark & logo, characters and elements are trademarks of The Jim Henson Company. All Rights Reserved. BOOM! Studios™ and the BOOM! logo are trademarks of Boom Entertainment, Inc., registered in various countries and categories. All rights reserved. The characters and events depicted herein are fictional. Any similarity to actual persons, demons, anti-Christs, aliens, vampires, face-suckers or political figures, whether living, dead or undead, or to any actual or supernatural events is coincidental and unintentional. So don't come whining to us.

Office of publication: 6310 San Vicente Blvd, Ste 404, Los Angeles, CA 90048-5457.

First Edition: September 2009

10 9 8 7 6 5 4 3 2 1
PRINTED IN KOREA

FARSCAPE™

Farscape created by: ROCKNE S. O'BANNON

Story: ROCKNE S. O'BANNON
Script: KEITH R.A. DECANDIDO
Artist: WILL SLINEY
Colorist: ZAC ATKINSON
Letterer: ED DUKESHIRE

Editor: IAN BRILL
Managing Editor: MATT GAGNON

Executive Producer: ROCKNE S. O'BANNON

Cover Artist: JOE CORRONEY

Jim Henson
THE JIM HENSON COMPANY

RHI ENTERTAINMENT

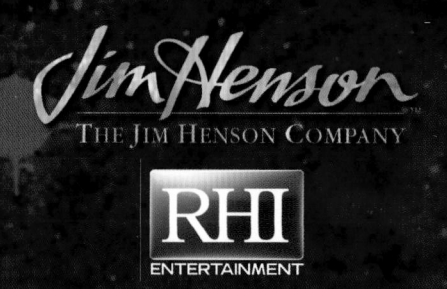

Special Thanks:
Brian Henson, Lisa Henson, Jim Formanek, Nicole Goldman, Joe LeFavi, Maryanne Pittman, Allyson Smith

BOOK ONE

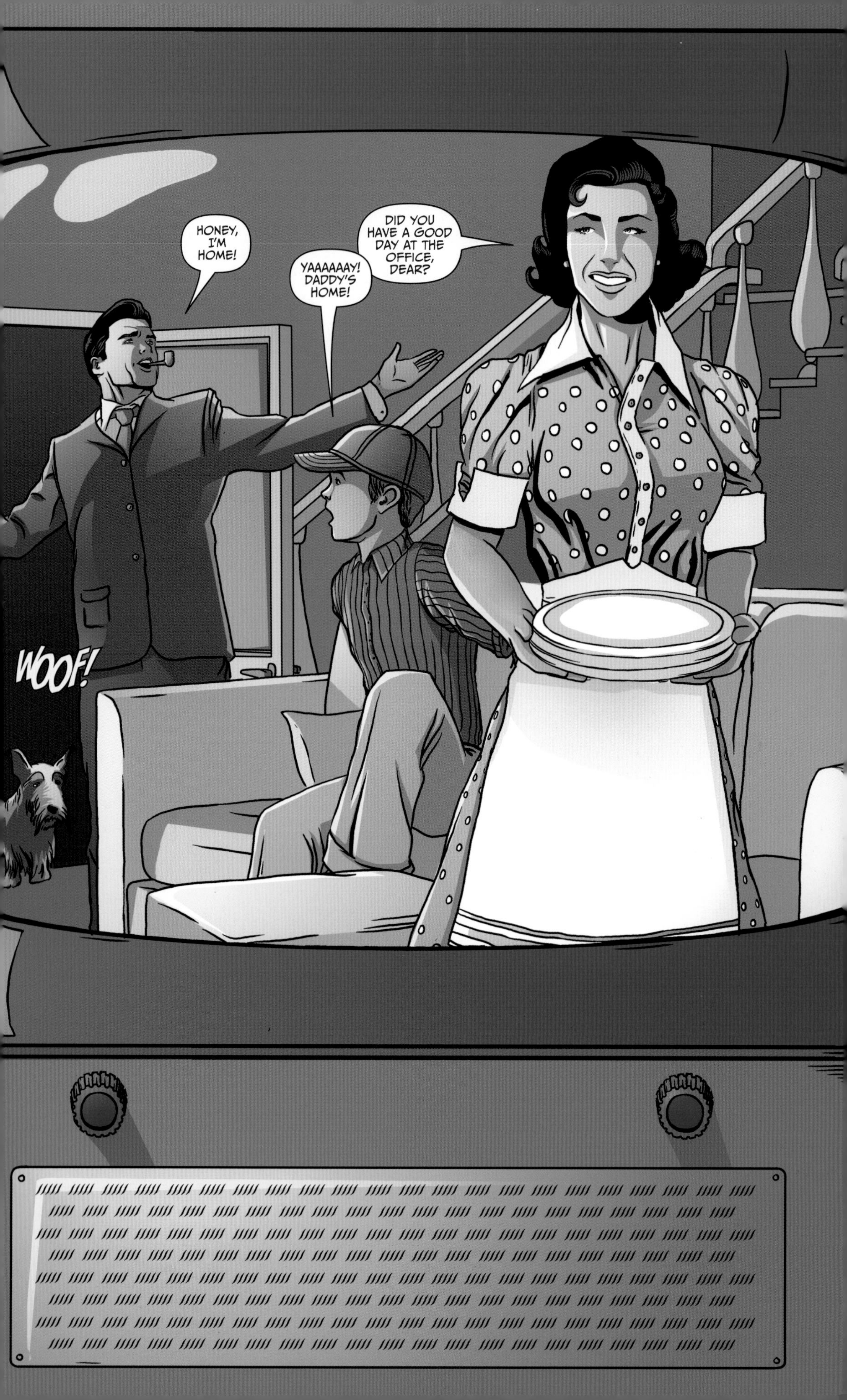
HONEY, I'M HOME!
YAAAAAAY! DADDY'S HOME!
DID YOU HAVE A GOOD DAY AT THE OFFICE, DEAR?
WOOF!

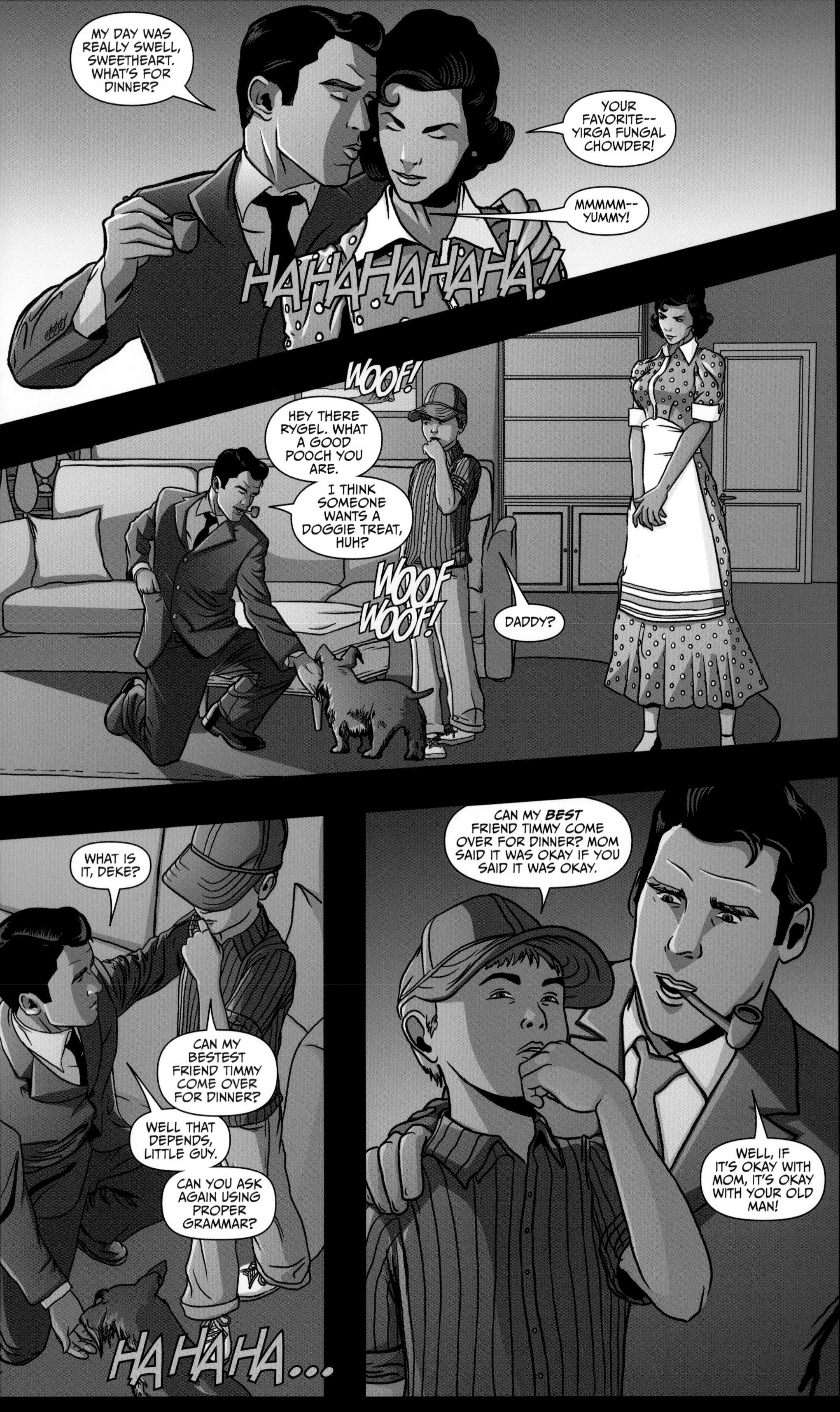
MY DAY WAS REALLY SWELL, SWEETHEART. WHAT'S FOR DINNER?
YOUR FAVORITE-- YIRGA FUNGAL CHOWDER!
MMMMM-- YUMMY!
HAHAHAHAHAHA!
WOOF!
HEY THERE RYGEL. WHAT A GOOD POOCH YOU ARE.
I THINK SOMEONE WANTS A DOGGIE TREAT, HUH?
WOOF WOOF!
DADDY?
WHAT IS IT, DEKE?
CAN MY BESTEST FRIEND TIMMY COME OVER FOR DINNER?
WELL THAT DEPENDS, LITTLE GUY.
CAN YOU ASK AGAIN USING PROPER GRAMMAR?
HA HA HA...
CAN MY BEST FRIEND TIMMY COME OVER FOR DINNER? MOM SAID IT WAS OKAY IF YOU SAID IT WAS OKAY.
WELL, IF IT'S OKAY WITH MOM, IT'S OKAY WITH YOUR OLD MAN!

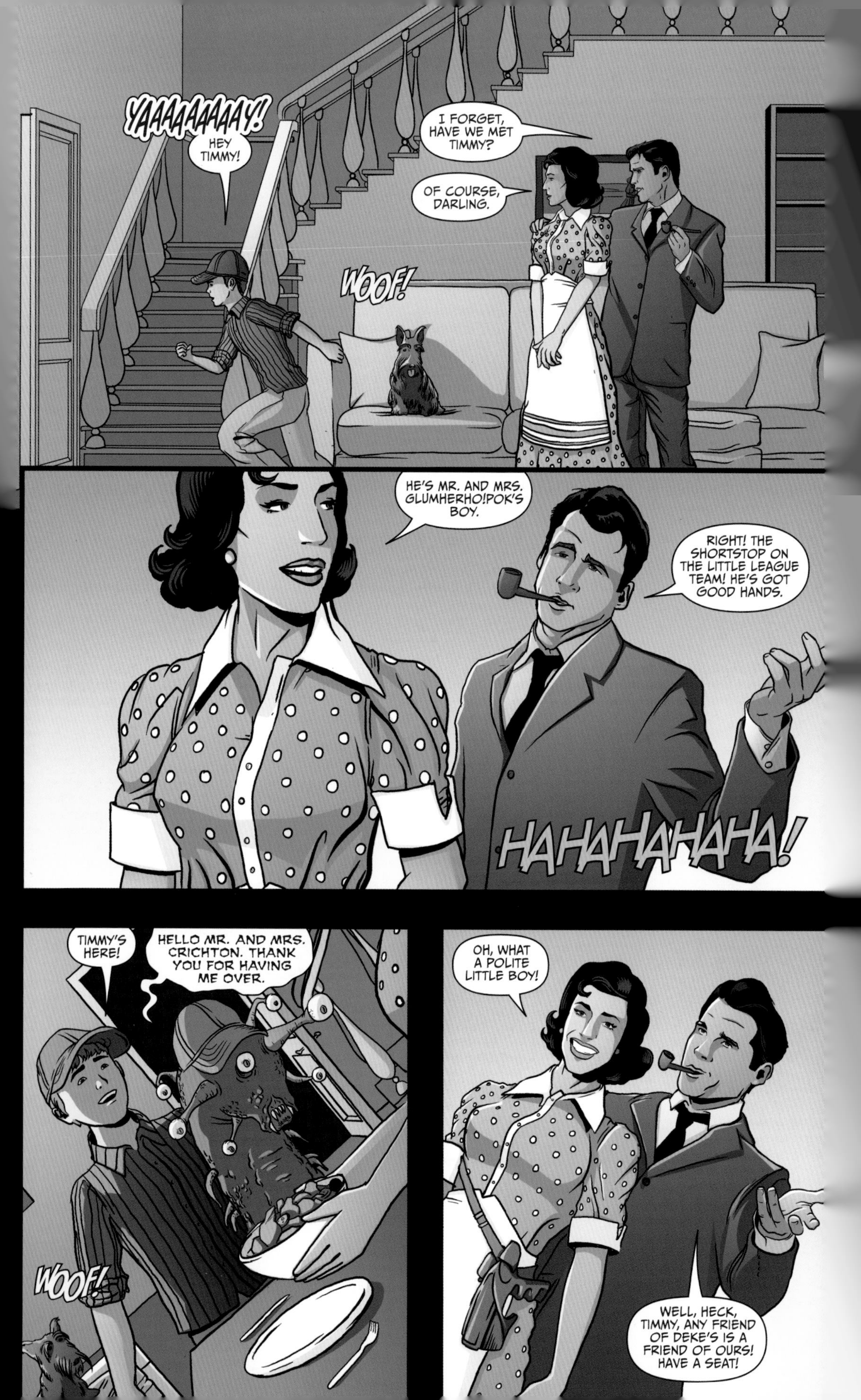
YAAAAAAAAY!
HEY TIMMY!
I FORGET, HAVE WE MET TIMMY?
OF COURSE, DARLING.
WOOF!
HE'S MR. AND MRS. GLUMHERHO!POK'S BOY.
RIGHT! THE SHORTSTOP ON THE LITTLE LEAGUE TEAM! HE'S GOT GOOD HANDS.
HAHAHAHAHA!
TIMMY'S HERE!
HELLO MR. AND MRS. CRICHTON. THANK YOU FOR HAVING ME OVER.
WOOF!
OH, WHAT A POLITE LITTLE BOY!
WELL, HECK, TIMMY, ANY FRIEND OF DEKE'S IS A FRIEND OF OURS! HAVE A SEAT!

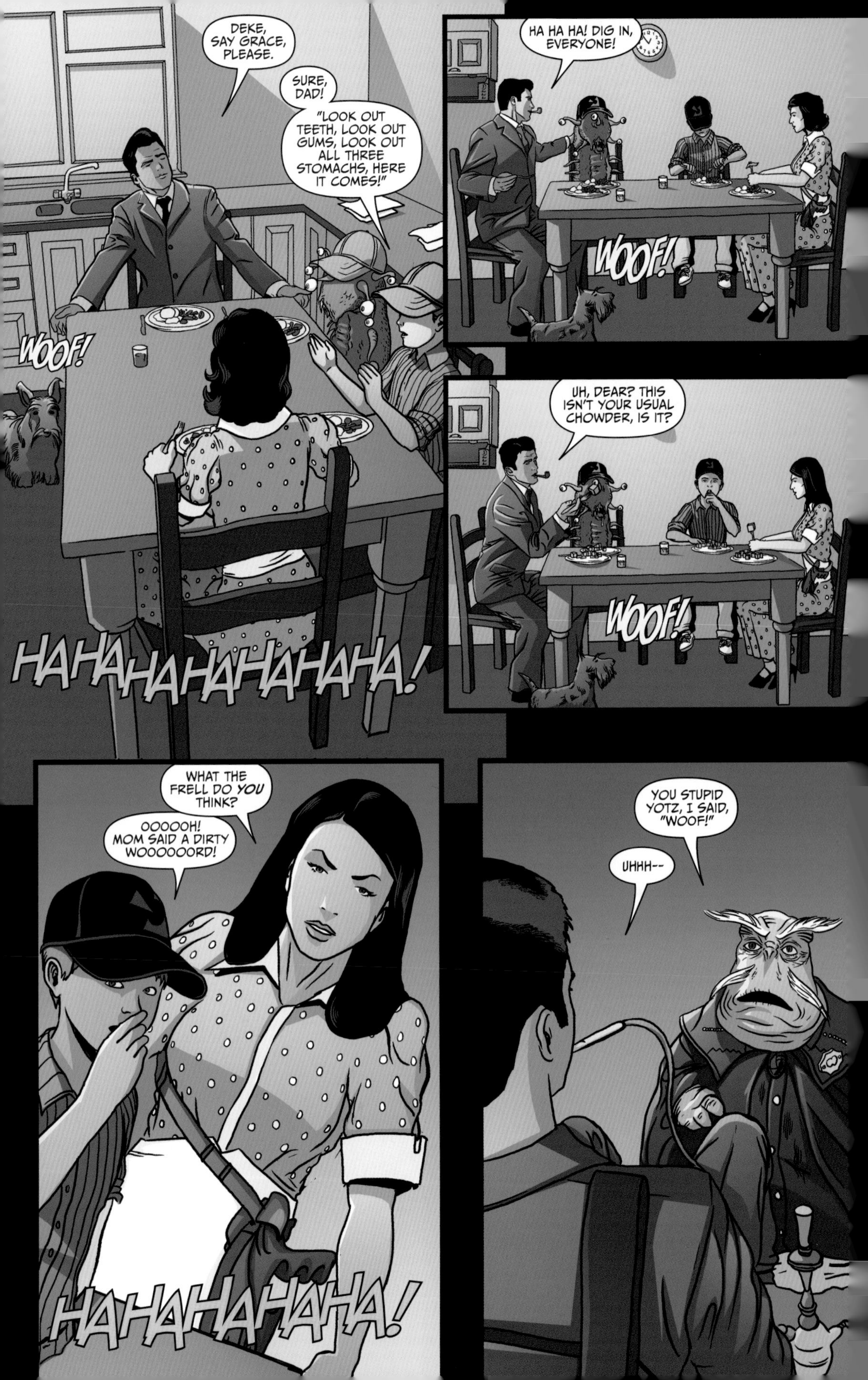
DEKE, SAY GRACE, PLEASE.
SURE, DAD!
"LOOK OUT TEETH, LOOK OUT GUMS, LOOK OUT ALL THREE STOMACHS, HERE IT COMES!"
WOOF!
HAHAHAHAHAHAHAHA!
HA HA HA! DIG IN, EVERYONE!
WOOF!
UH, DEAR? THIS ISN'T YOUR USUAL CHOWDER, IS IT?
WOOF!
WHAT THE FRELL DO YOU THINK?
OOOOOH! MOM SAID A DIRTY WOOOOOORD!
HAHAHAHAHAHA!
YOU STUPID YOTZ, I SAID, "WOOF!"
UHHH--

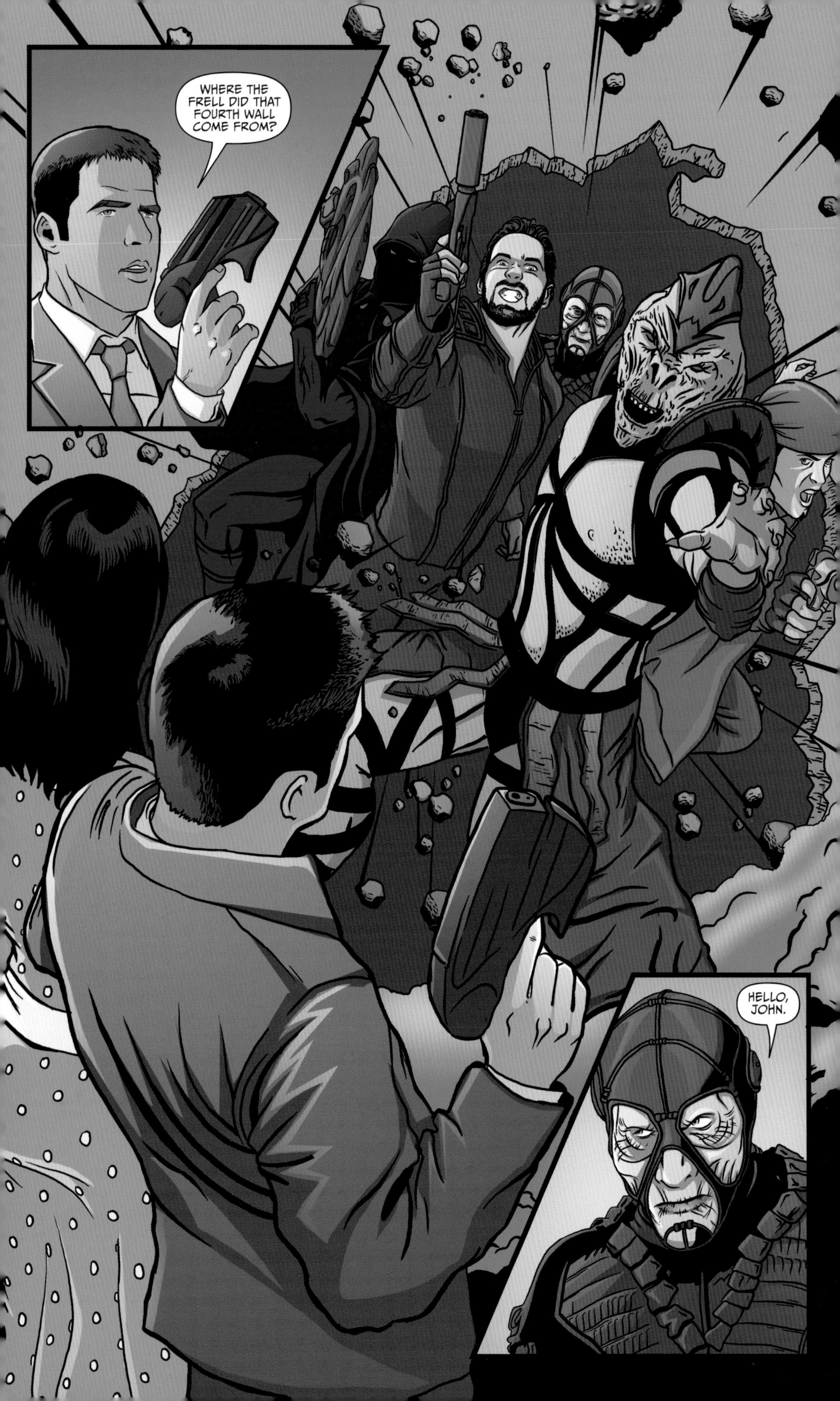
WHERE THE FRELL DID THAT FOURTH WALL COME FROM?
HELLO, JOHN.

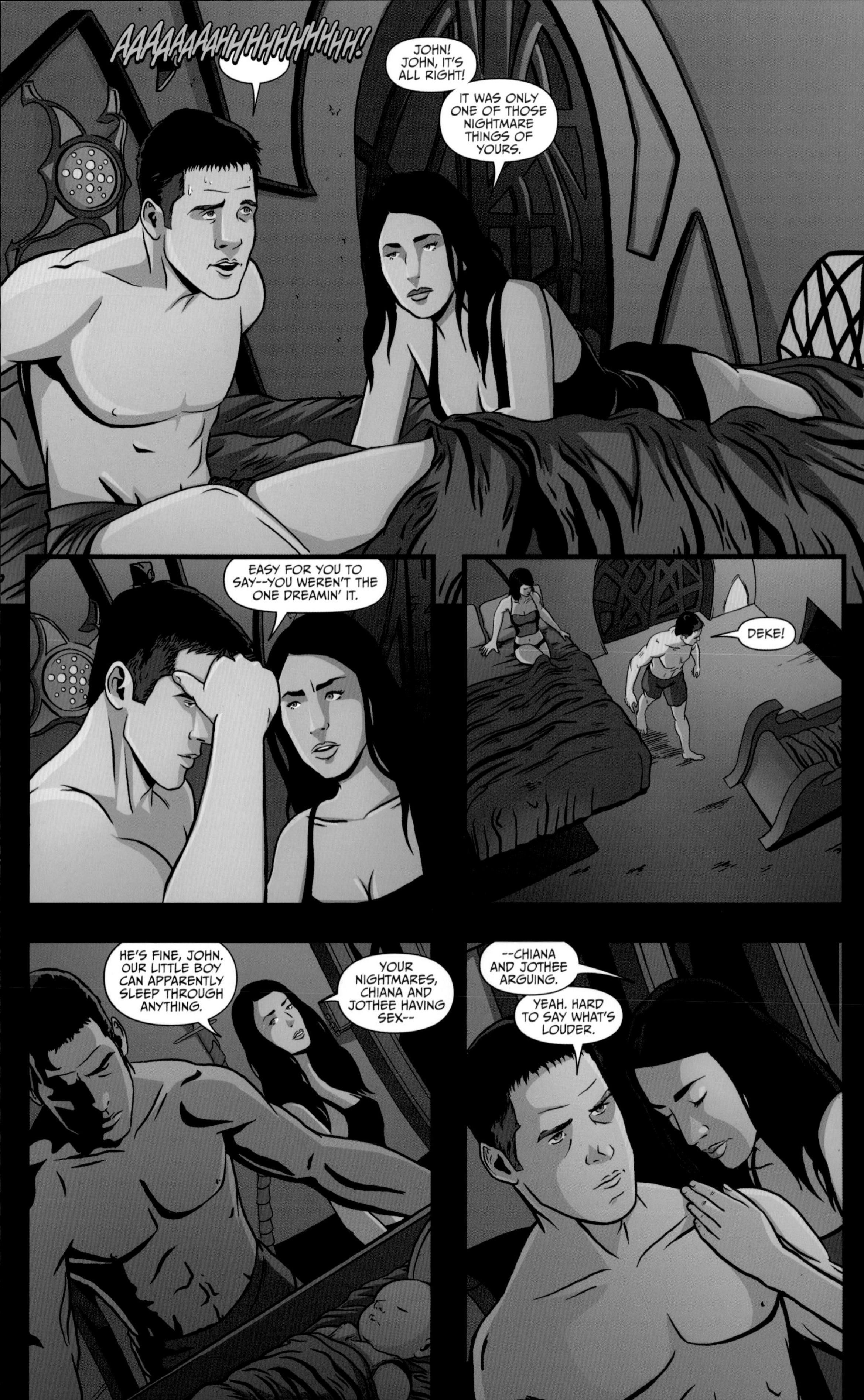
AAAAAAAAHHHHHHHHH!
JOHN! JOHN, IT'S ALL RIGHT!
IT WAS ONLY ONE OF THOSE NIGHTMARE THINGS OF YOURS.
EASY FOR YOU TO SAY--YOU WEREN'T THE ONE DREAMIN' IT.
DEKE!
HE'S FINE, JOHN. OUR LITTLE BOY CAN APPARENTLY SLEEP THROUGH ANYTHING.
YOUR NIGHTMARES, CHIANA AND JOTHEE HAVING SEX--
--CHIANA AND JOTHEE ARGUING.
YEAH. HARD TO SAY WHAT'S LOUDER.

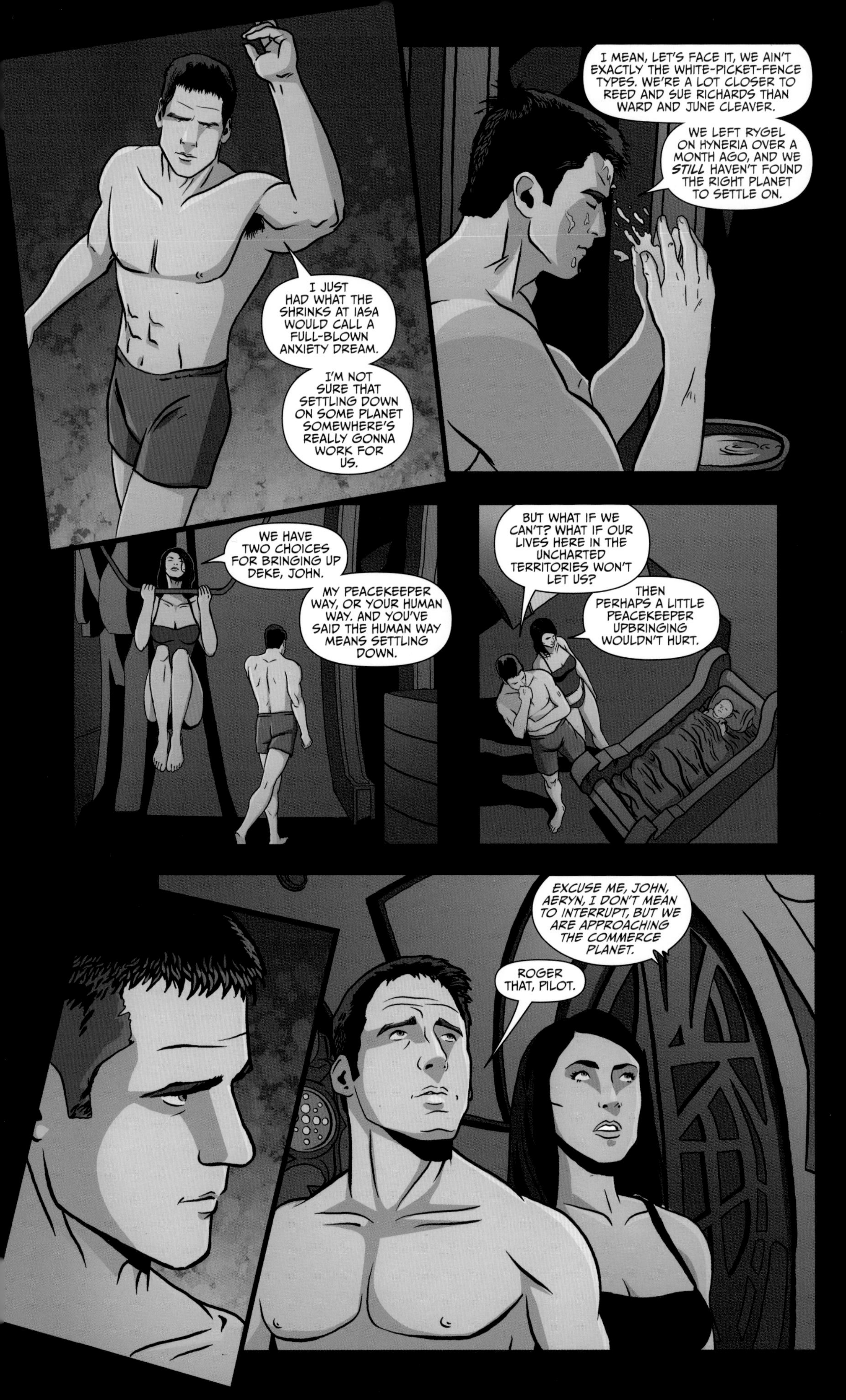
I JUST HAD WHAT THE SHRINKS AT IASA WOULD CALL A FULL-BLOWN ANXIETY DREAM.
I'M NOT SURE THAT SETTLING DOWN ON SOME PLANET SOMEWHERE'S REALLY GONNA WORK FOR US.
I MEAN, LET'S FACE IT, WE AIN'T EXACTLY THE WHITE-PICKET-FENCE TYPES. WE'RE A LOT CLOSER TO REED AND SUE RICHARDS THAN WARD AND JUNE CLEAVER.
WE LEFT RYGEL ON HYNERIA OVER A MONTH AGO, AND WE *STILL* HAVEN'T FOUND THE RIGHT PLANET TO SETTLE ON.
WE HAVE TWO CHOICES FOR BRINGING UP DEKE, JOHN.
MY PEACEKEEPER WAY, OR YOUR HUMAN WAY. AND YOU'VE SAID THE HUMAN WAY MEANS SETTLING DOWN.
BUT WHAT IF WE CAN'T? WHAT IF OUR LIVES HERE IN THE UNCHARTED TERRITORIES WON'T LET US?
THEN PERHAPS A LITTLE PEACEKEEPER UPBRINGING WOULDN'T HURT.
EXCUSE ME, JOHN, AERYN, I DON'T MEAN TO INTERRUPT, BUT WE ARE APPROACHING THE COMMERCE PLANET.
ROGER THAT, PILOT.

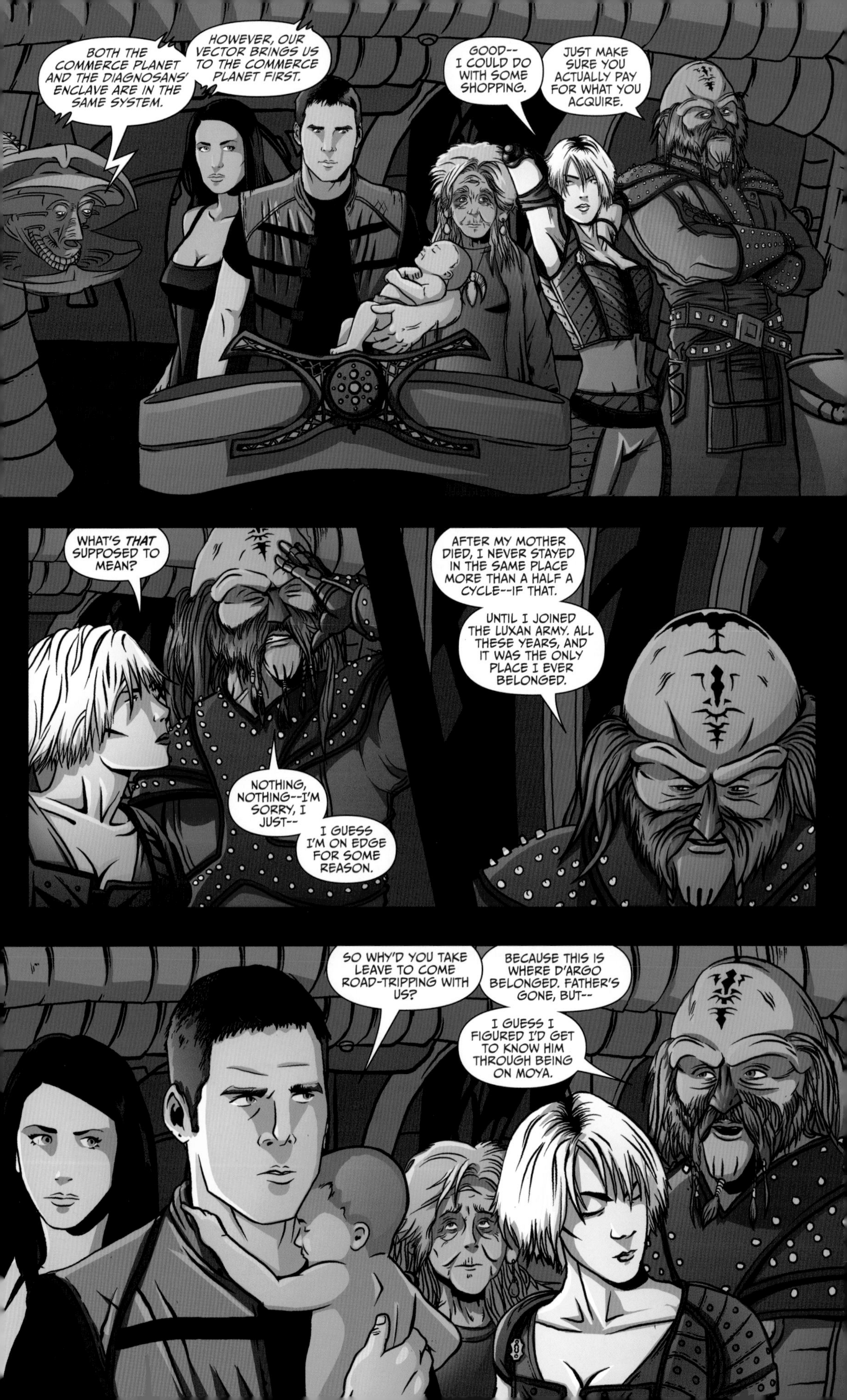
BOTH THE COMMERCE PLANET AND THE DIAGNOSANS' ENCLAVE ARE IN THE SAME SYSTEM.
HOWEVER, OUR VECTOR BRINGS US TO THE COMMERCE PLANET FIRST.
GOOD-- I COULD DO WITH SOME SHOPPING.
JUST MAKE SURE YOU ACTUALLY PAY FOR WHAT YOU ACQUIRE.
WHAT'S *THAT* SUPPOSED TO MEAN?
NOTHING, NOTHING--I'M SORRY, I JUST--
I GUESS I'M ON EDGE FOR SOME REASON.
AFTER MY MOTHER DIED, I NEVER STAYED IN THE SAME PLACE MORE THAN A HALF A CYCLE--IF THAT.
UNTIL I JOINED THE LUXAN ARMY. ALL THESE YEARS, AND IT WAS THE ONLY PLACE I EVER BELONGED.
SO WHY'D YOU TAKE LEAVE TO COME ROAD-TRIPPING WITH US?
BECAUSE THIS IS WHERE D'ARGO BELONGED. FATHER'S GONE, BUT--
I GUESS I FIGURED I'D GET TO KNOW HIM THROUGH BEING ON MOYA.

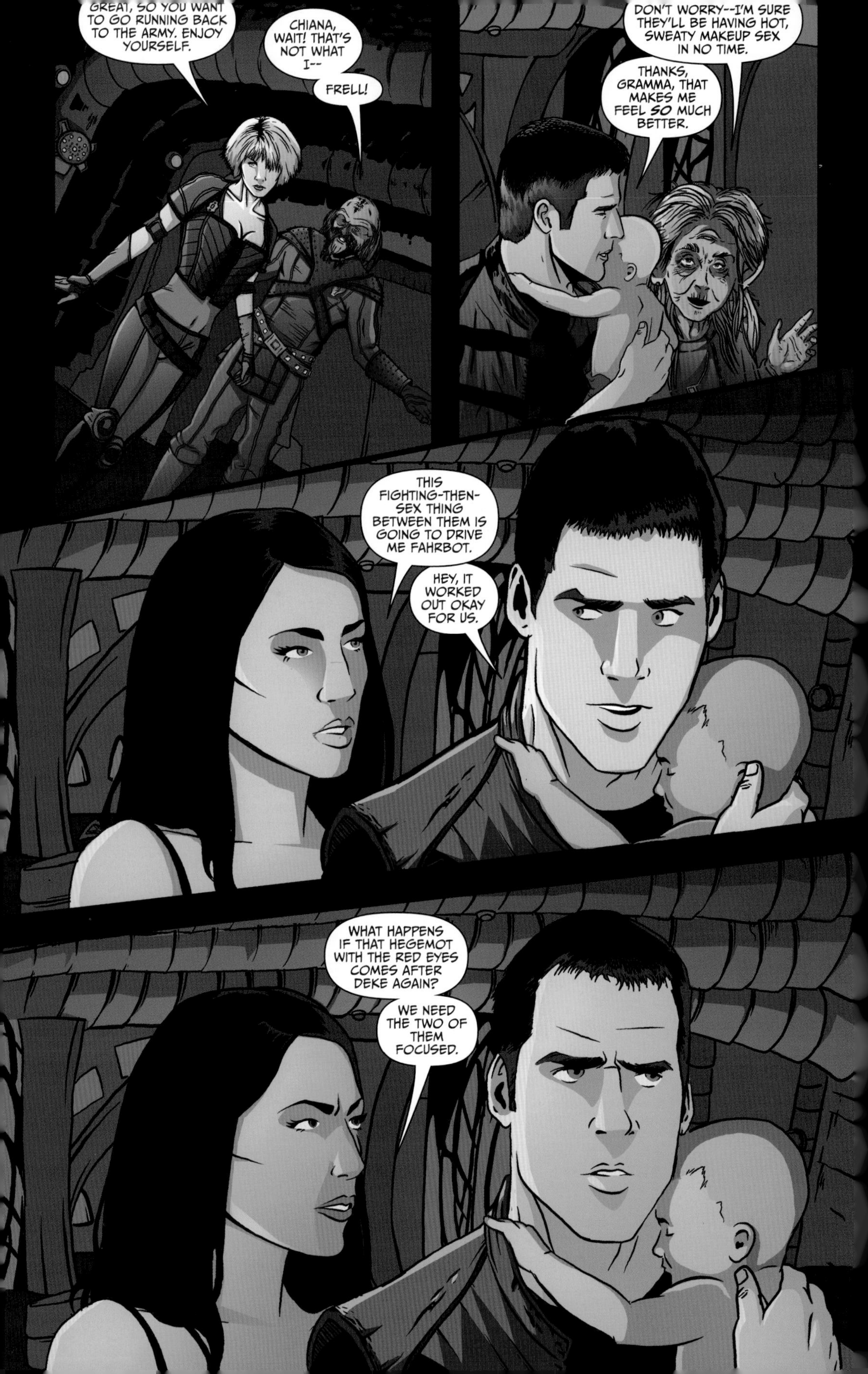
GREAT, SO YOU WANT TO GO RUNNING BACK TO THE ARMY. ENJOY YOURSELF.
CHIANA, WAIT! THAT'S NOT WHAT I--
FRELL!
DON'T WORRY--I'M SURE THEY'LL BE HAVING HOT, SWEATY MAKEUP SEX IN NO TIME.
THANKS, GRAMMA, THAT MAKES ME FEEL **SO** MUCH BETTER.
THIS FIGHTING-THEN-SEX THING BETWEEN THEM IS GOING TO DRIVE ME FAHRBOT.
HEY, IT WORKED OUT OKAY FOR US.
WHAT HAPPENS IF THAT HEGEMOT WITH THE RED EYES COMES AFTER DEKE AGAIN?
WE NEED THE TWO OF THEM FOCUSED.

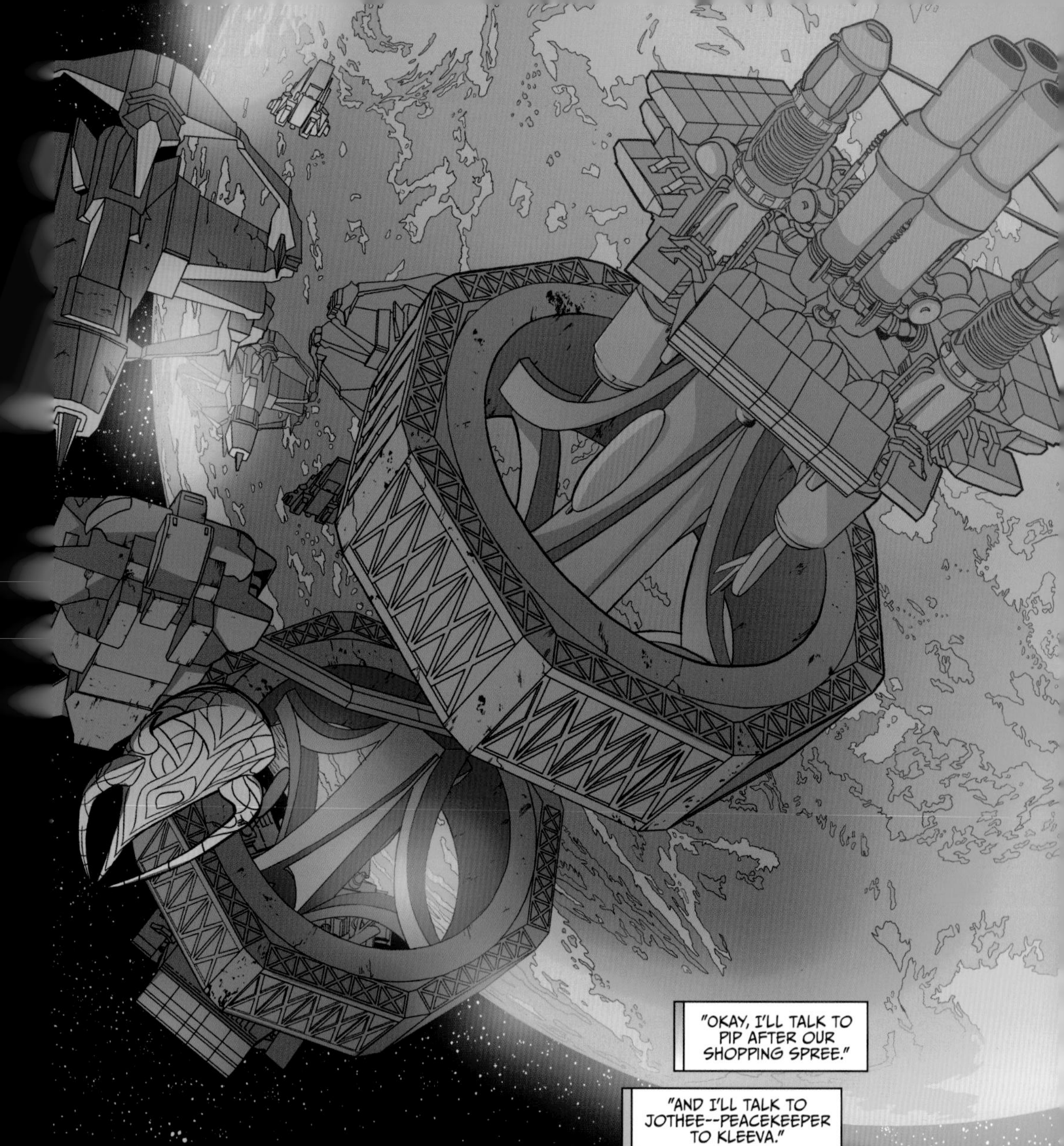
"OKAY, I'LL TALK TO PIP AFTER OUR SHOPPING SPREE."
"AND I'LL TALK TO JOTHEE--PEACEKEEPER TO KLEEVA."
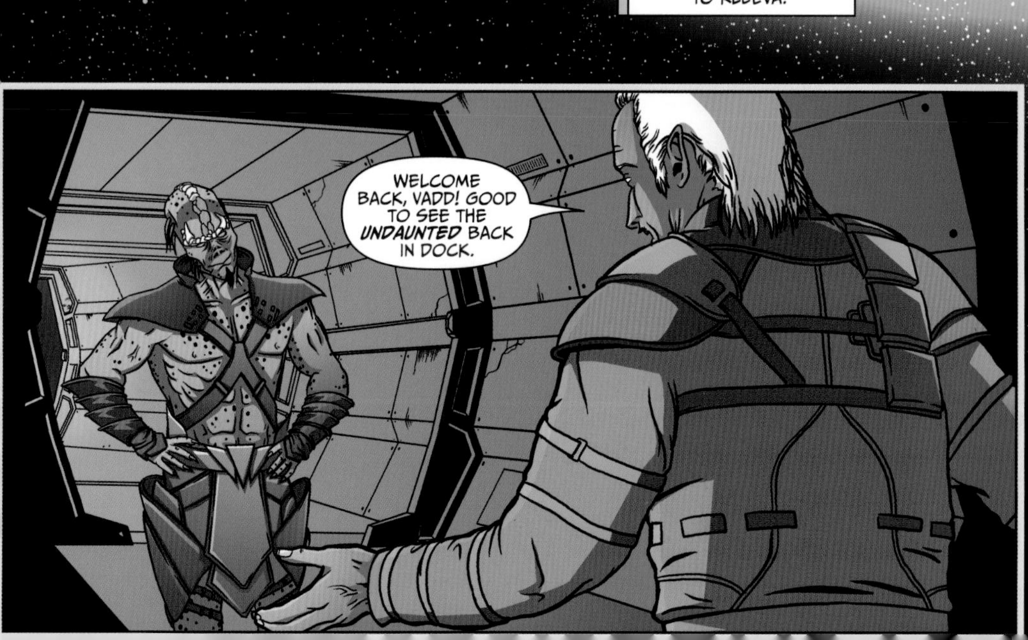
WELCOME BACK, VADD! GOOD TO SEE THE *UNDAUNTED* BACK IN DOCK.

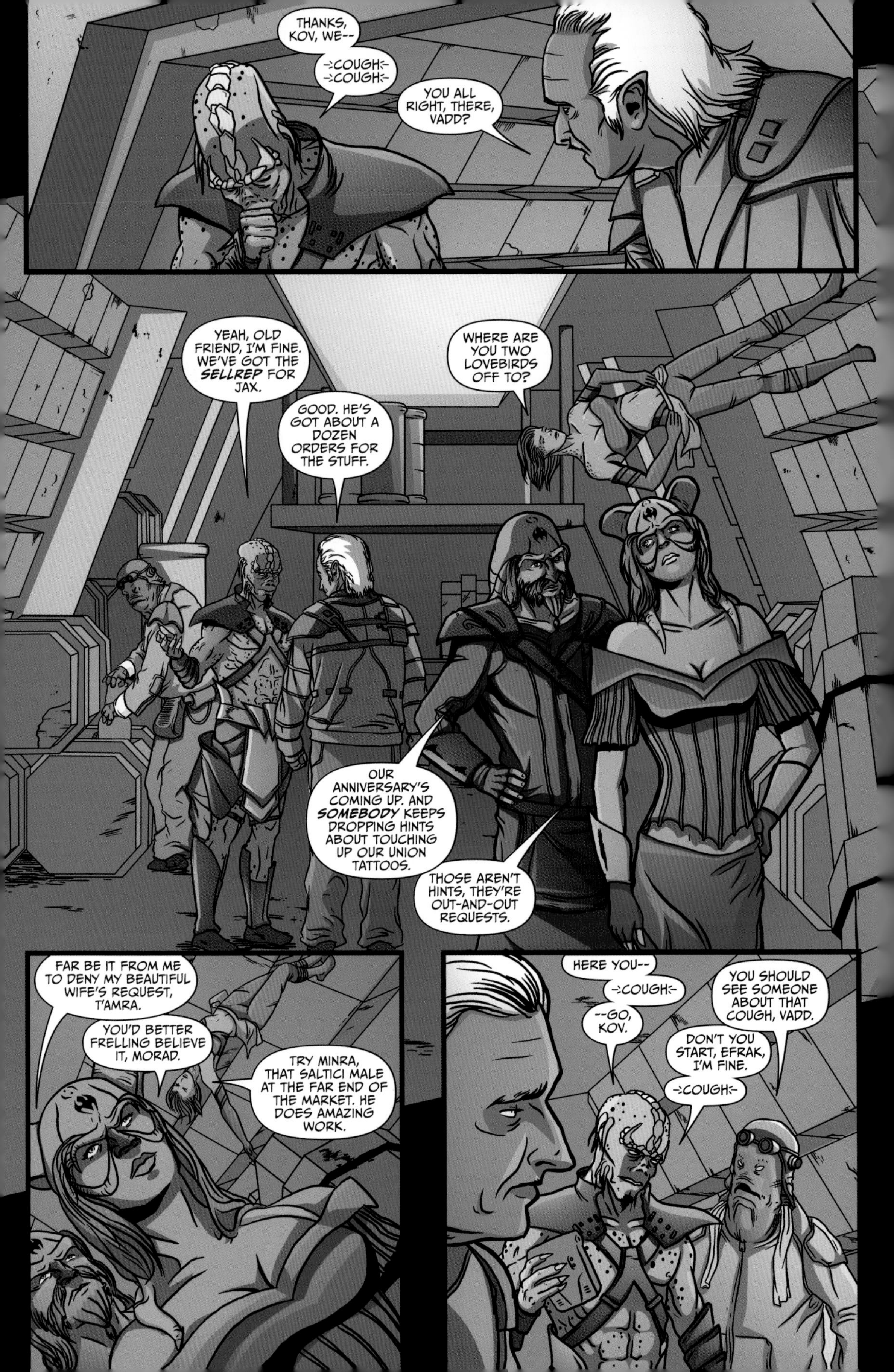

THANKS, KOV, WE--
-:-COUGH-:- -:-COUGH-:-
YOU ALL RIGHT, THERE, VADD?
YEAH, OLD FRIEND, I'M FINE. WE'VE GOT THE **SELLREP** FOR JAX.
GOOD. HE'S GOT ABOUT A DOZEN ORDERS FOR THE STUFF.
WHERE ARE YOU TWO LOVEBIRDS OFF TO?
OUR ANNIVERSARY'S COMING UP. AND **SOMEBODY** KEEPS DROPPING HINTS ABOUT TOUCHING UP OUR UNION TATTOOS.
THOSE AREN'T HINTS, THEY'RE OUT-AND-OUT REQUESTS.
FAR BE IT FROM ME TO DENY MY BEAUTIFUL WIFE'S REQUEST, T'AMRA.
YOU'D BETTER FRELLING BELIEVE IT, MORAD.
TRY MINRA, THAT SALTICI MALE AT THE FAR END OF THE MARKET. HE DOES AMAZING WORK.
HERE YOU--
-:-COUGH-:-
--GO, KOV.
YOU SHOULD SEE SOMEONE ABOUT THAT COUGH, VADD.
DON'T YOU START, EFRAK, I'M FINE.
-:-COUGH-:-

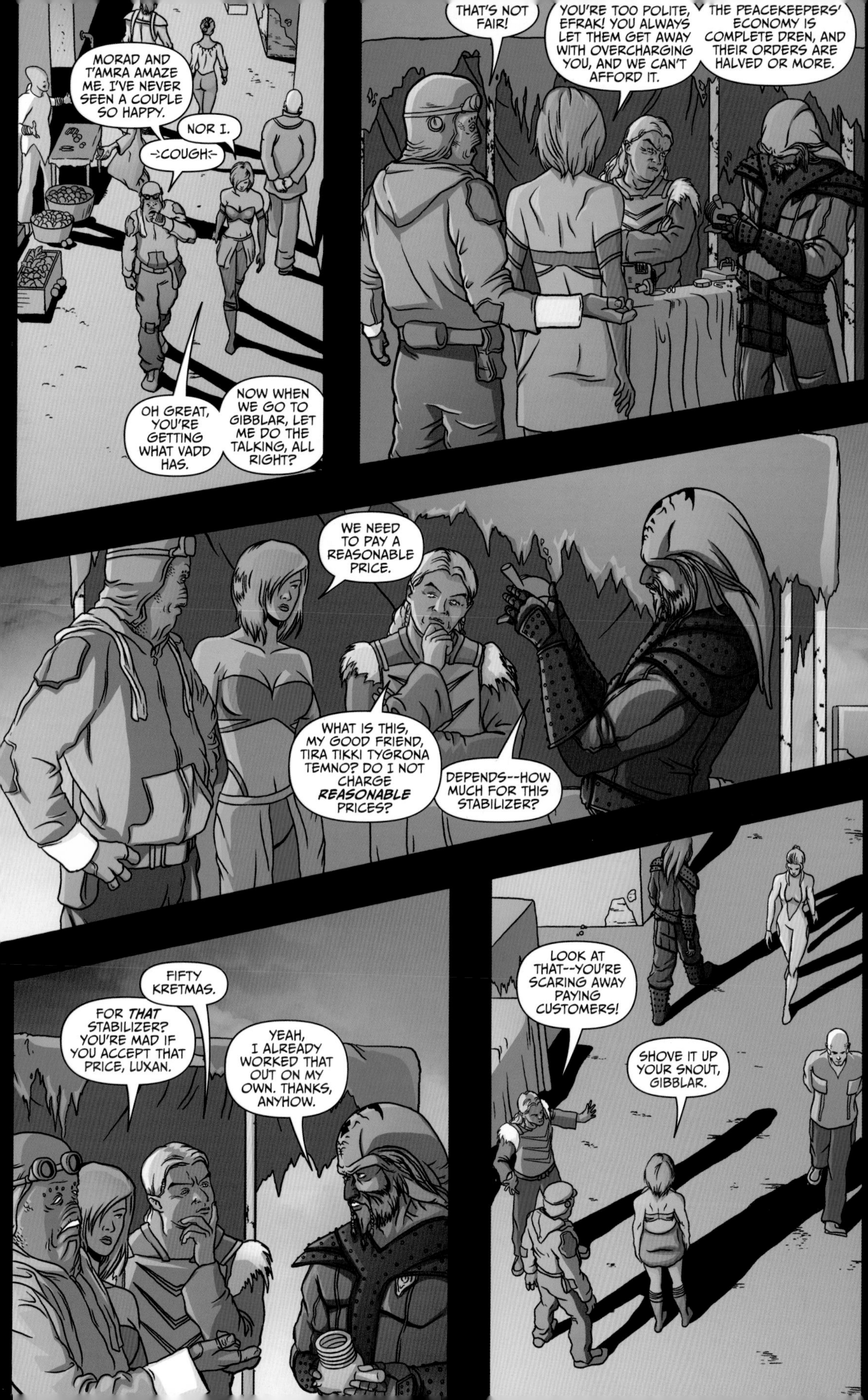
MORAD AND T'AMRA AMAZE ME. I'VE NEVER SEEN A COUPLE SO HAPPY.
NOR I.
-:-COUGH-:-
NOW WHEN WE GO TO GIBBLAR, LET ME DO THE TALKING, ALL RIGHT?
OH GREAT, YOU'RE GETTING WHAT VADD HAS.
THAT'S NOT FAIR!
YOU'RE TOO POLITE, EFRAK! YOU ALWAYS LET THEM GET AWAY WITH OVERCHARGING YOU, AND WE CAN'T AFFORD IT.
THE PEACEKEEPERS' ECONOMY IS COMPLETE DREN, AND THEIR ORDERS ARE HALVED OR MORE.
WE NEED TO PAY A REASONABLE PRICE.
WHAT IS THIS, MY GOOD FRIEND, TIRA TIKKI TYGRONA TEMNO? DO I NOT CHARGE ***REASONABLE*** PRICES?
DEPENDS--HOW MUCH FOR THIS STABILIZER?
FIFTY KRETMAS.
FOR ***THAT*** STABILIZER? YOU'RE MAD IF YOU ACCEPT THAT PRICE, LUXAN.
YEAH, I ALREADY WORKED THAT OUT ON MY OWN. THANKS, ANYHOW.
LOOK AT THAT--YOU'RE SCARING AWAY PAYING CUSTOMERS!
SHOVE IT UP YOUR SNOUT, GIBBLAR.

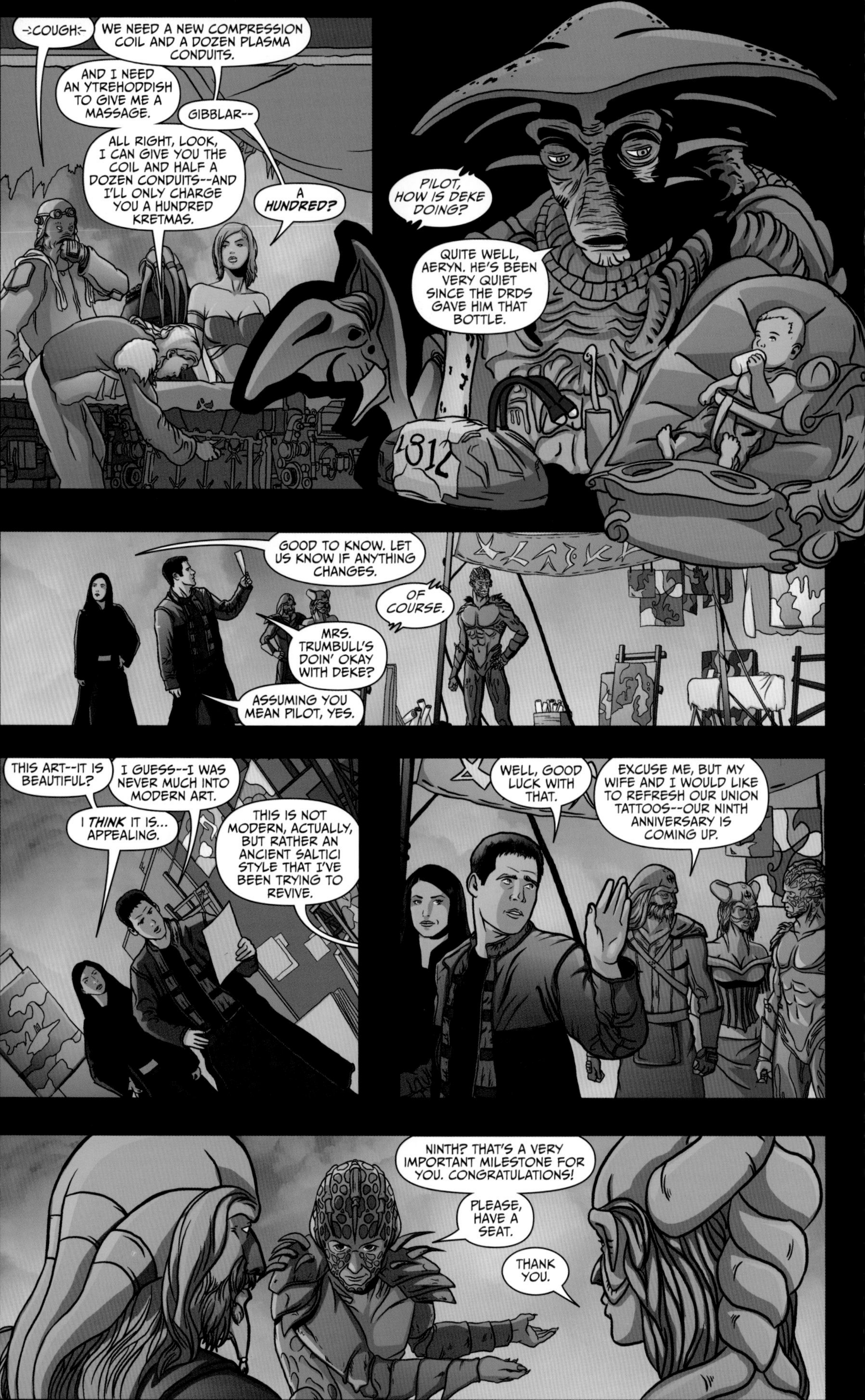

~COUGH~
WE NEED A NEW COMPRESSION COIL AND A DOZEN PLASMA CONDUITS.
AND I NEED AN YTREHODDISH TO GIVE ME A MASSAGE.
GIBBLAR--
ALL RIGHT, LOOK, I CAN GIVE YOU THE COIL AND HALF A DOZEN CONDUITS--AND I'LL ONLY CHARGE YOU A HUNDRED KRETMAS.
A *HUNDRED?*
PILOT, HOW IS DEKE DOING?
QUITE WELL, AERYN. HE'S BEEN VERY QUIET SINCE THE DRDS GAVE HIM THAT BOTTLE.
1812
GOOD TO KNOW. LET US KNOW IF ANYTHING CHANGES.
OF COURSE.
MRS. TRUMBULL'S DOIN' OKAY WITH DEKE?
ASSUMING YOU MEAN PILOT, YES.
THIS ART--IT IS BEAUTIFUL?
I GUESS--I WAS NEVER MUCH INTO MODERN ART.
I ***THINK*** IT IS... APPEALING.
THIS IS NOT MODERN, ACTUALLY, BUT RATHER AN ANCIENT SALTICI STYLE THAT I'VE BEEN TRYING TO REVIVE.
WELL, GOOD LUCK WITH THAT.
EXCUSE ME, BUT MY WIFE AND I WOULD LIKE TO REFRESH OUR UNION TATTOOS--OUR NINTH ANNIVERSARY IS COMING UP.
NINTH? THAT'S A VERY IMPORTANT MILESTONE FOR YOU. CONGRATULATIONS!
PLEASE, HAVE A SEAT.
THANK YOU.

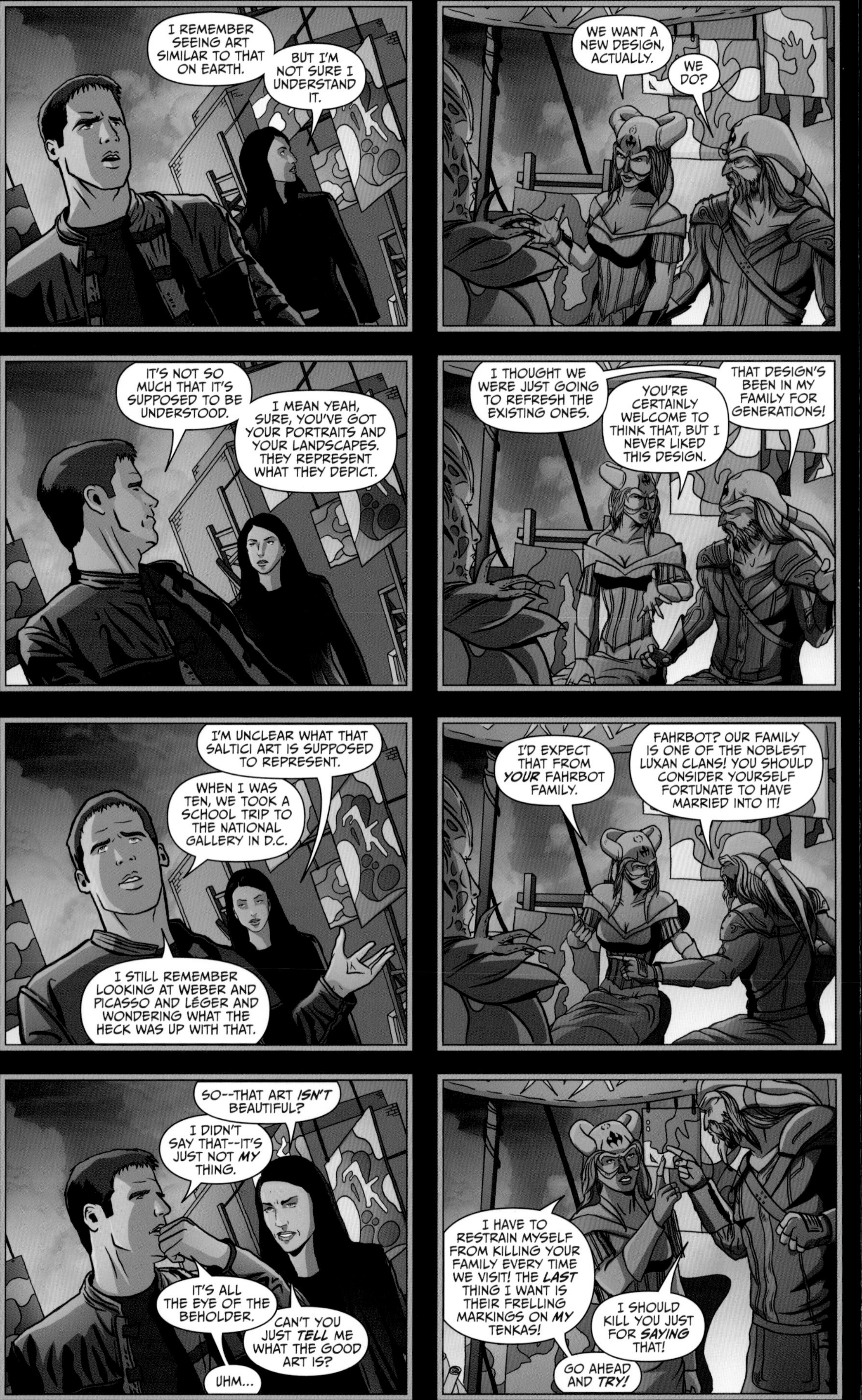
I REMEMBER SEEING ART SIMILAR TO THAT ON EARTH.
BUT I'M NOT SURE I UNDERSTAND IT.
IT'S NOT SO MUCH THAT IT'S SUPPOSED TO BE UNDERSTOOD.
I MEAN YEAH, SURE, YOU'VE GOT YOUR PORTRAITS AND YOUR LANDSCAPES. THEY REPRESENT WHAT THEY DEPICT.
I'M UNCLEAR WHAT THAT SALTICI ART IS SUPPOSED TO REPRESENT.
WHEN I WAS TEN, WE TOOK A SCHOOL TRIP TO THE NATIONAL GALLERY IN D.C.
I STILL REMEMBER LOOKING AT WEBER AND PICASSO AND LÉGER AND WONDERING WHAT THE HECK WAS UP WITH THAT.
SO--THAT ART *ISN'T* BEAUTIFUL?
I DIDN'T SAY THAT--IT'S JUST NOT *MY* THING.
IT'S ALL THE EYE OF THE BEHOLDER.
CAN'T YOU JUST *TELL* ME WHAT THE GOOD ART IS?
UHM...
WE WANT A NEW DESIGN, ACTUALLY.
WE DO?
I THOUGHT WE WERE JUST GOING TO REFRESH THE EXISTING ONES.
YOU'RE CERTAINLY WELCOME TO THINK THAT, BUT I NEVER LIKED THIS DESIGN.
THAT DESIGN'S BEEN IN MY FAMILY FOR GENERATIONS!
I'D EXPECT THAT FROM *YOUR* FAHRBOT FAMILY.
FAHRBOT? OUR FAMILY IS ONE OF THE NOBLEST LUXAN CLANS! YOU SHOULD CONSIDER YOURSELF FORTUNATE TO HAVE MARRIED INTO IT!
I HAVE TO RESTRAIN MYSELF FROM KILLING YOUR FAMILY EVERY TIME WE VISIT! THE *LAST* THING I WANT IS THEIR FRELLING MARKINGS ON *MY* TENKAS!
I SHOULD KILL YOU JUST FOR *SAYING* THAT!
GO AHEAD AND *TRY!*

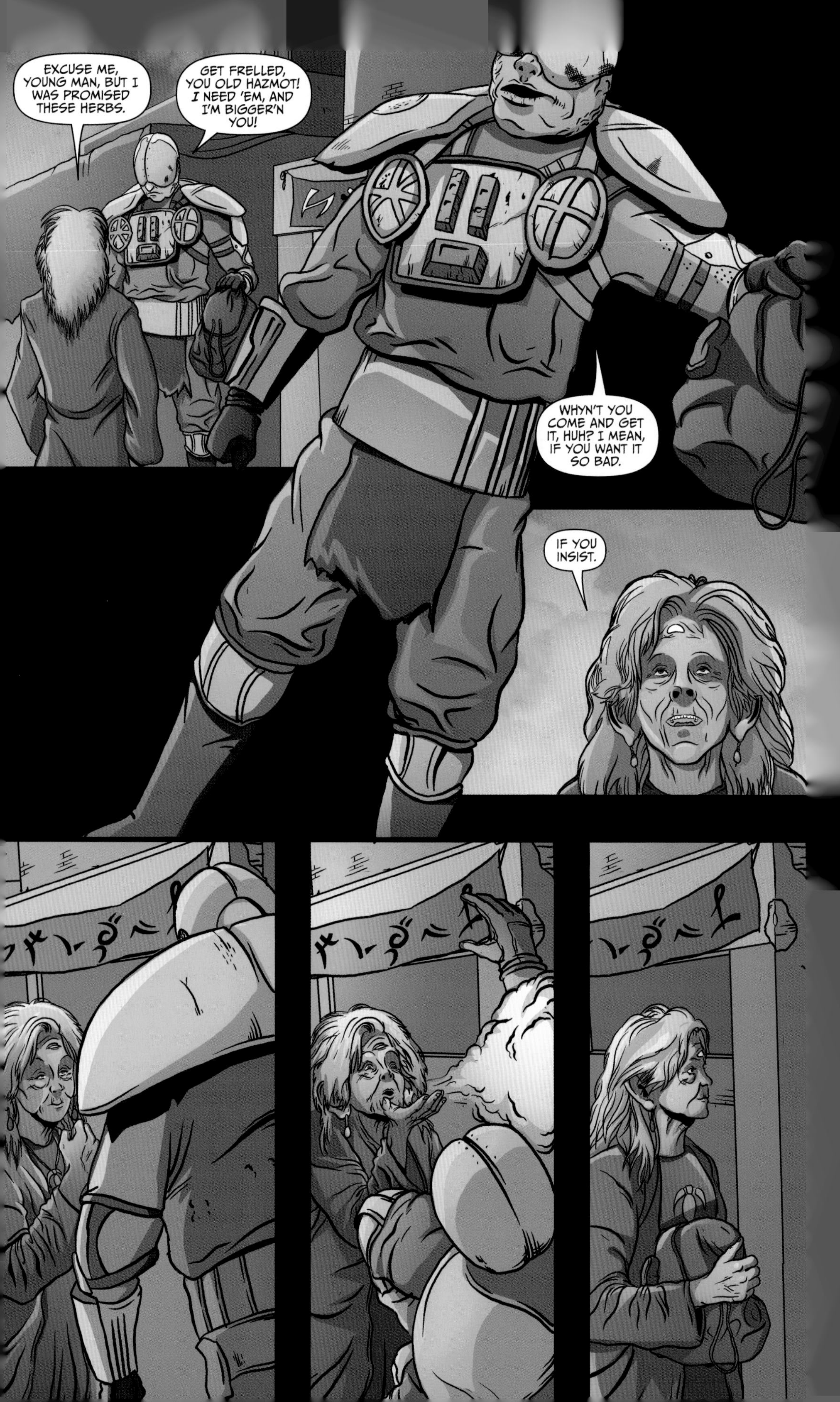
EXCUSE ME, YOUNG MAN, BUT I WAS PROMISED THESE HERBS.
GET FRELLED, YOU OLD HAZMOT! I NEED 'EM, AND I'M BIGGER'N YOU!
WHYN'T YOU COME AND GET IT, HUH? I MEAN, IF YOU WANT IT SO BAD.
IF YOU INSIST.

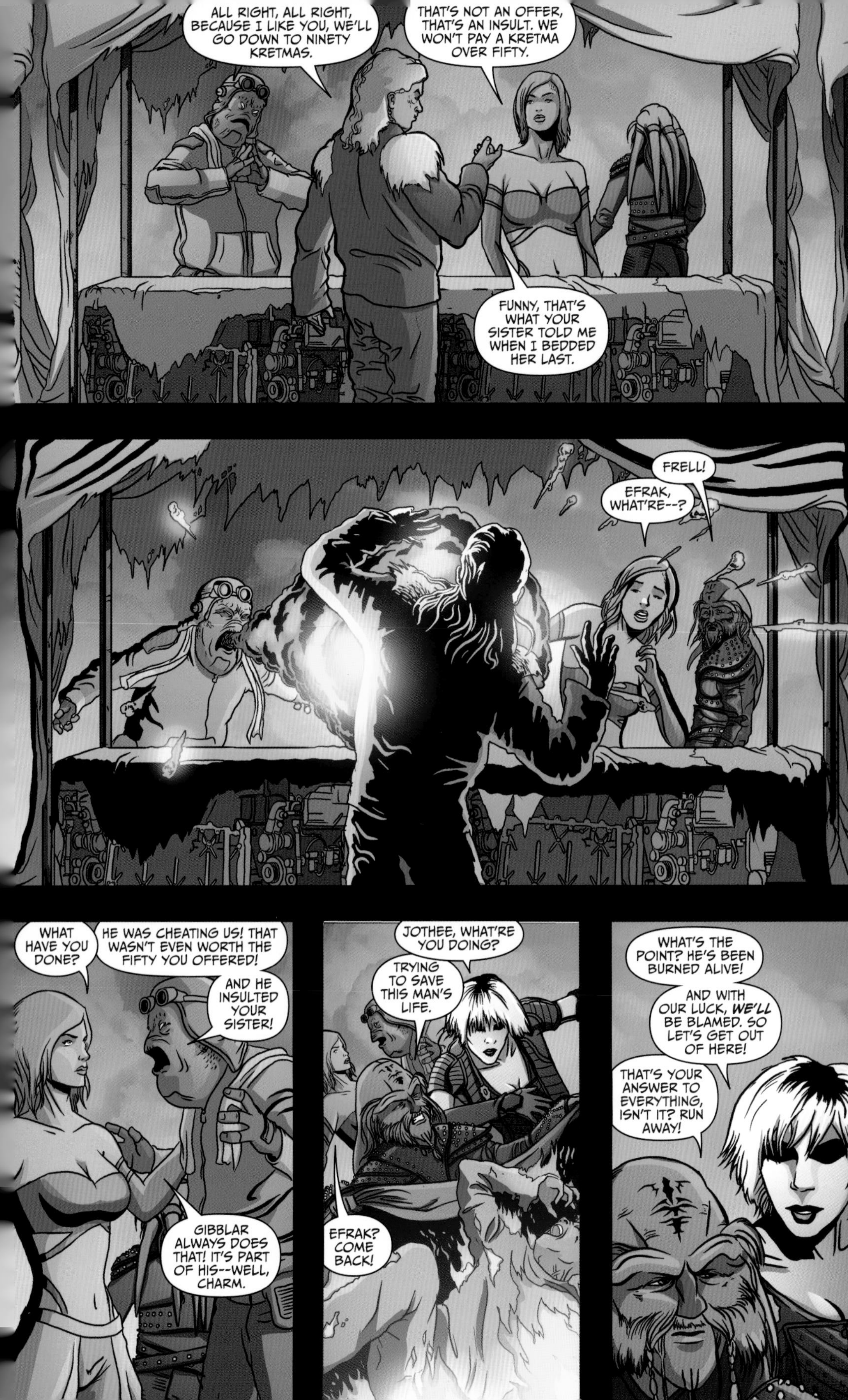
ALL RIGHT, ALL RIGHT, BECAUSE I LIKE YOU, WE'LL GO DOWN TO NINETY KRETMAS.
THAT'S NOT AN OFFER, THAT'S AN INSULT. WE WON'T PAY A KRETMA OVER FIFTY.
FUNNY, THAT'S WHAT YOUR SISTER TOLD ME WHEN I BEDDED HER LAST.
FRELL!
EFRAK, WHAT'RE--?
WHAT HAVE YOU DONE?
HE WAS CHEATING US! THAT WASN'T EVEN WORTH THE FIFTY YOU OFFERED!
AND HE INSULTED YOUR SISTER!
GIBBLAR ALWAYS DOES THAT! IT'S PART OF HIS--WELL, CHARM.
JOTHEE, WHAT'RE YOU DOING?
TRYING TO SAVE THIS MAN'S LIFE.
EFRAK? COME BACK!
WHAT'S THE POINT? HE'S BEEN BURNED ALIVE!
AND WITH OUR LUCK, *WE'LL* BE BLAMED. SO LET'S GET OUT OF HERE!
THAT'S YOUR ANSWER TO EVERYTHING, ISN'T IT? RUN AWAY!

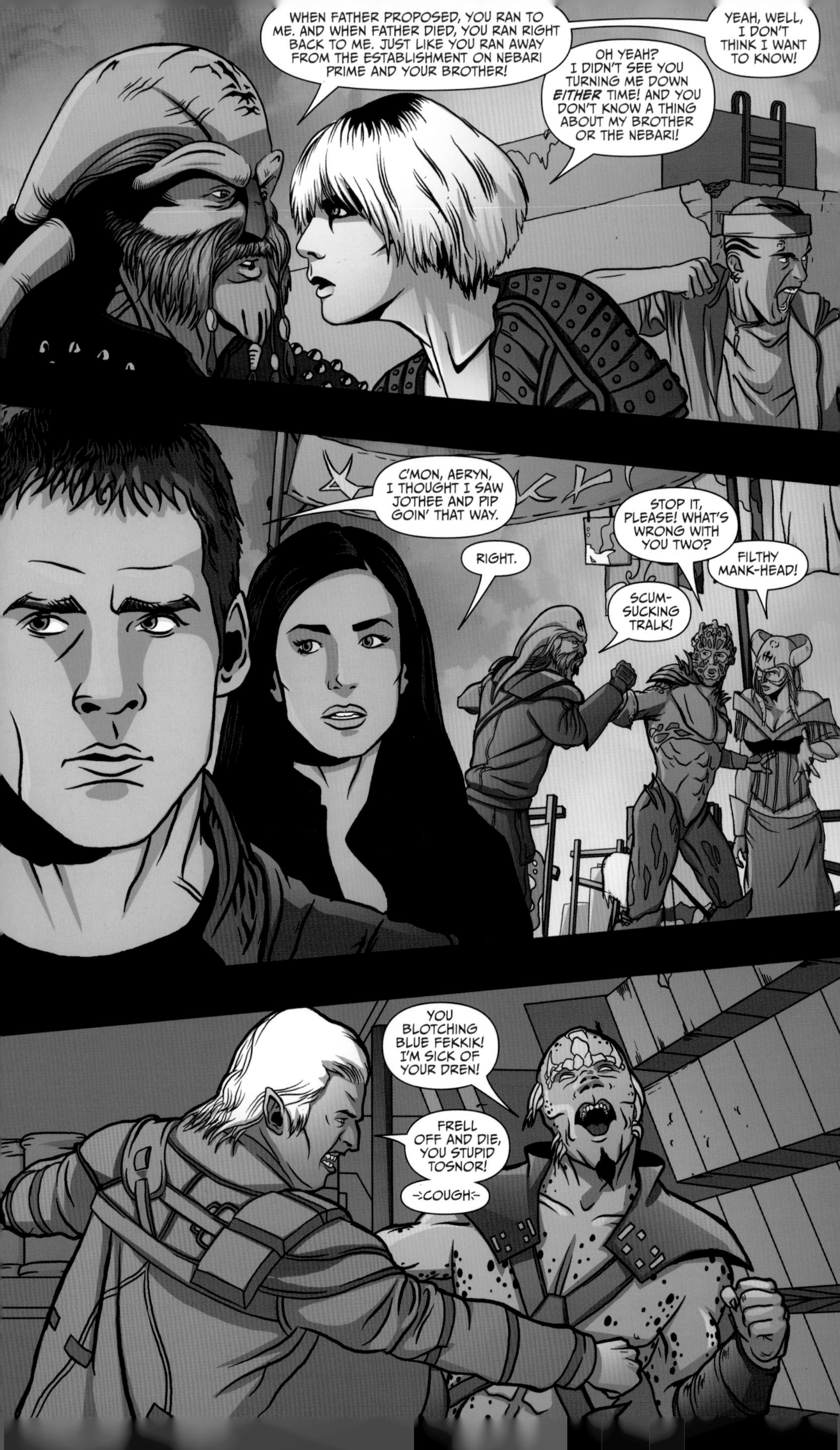
WHEN FATHER PROPOSED, YOU RAN TO ME. AND WHEN FATHER DIED, YOU RAN RIGHT BACK TO ME. JUST LIKE YOU RAN AWAY FROM THE ESTABLISHMENT ON NEBARI PRIME AND YOUR BROTHER!
OH YEAH? I DIDN'T SEE YOU TURNING ME DOWN *EITHER* TIME! AND YOU DON'T KNOW A THING ABOUT MY BROTHER OR THE NEBARI!
YEAH, WELL, I DON'T THINK I WANT TO KNOW!
C'MON, AERYN, I THOUGHT I SAW JOTHEE AND PIP GOIN' THAT WAY.
RIGHT.
STOP IT, PLEASE! WHAT'S WRONG WITH YOU TWO?
FILTHY MANK-HEAD!
SCUM-SUCKING TRALK!
YOU BLOTCHING BLUE FEKKIK! I'M SICK OF YOUR DREN!
FRELL OFF AND DIE, YOU STUPID TOSNOR!
-COUGH-

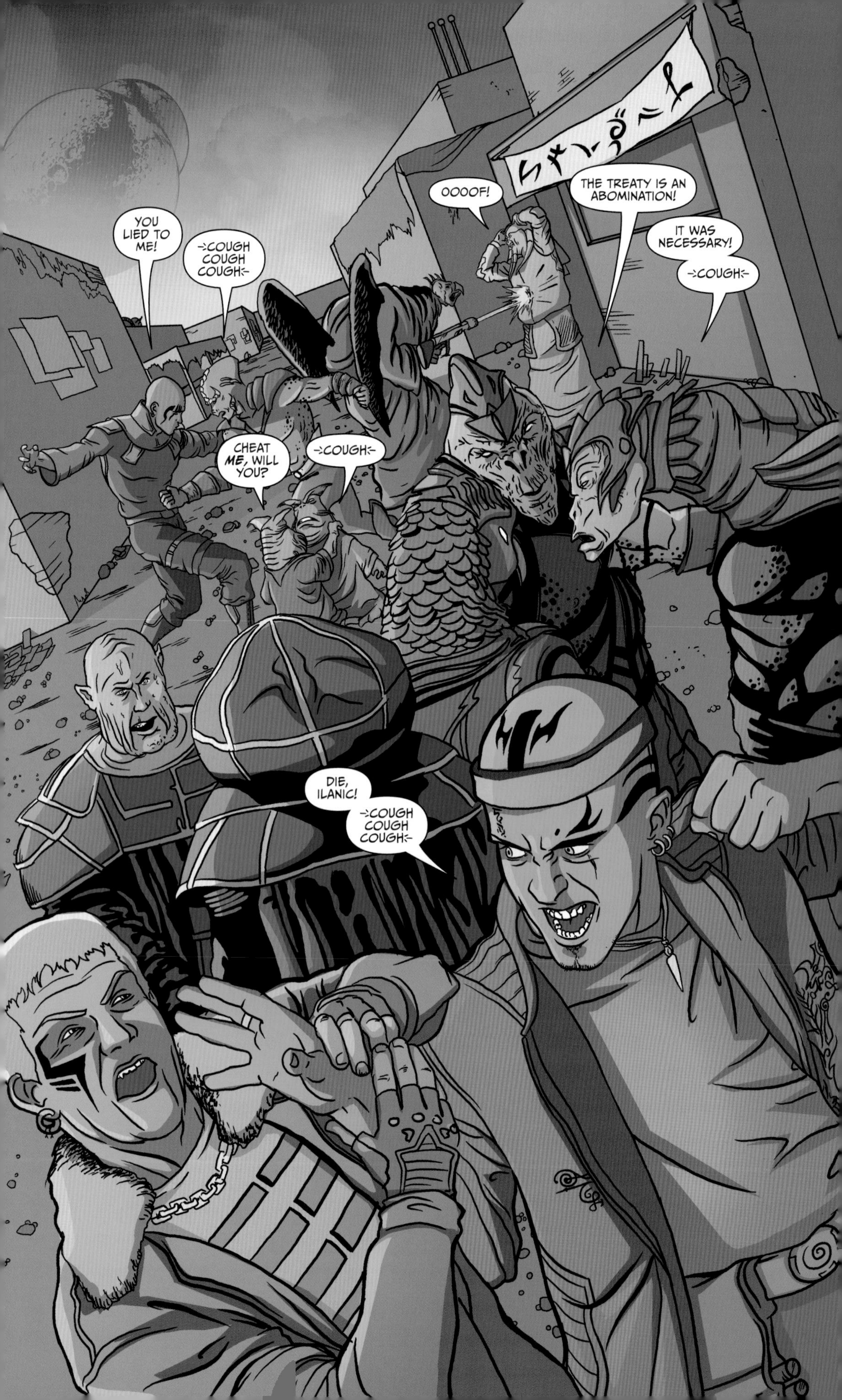

YOU LIED TO ME!
-:-COUGH COUGH COUGH-:-
OOOOF!
THE TREATY IS AN ABOMINATION!
IT WAS NECESSARY!
-:-COUGH-:-
CHEAT *ME*, WILL YOU?
-:-COUGH-:-
DIE, ILANIC!
-:-COUGH COUGH COUGH-:-

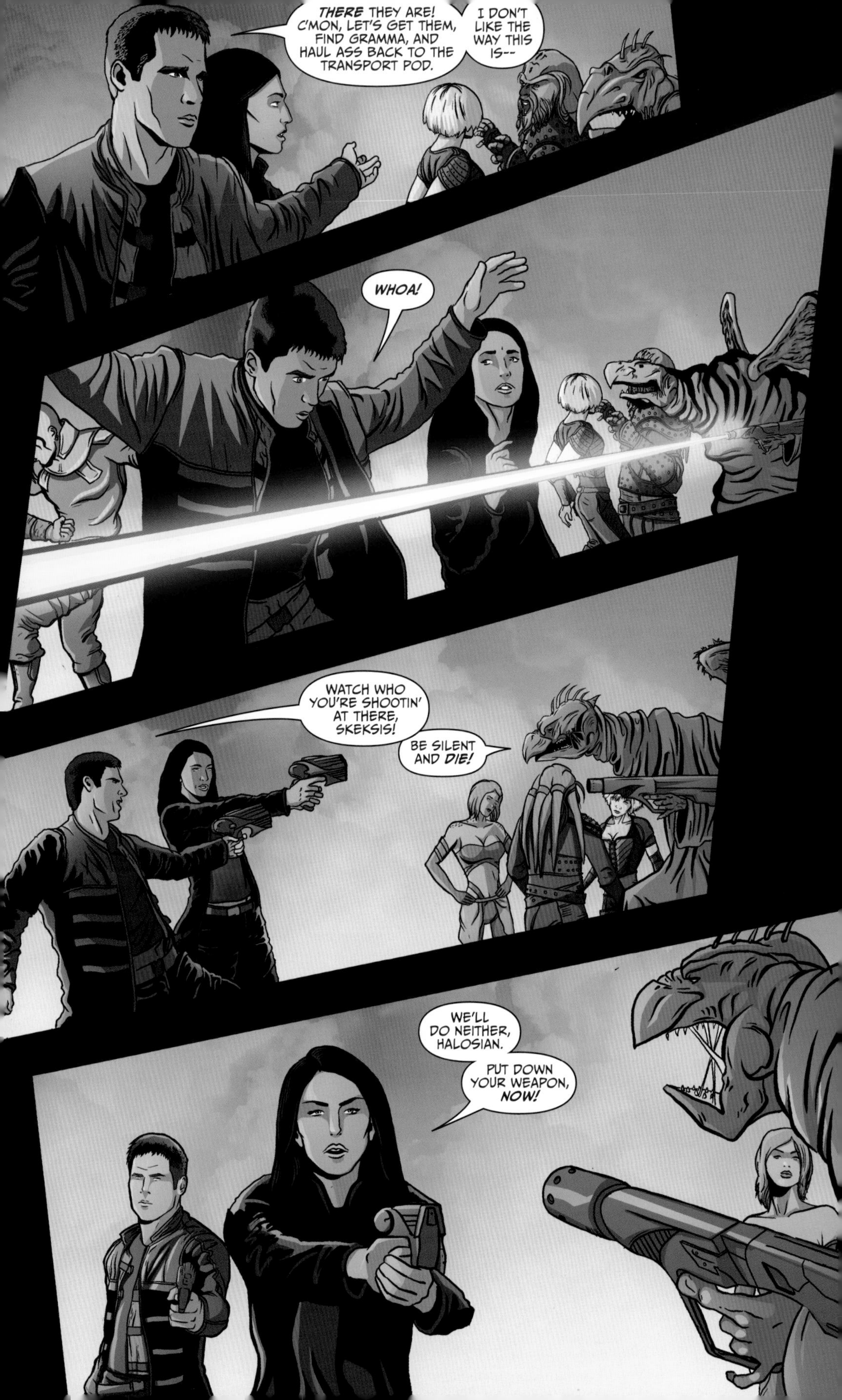
THERE THEY ARE! C'MON, LET'S GET THEM, FIND GRAMMA, AND HAUL ASS BACK TO THE TRANSPORT POD.
I DON'T LIKE THE WAY THIS IS--
WHOA!
WATCH WHO YOU'RE SHOOTIN' AT THERE, SKEKSIS!
BE SILENT AND DIE!
WE'LL DO NEITHER, HALOSIAN.
PUT DOWN YOUR WEAPON, NOW!

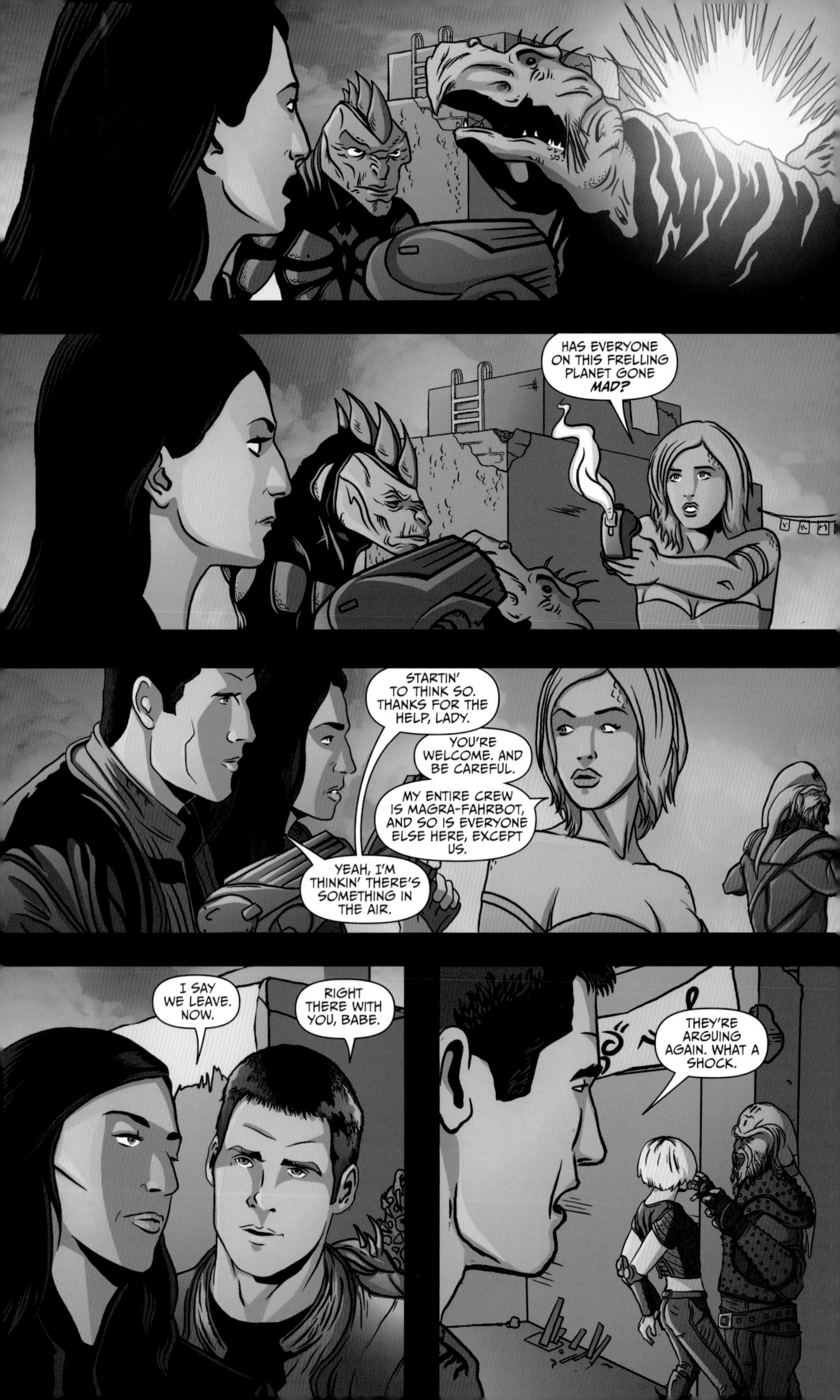
HAS EVERYONE ON THIS FRELLING PLANET GONE *MAD?*
STARTIN' TO THINK SO. THANKS FOR THE HELP, LADY.
YOU'RE WELCOME. AND BE CAREFUL.
MY ENTIRE CREW IS MAGRA-FAHRBOT, AND SO IS EVERYONE ELSE HERE, EXCEPT US.
YEAH, I'M THINKIN' THERE'S SOMETHING IN THE AIR.
I SAY WE LEAVE. NOW.
RIGHT THERE WITH YOU, BABE.
THEY'RE ARGUING AGAIN. WHAT A SHOCK.

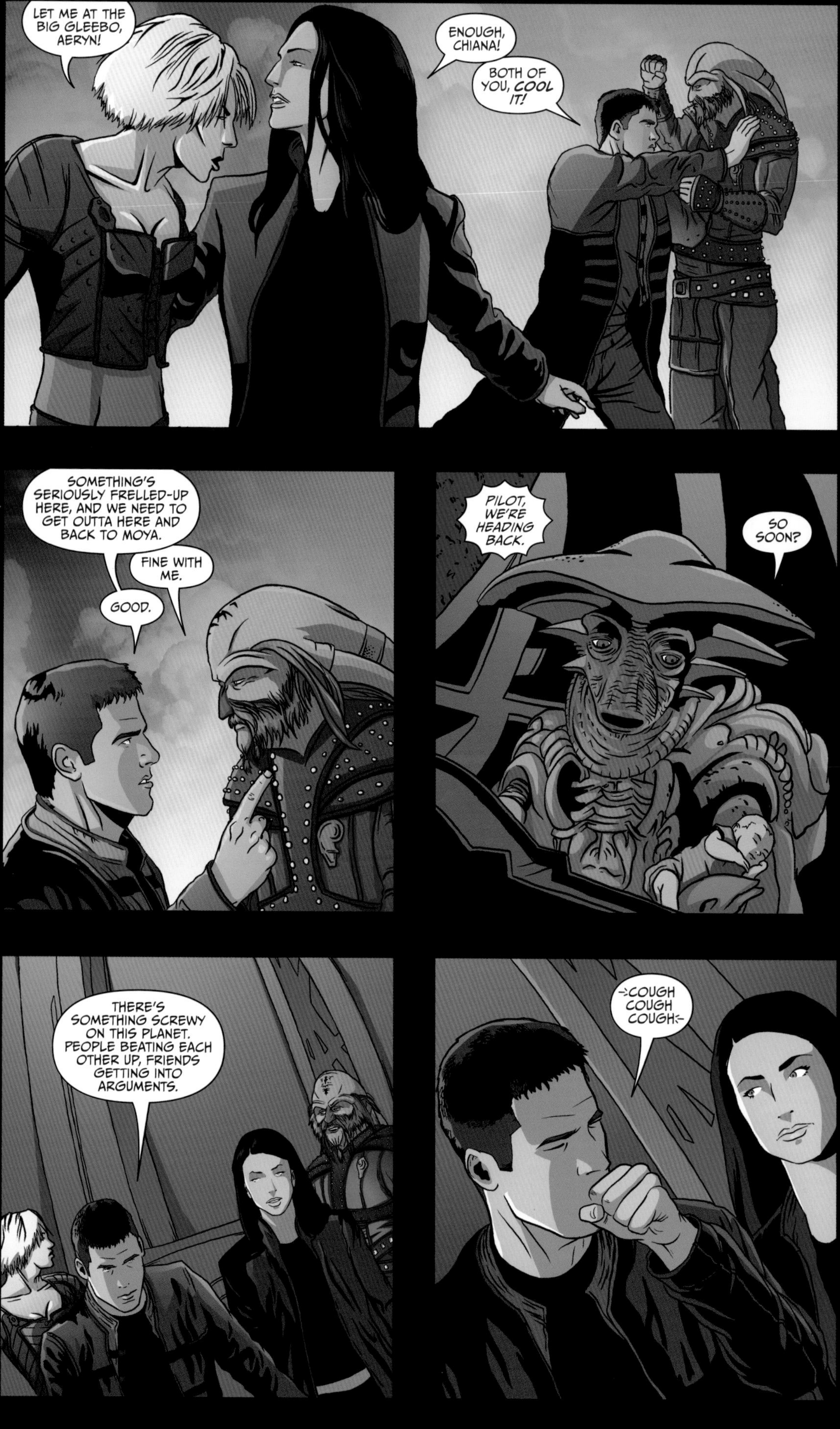
LET ME AT THE BIG GLEEBO, AERYN!
ENOUGH, CHIANA!
BOTH OF YOU, **COOL** IT!
SOMETHING'S SERIOUSLY FRELLED-UP HERE, AND WE NEED TO GET OUTTA HERE AND BACK TO MOYA.
FINE WITH ME.
GOOD.
PILOT, WE'RE HEADING BACK.
SO SOON?
THERE'S SOMETHING SCREWY ON THIS PLANET. PEOPLE BEATING EACH OTHER UP, FRIENDS GETTING INTO ARGUMENTS.
COUGH COUGH COUGH

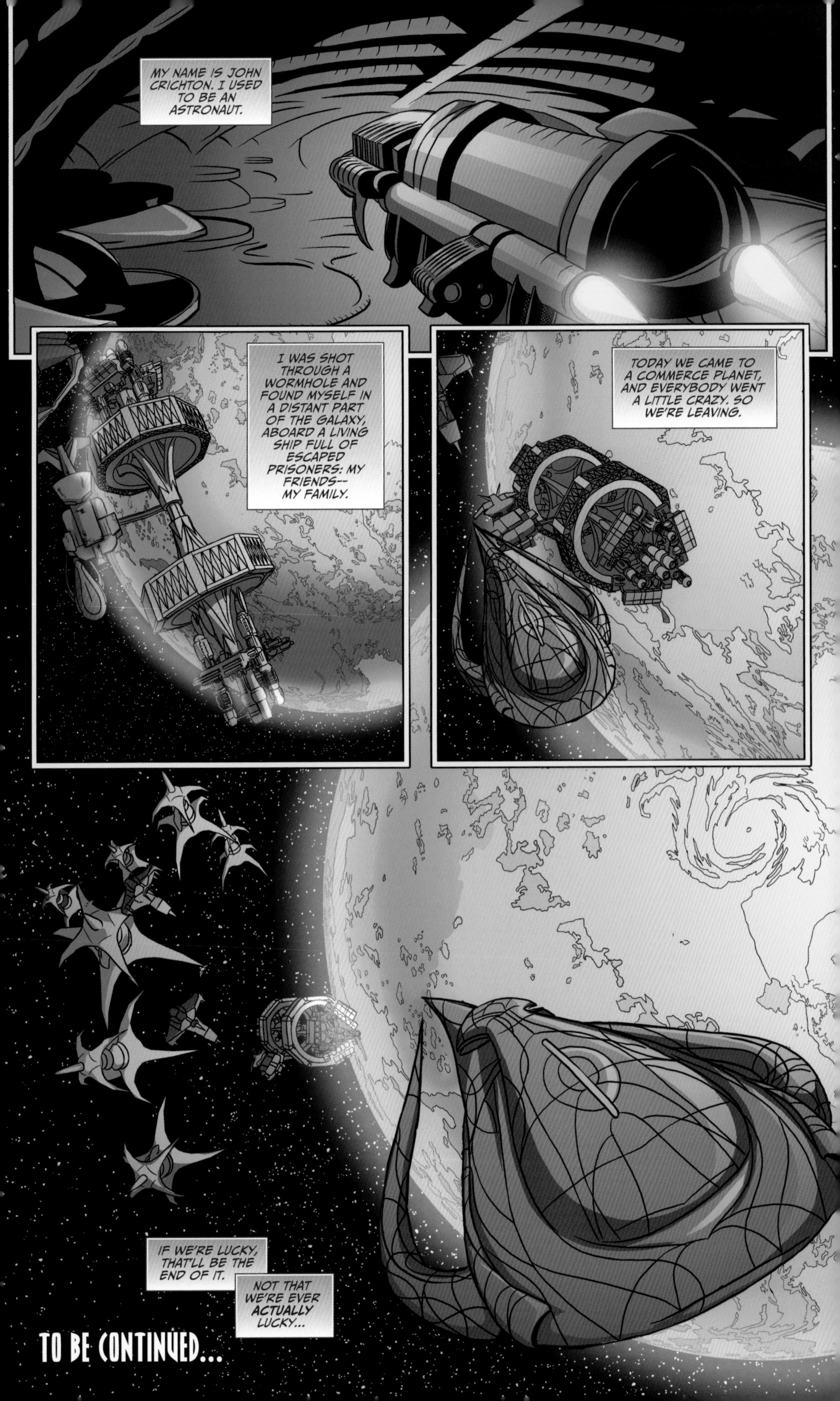
MY NAME IS JOHN CRICHTON. I USED TO BE AN ASTRONAUT.
I WAS SHOT THROUGH A WORMHOLE AND FOUND MYSELF IN A DISTANT PART OF THE GALAXY, ABOARD A LIVING SHIP FULL OF ESCAPED PRISONERS: MY FRIENDS-- MY FAMILY.
TODAY WE CAME TO A COMMERCE PLANET, AND EVERYBODY WENT A LITTLE CRAZY. SO WE'RE LEAVING.
IF WE'RE LUCKY, THAT'LL BE THE END OF IT.
NOT THAT WE'RE EVER ACTUALLY LUCKY...
TO BE CONTINUED...

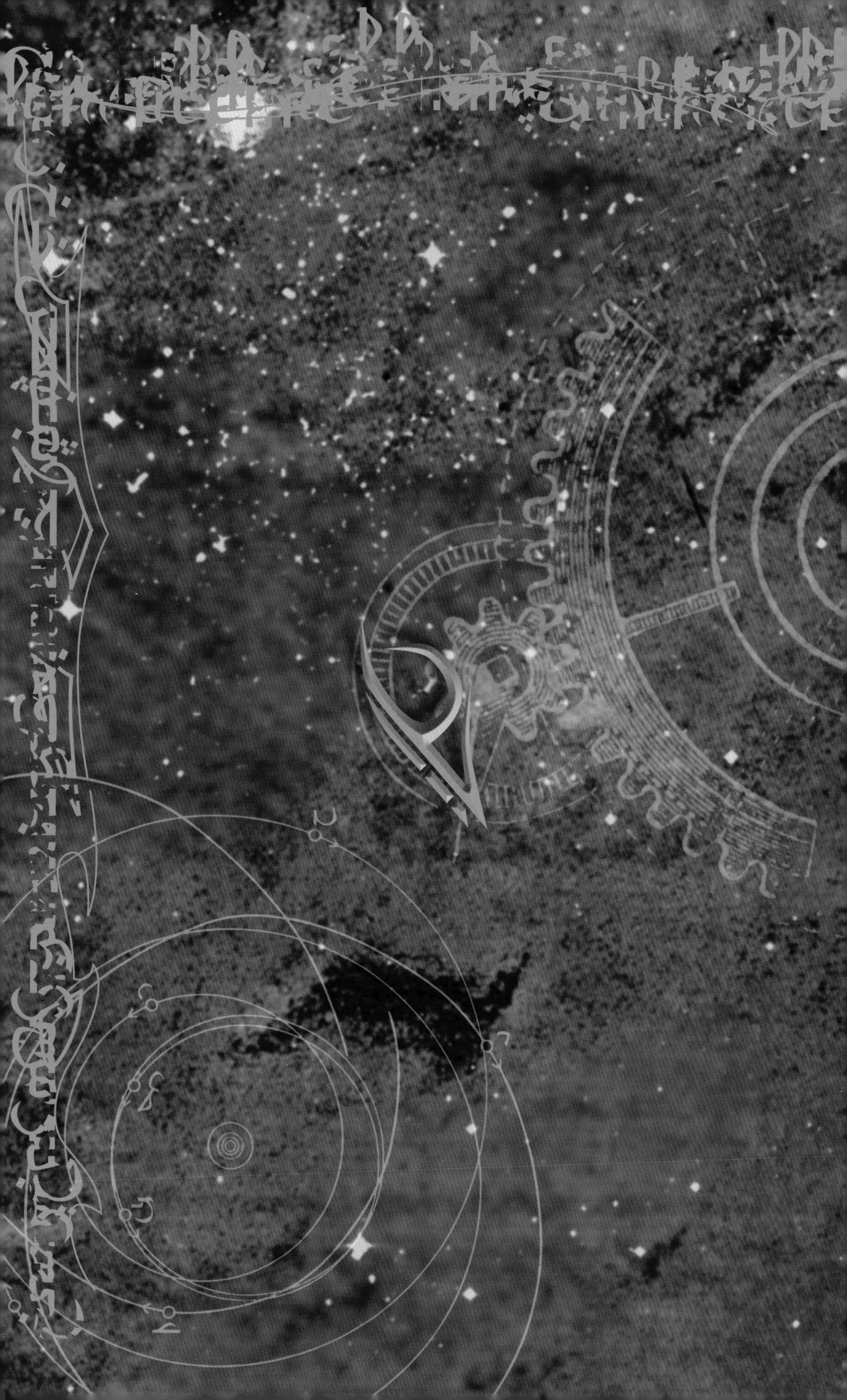

BOOK TWO

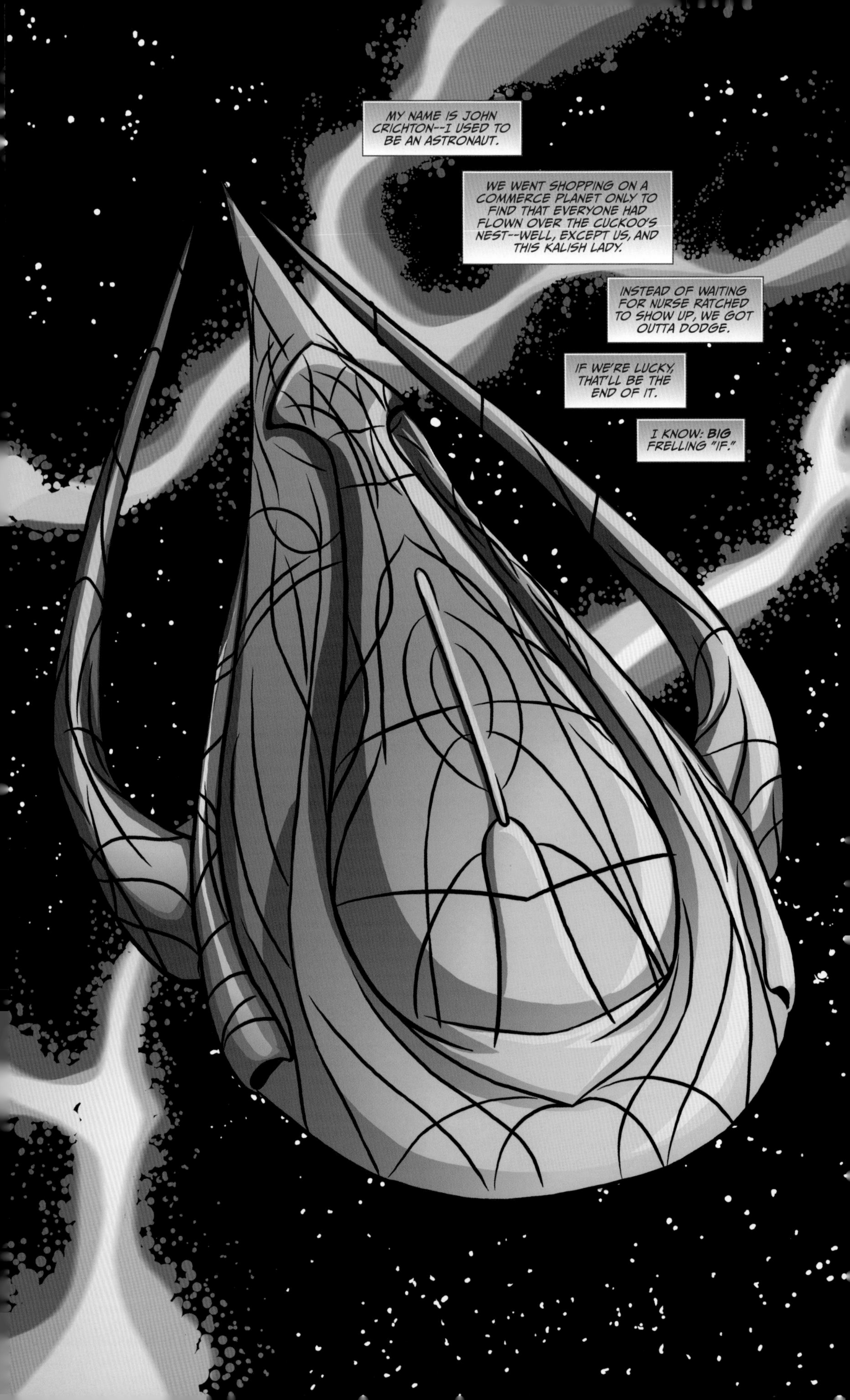
MY NAME IS JOHN CRICHTON--I USED TO BE AN ASTRONAUT.
WE WENT SHOPPING ON A COMMERCE PLANET ONLY TO FIND THAT EVERYONE HAD FLOWN OVER THE CUCKOO'S NEST--WELL, EXCEPT US, AND THIS KALISH LADY.
INSTEAD OF WAITING FOR NURSE RATCHED TO SHOW UP, WE GOT OUTTA DODGE.
IF WE'RE LUCKY, THAT'LL BE THE END OF IT.
I KNOW: BIG FRELLING "IF."

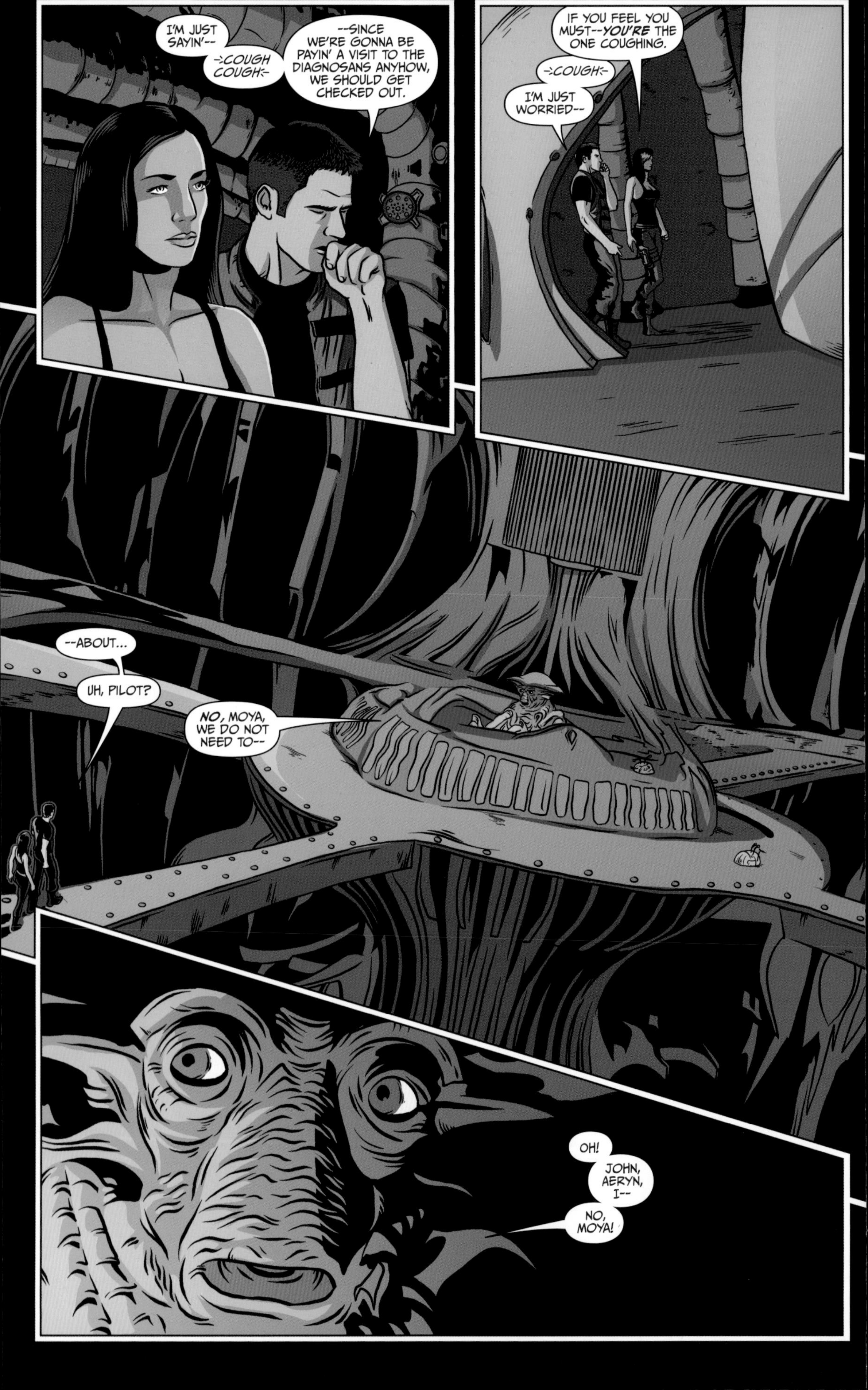
I'M JUST SAYIN'--
COUGH COUGH
--SINCE WE'RE GONNA BE PAYIN' A VISIT TO THE DIAGNOSANS ANYHOW, WE SHOULD GET CHECKED OUT.
IF YOU FEEL YOU MUST--*YOU'RE* THE ONE COUGHING.
COUGH
I'M JUST WORRIED--
--ABOUT...
UH, PILOT?
NO, MOYA, WE DO NOT NEED TO--
OH!
JOHN, AERYN, I--
NO, MOYA!

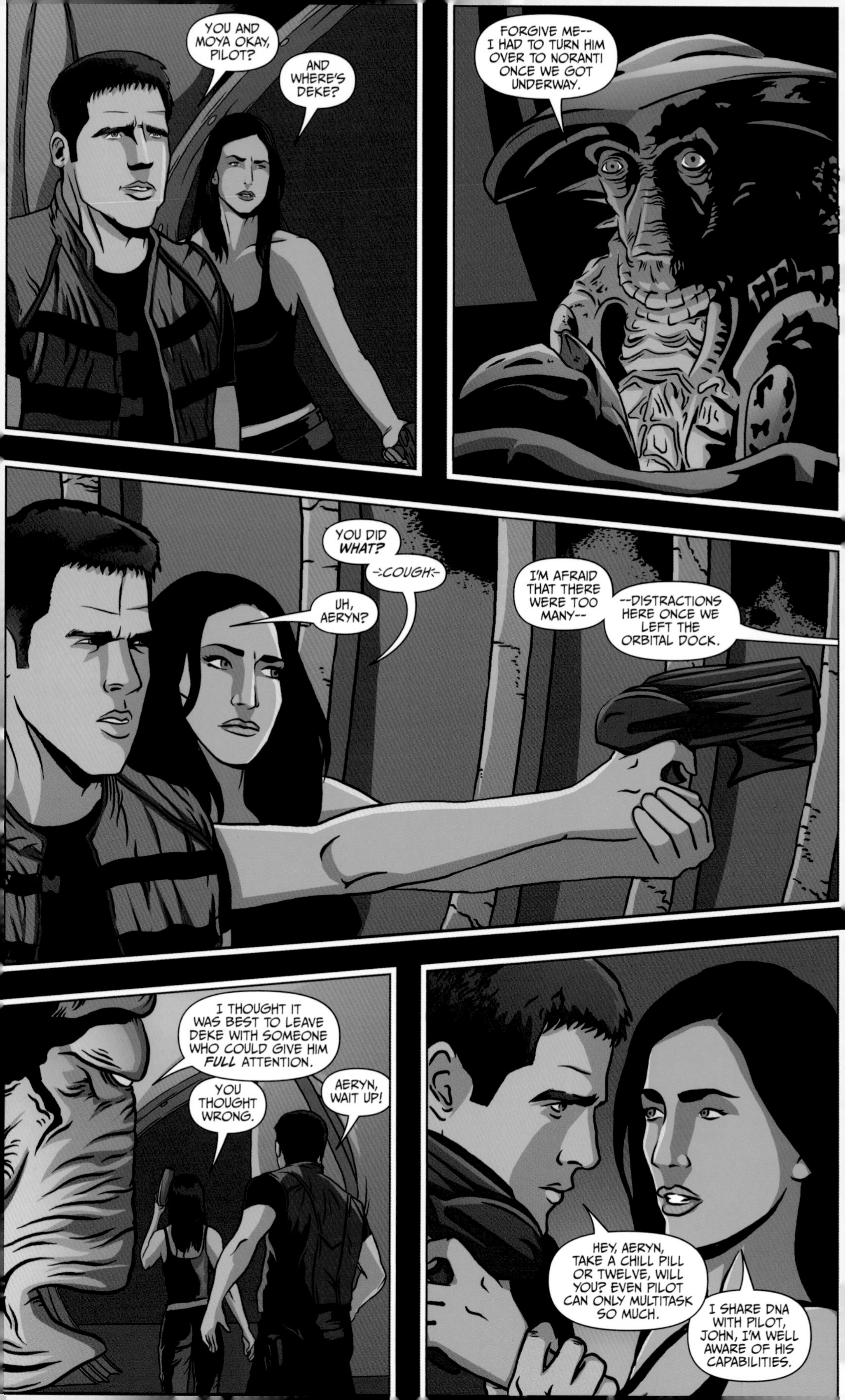
YOU AND MOYA OKAY, PILOT?
AND WHERE'S DEKE?
FORGIVE ME-- I HAD TO TURN HIM OVER TO NORANTI ONCE WE GOT UNDERWAY.
YOU DID **WHAT?**
-:-COUGH-:-
UH, AERYN?
I'M AFRAID THAT THERE WERE TOO MANY--
--DISTRACTIONS HERE ONCE WE LEFT THE ORBITAL DOCK.
I THOUGHT IT WAS BEST TO LEAVE DEKE WITH SOMEONE WHO COULD GIVE HIM **FULL** ATTENTION.
YOU THOUGHT WRONG.
AERYN, WAIT UP!
HEY, AERYN, TAKE A CHILL PILL OR TWELVE, WILL YOU? EVEN PILOT CAN ONLY MULTITASK SO MUCH.
I SHARE DNA WITH PILOT, JOHN, I'M WELL AWARE OF HIS CAPABILITIES.

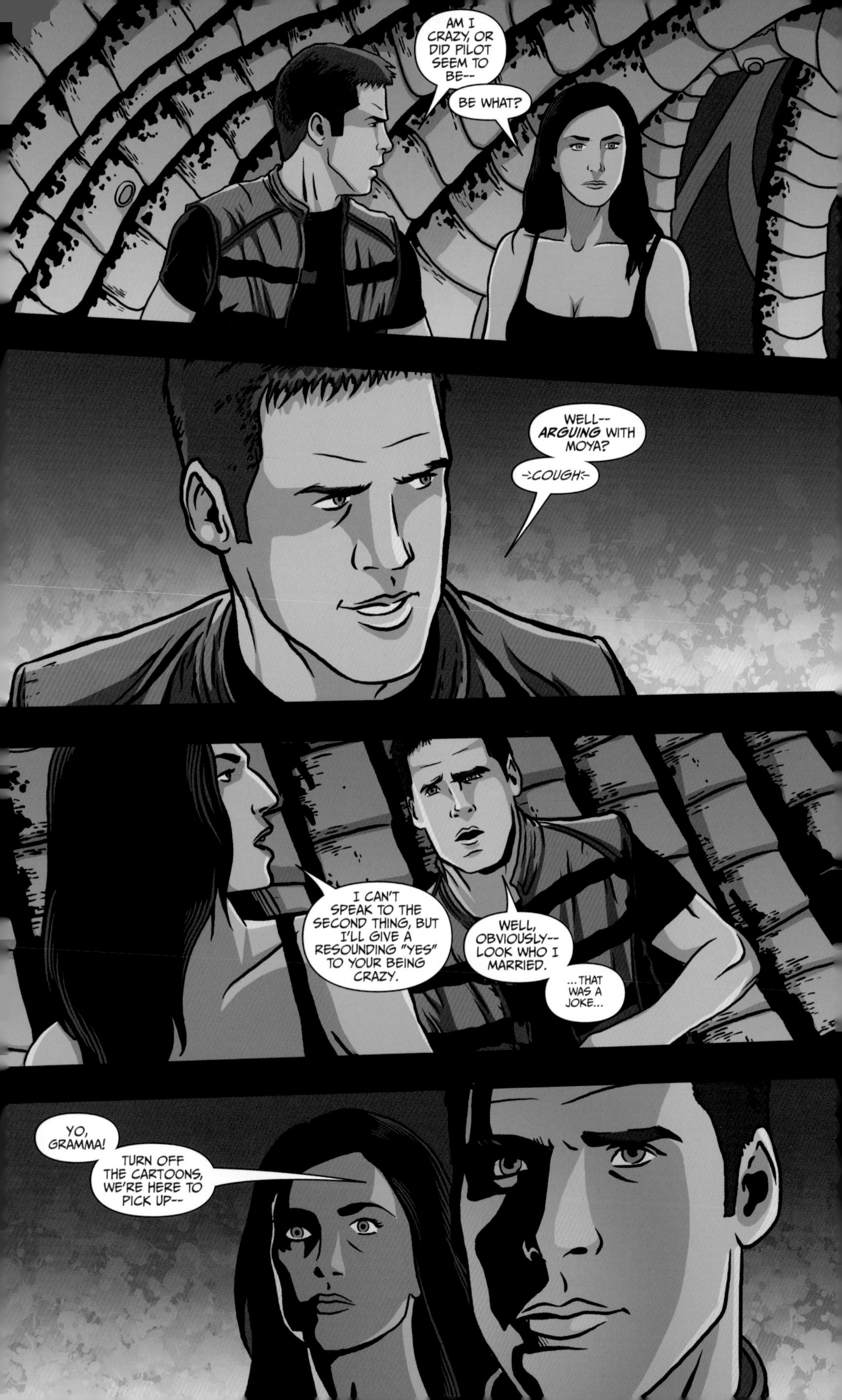
AM I CRAZY, OR DID PILOT SEEM TO BE--
BE WHAT?
WELL-- ARGUING WITH MOYA?
-COUGH-
I CAN'T SPEAK TO THE SECOND THING, BUT I'LL GIVE A RESOUNDING "YES" TO YOUR BEING CRAZY.
WELL, OBVIOUSLY-- LOOK WHO I MARRIED.
...THAT WAS A JOKE...
YO, GRAMMA!
TURN OFF THE CARTOONS, WE'RE HERE TO PICK UP--

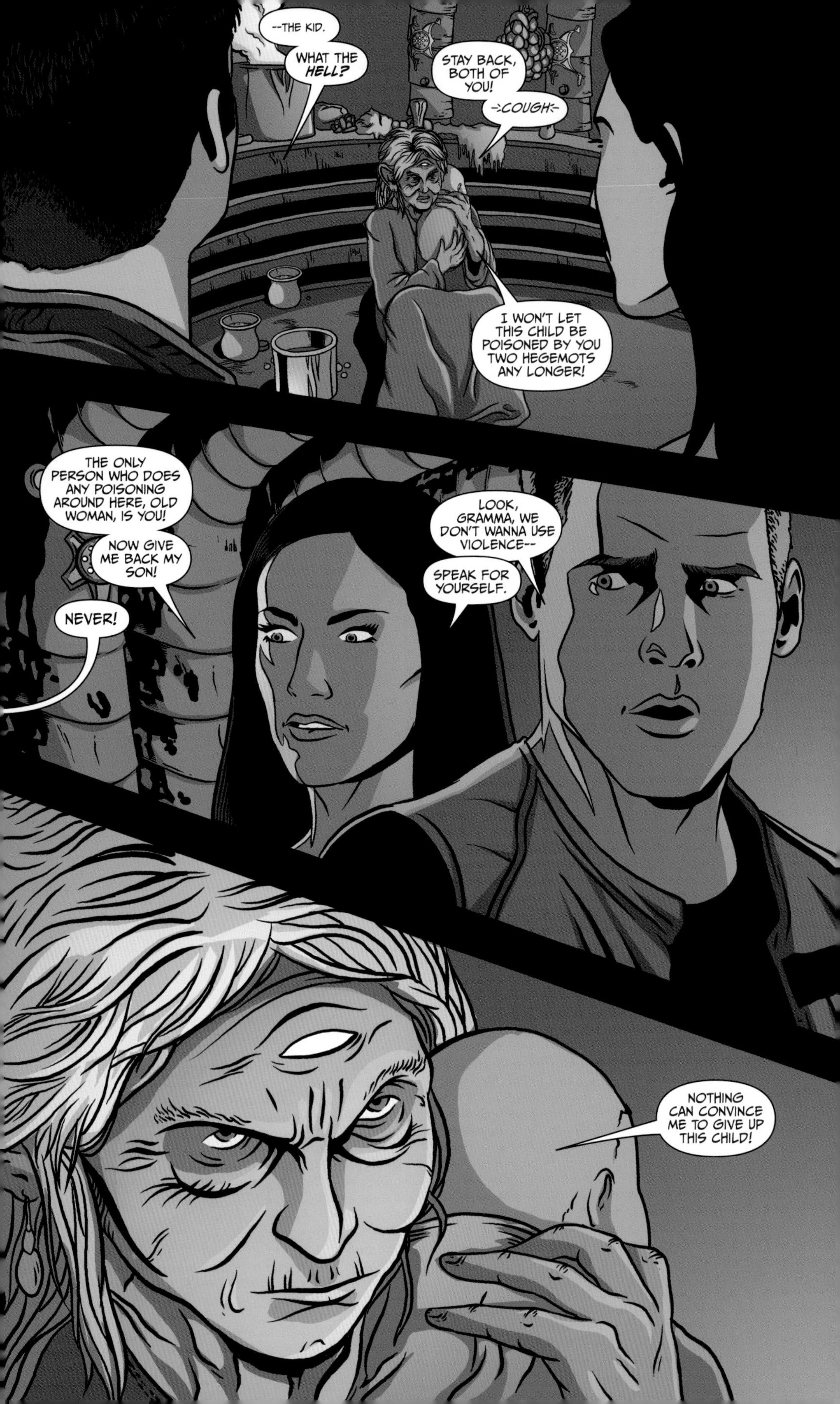
--THE KID.
WHAT THE HELL?
STAY BACK, BOTH OF YOU!
-:COUGH:-
I WON'T LET THIS CHILD BE POISONED BY YOU TWO HEGEMOTS ANY LONGER!
THE ONLY PERSON WHO DOES ANY POISONING AROUND HERE, OLD WOMAN, IS YOU!
NOW GIVE ME BACK MY SON!
NEVER!
LOOK, GRAMMA, WE DON'T WANNA USE VIOLENCE--
SPEAK FOR YOURSELF.
NOTHING CAN CONVINCE ME TO GIVE UP THIS CHILD!

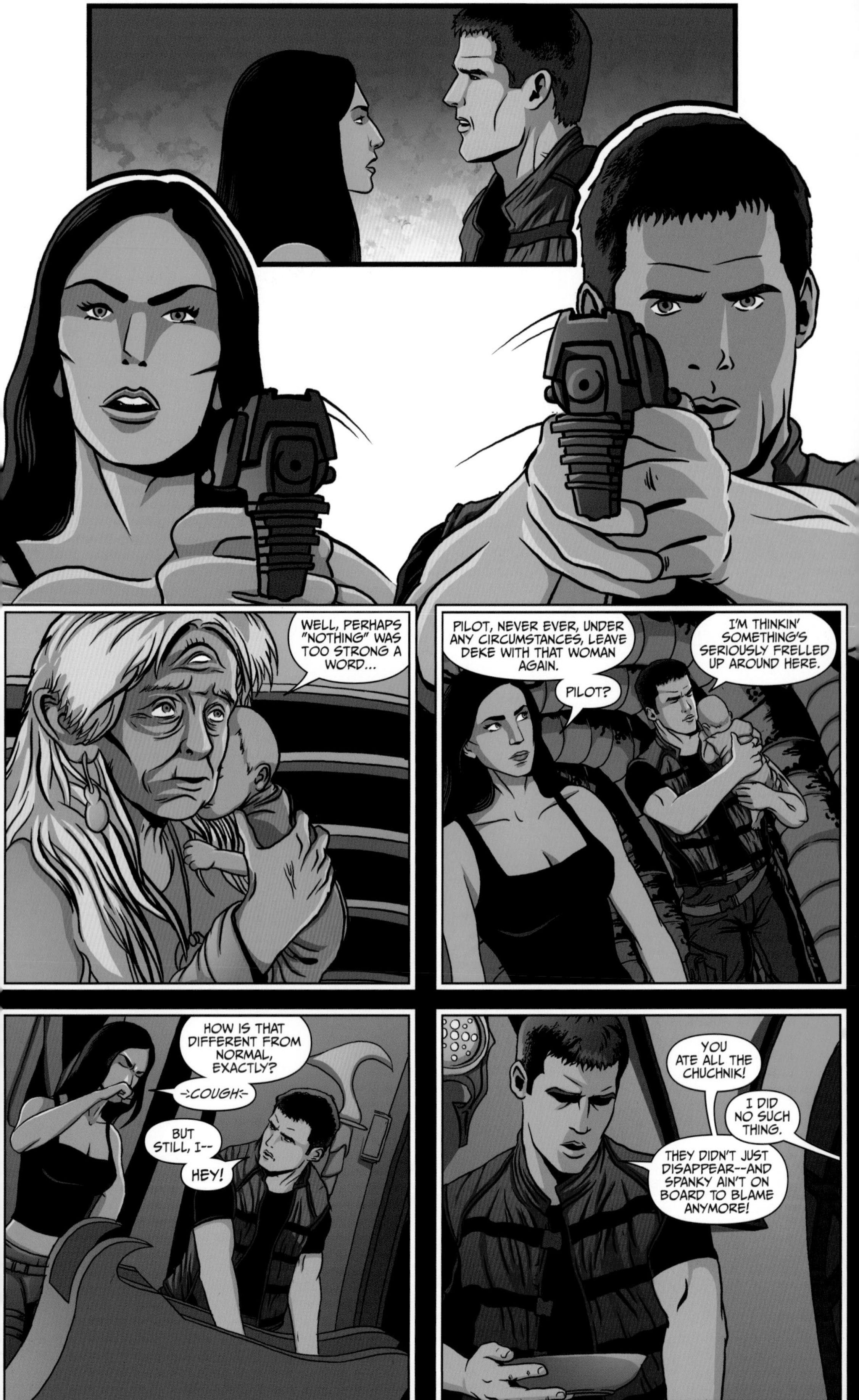
WELL, PERHAPS "NOTHING" WAS TOO STRONG A WORD...
PILOT, NEVER EVER, UNDER ANY CIRCUMSTANCES, LEAVE DEKE WITH THAT WOMAN AGAIN.
PILOT?
I'M THINKIN' SOMETHING'S SERIOUSLY FRELLED UP AROUND HERE.
HOW IS THAT DIFFERENT FROM NORMAL, EXACTLY?
-:-COUGH-:-
BUT STILL, I--
HEY!
YOU ATE ALL THE CHUCHNIK!
I DID NO SUCH THING.
THEY DIDN'T JUST DISAPPEAR--AND SPANKY AIN'T ON BOARD TO BLAME ANYMORE!

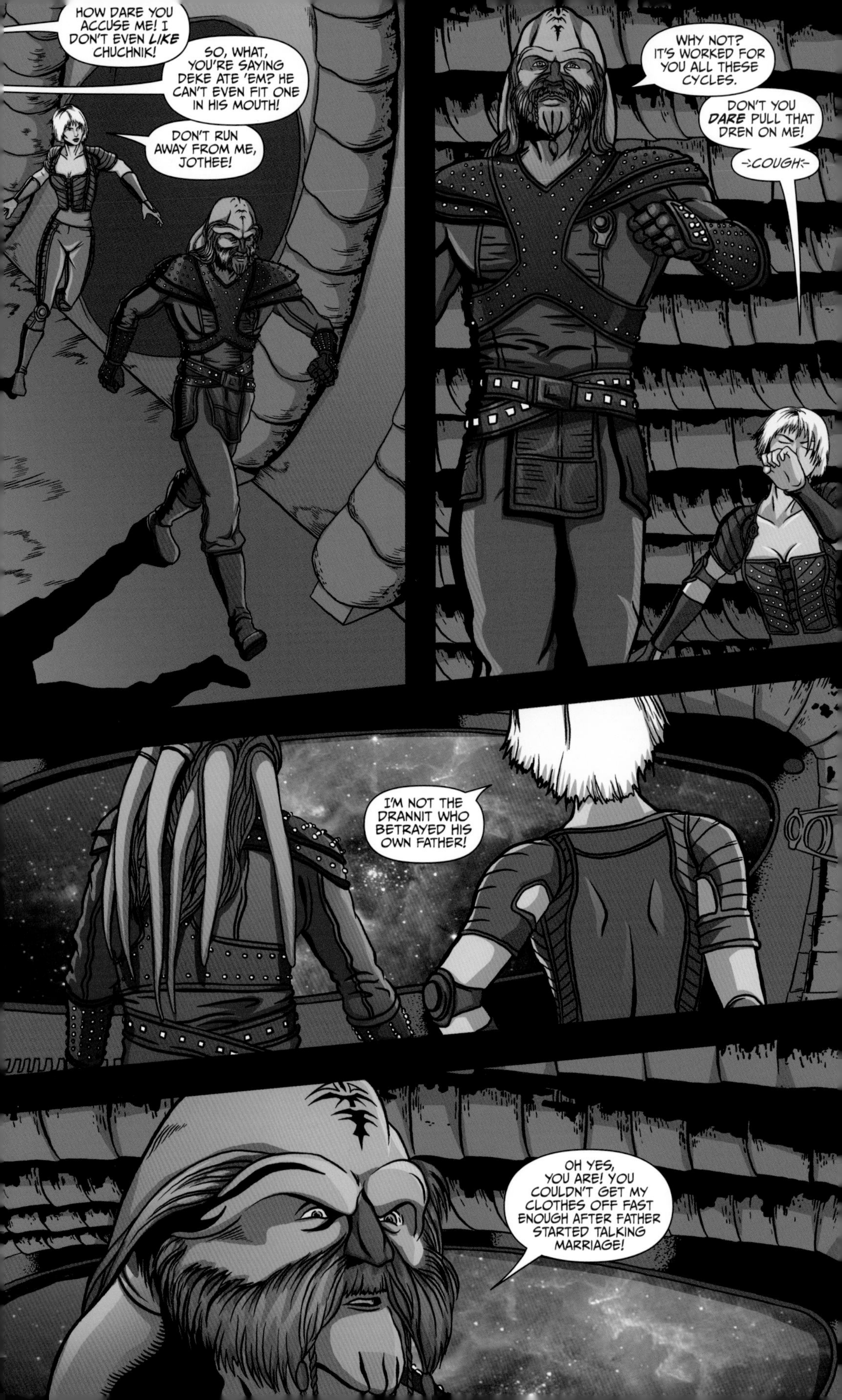
HOW DARE YOU ACCUSE ME! I DON'T EVEN ***LIKE*** CHUCHNIK!
SO, WHAT, YOU'RE SAYING DEKE ATE 'EM? HE CAN'T EVEN FIT ONE IN HIS MOUTH!
DON'T RUN AWAY FROM ME, JOTHEE!
WHY NOT? IT'S WORKED FOR YOU ALL THESE CYCLES.
DON'T YOU ***DARE*** PULL THAT DREN ON ME!
-:-COUGH-:-
I'M NOT THE DRANNIT WHO BETRAYED HIS OWN FATHER!
OH YES, YOU ARE! YOU COULDN'T GET MY CLOTHES OFF FAST ENOUGH AFTER FATHER STARTED TALKING MARRIAGE!

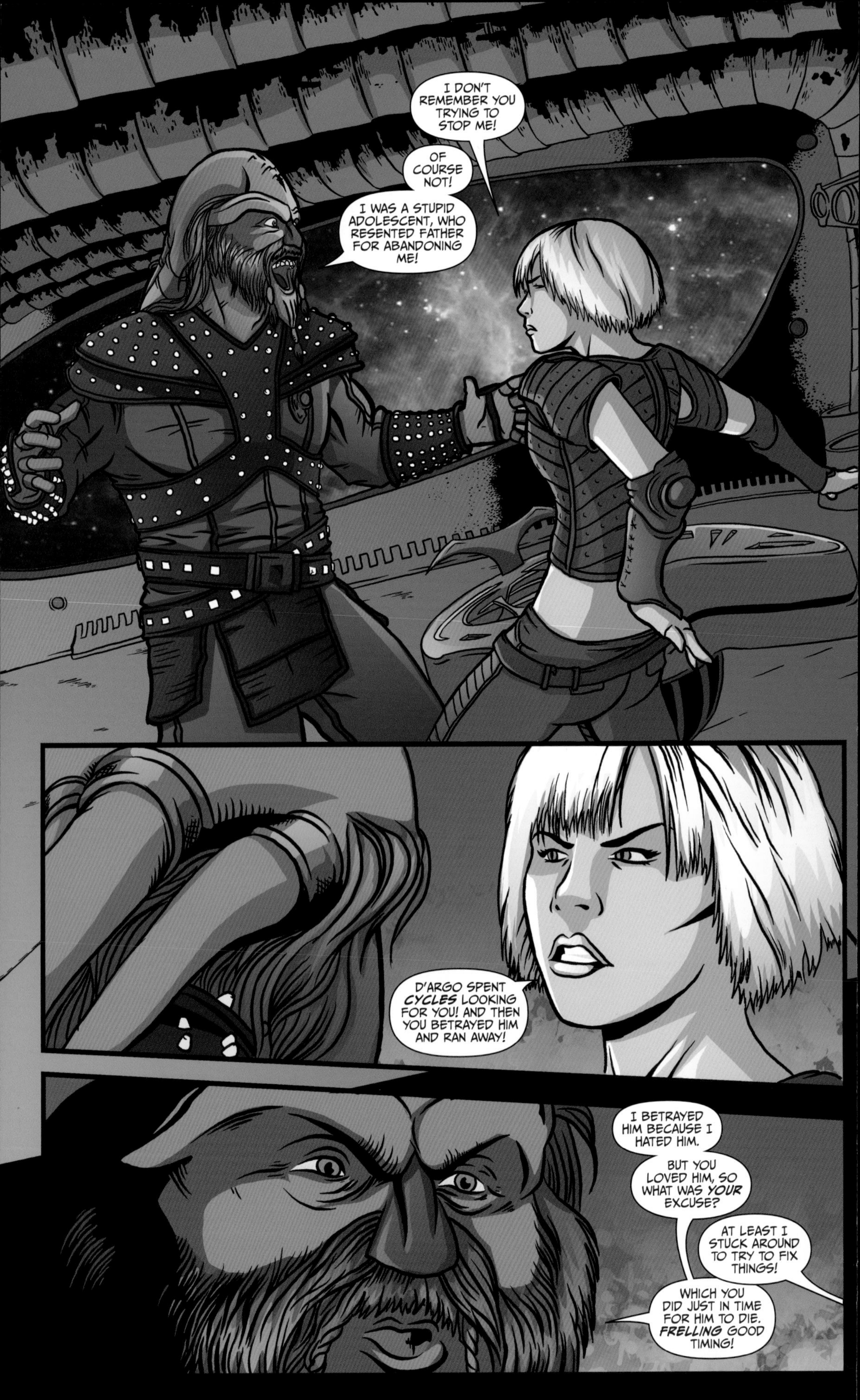
I DON'T REMEMBER YOU TRYING TO STOP ME!
OF COURSE NOT!
I WAS A STUPID ADOLESCENT, WHO RESENTED FATHER FOR ABANDONING ME!
D'ARGO SPENT *CYCLES* LOOKING FOR YOU! AND THEN YOU BETRAYED HIM AND RAN AWAY!
I BETRAYED HIM BECAUSE I HATED HIM.
BUT YOU LOVED HIM, SO WHAT WAS *YOUR* EXCUSE?
AT LEAST I STUCK AROUND TO TRY TO FIX THINGS!
WHICH YOU DID JUST IN TIME FOR HIM TO DIE. *FRELLING* GOOD TIMING!

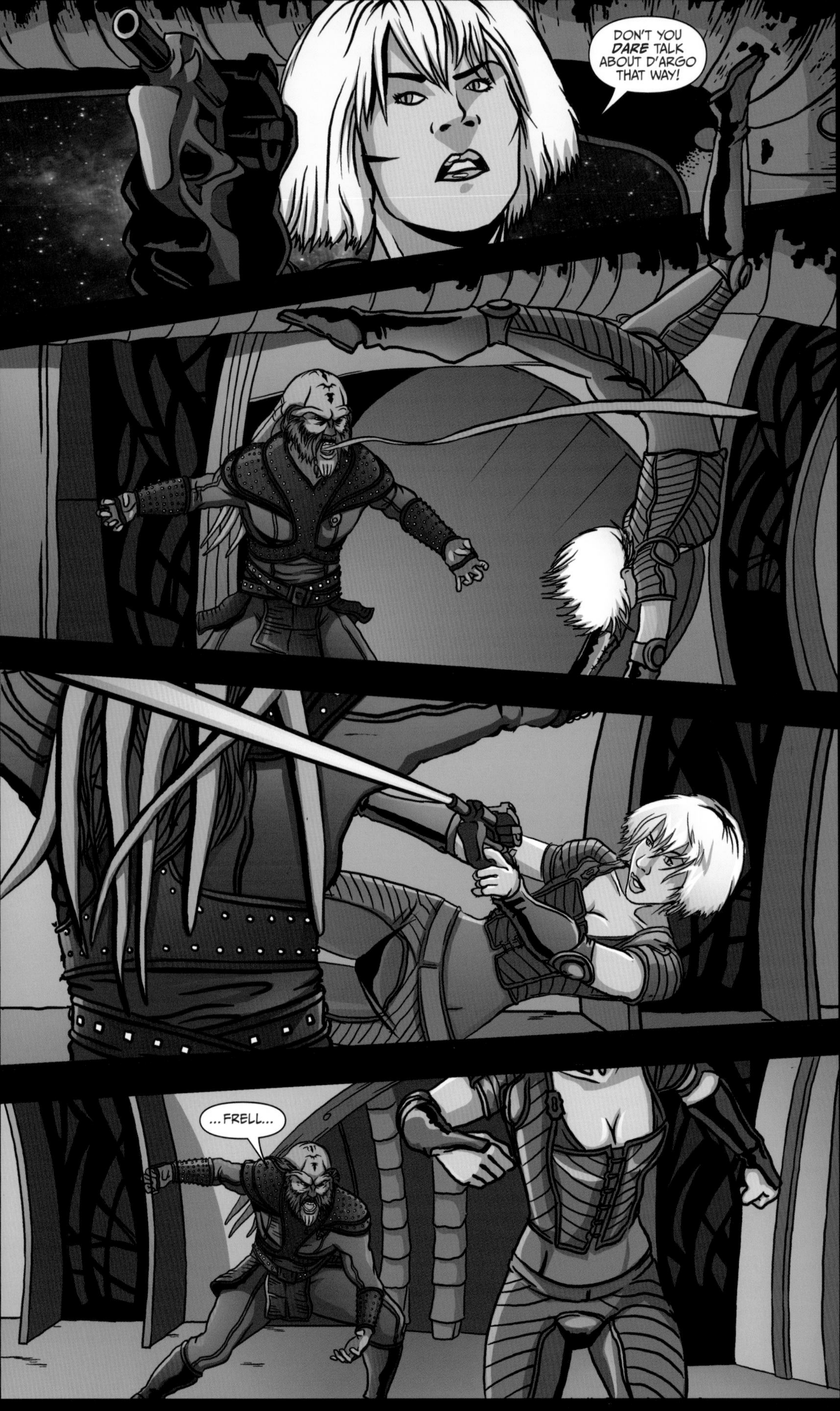
DON'T YOU *DARE* TALK ABOUT D'ARGO THAT WAY!
...FRELL...

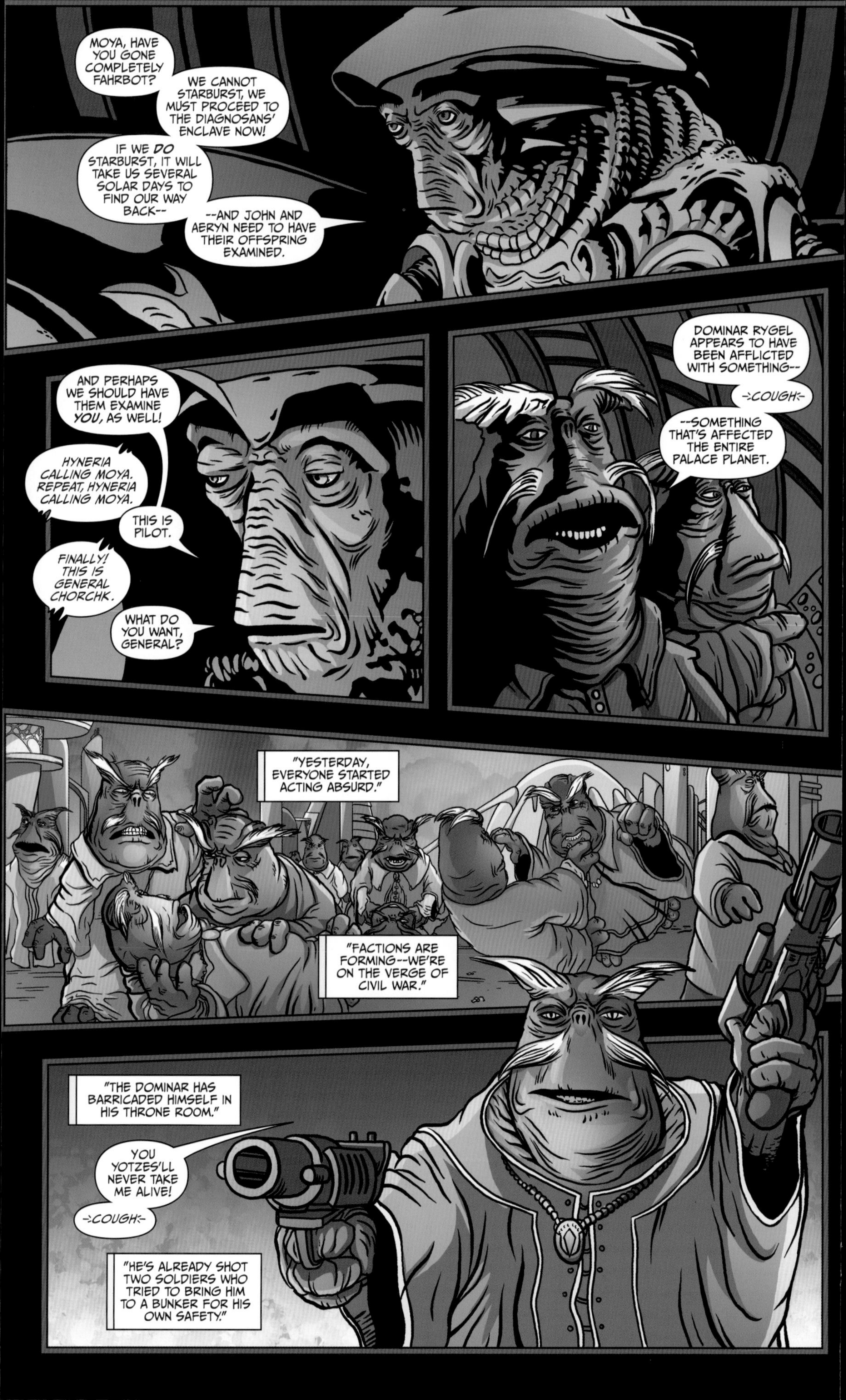
MOYA, HAVE YOU GONE COMPLETELY FAHRBOT?
WE CANNOT STARBURST, WE MUST PROCEED TO THE DIAGNOSANS' ENCLAVE NOW!
IF WE DO STARBURST, IT WILL TAKE US SEVERAL SOLAR DAYS TO FIND OUR WAY BACK--
--AND JOHN AND AERYN NEED TO HAVE THEIR OFFSPRING EXAMINED.
AND PERHAPS WE SHOULD HAVE THEM EXAMINE YOU, AS WELL!
HYNERIA CALLING MOYA. REPEAT, HYNERIA CALLING MOYA.
THIS IS PILOT.
FINALLY! THIS IS GENERAL CHORCHK.
WHAT DO YOU WANT, GENERAL?
DOMINAR RYGEL APPEARS TO HAVE BEEN AFFLICTED WITH SOMETHING--
-:COUGH:-
--SOMETHING THAT'S AFFECTED THE ENTIRE PALACE PLANET.
"YESTERDAY, EVERYONE STARTED ACTING ABSURD."
"FACTIONS ARE FORMING--WE'RE ON THE VERGE OF CIVIL WAR."
"THE DOMINAR HAS BARRICADED HIMSELF IN HIS THRONE ROOM."
YOU YOTZES'LL NEVER TAKE ME ALIVE!
-:COUGH:-
"HE'S ALREADY SHOT TWO SOLDIERS WHO TRIED TO BRING HIM TO A BUNKER FOR HIS OWN SAFETY."

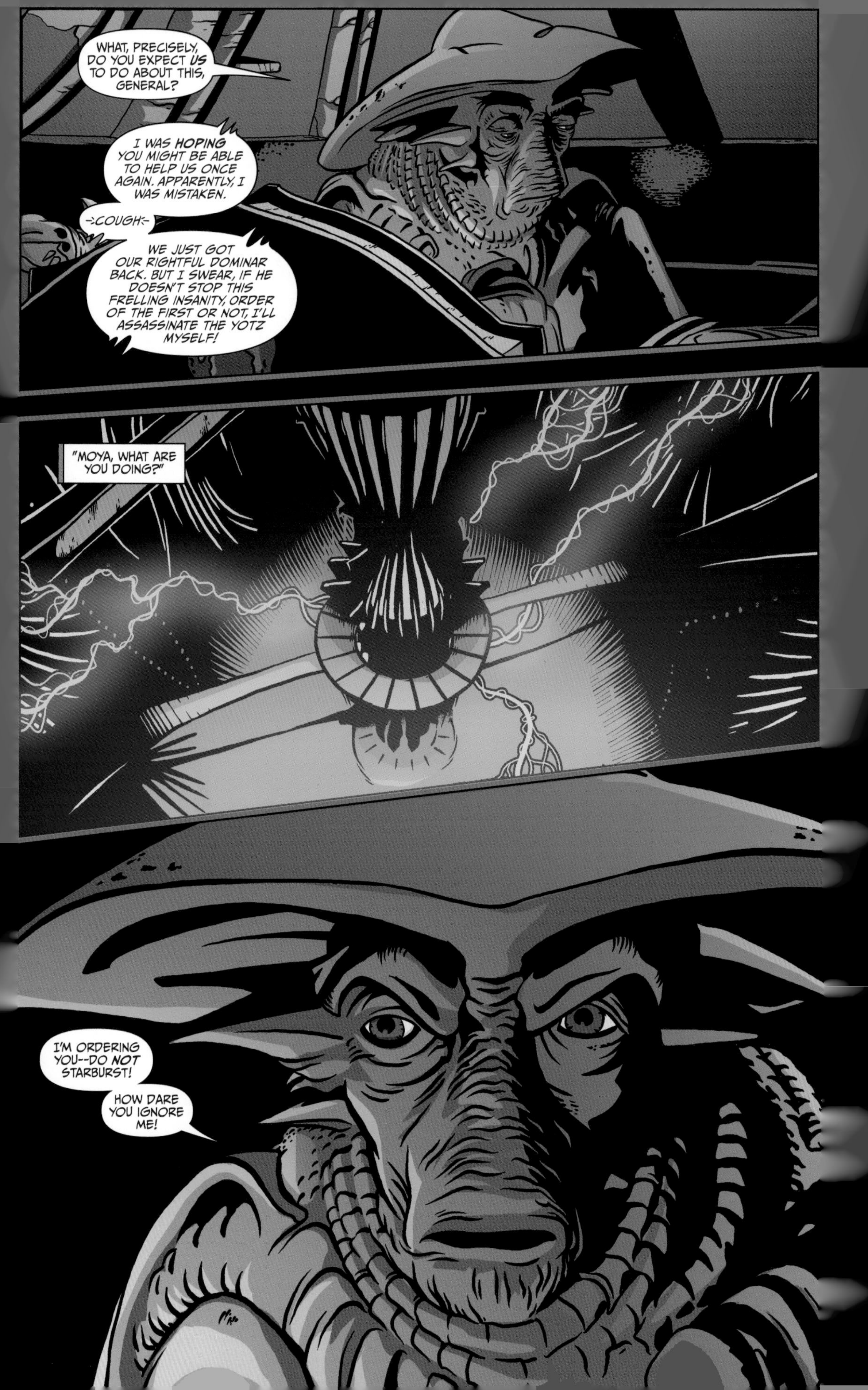
WHAT, PRECISELY, DO YOU EXPECT US TO DO ABOUT THIS, GENERAL?
I WAS HOPING YOU MIGHT BE ABLE TO HELP US ONCE AGAIN. APPARENTLY, I WAS MISTAKEN.
-COUGH-
WE JUST GOT OUR RIGHTFUL DOMINAR BACK. BUT I SWEAR, IF HE DOESN'T STOP THIS FRELLING INSANITY, ORDER OF THE FIRST OR NOT, I'LL ASSASSINATE THE YOTZ MYSELF!
"MOYA, WHAT ARE YOU DOING?"
I'M ORDERING YOU--DO NOT STARBURST!
HOW DARE YOU IGNORE ME!

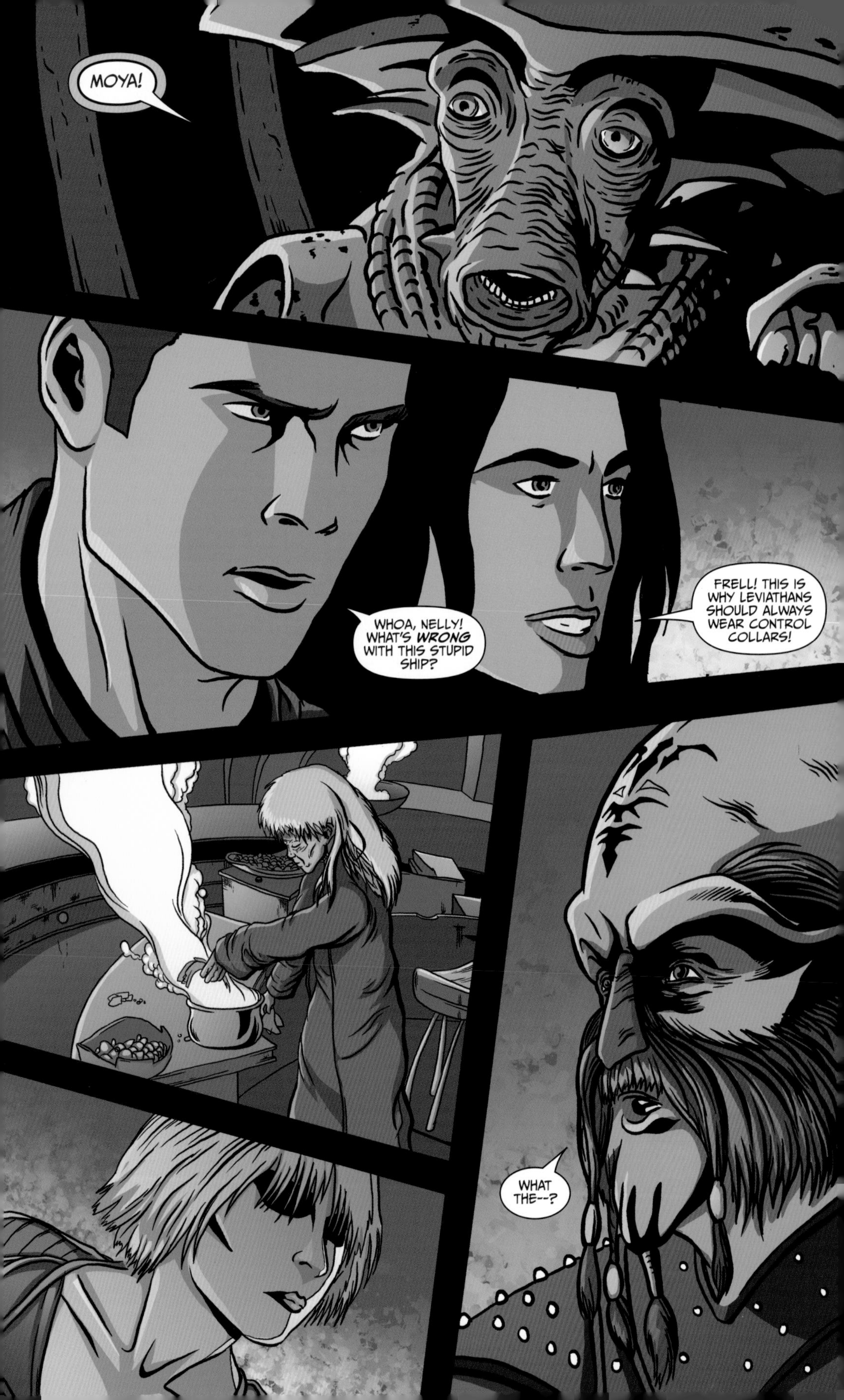
MOYA!
WHOA, NELLY! WHAT'S **WRONG** WITH THIS STUPID SHIP?
FRELL! THIS IS WHY LEVIATHANS SHOULD ALWAYS WEAR CONTROL COLLARS!
WHAT THE--?

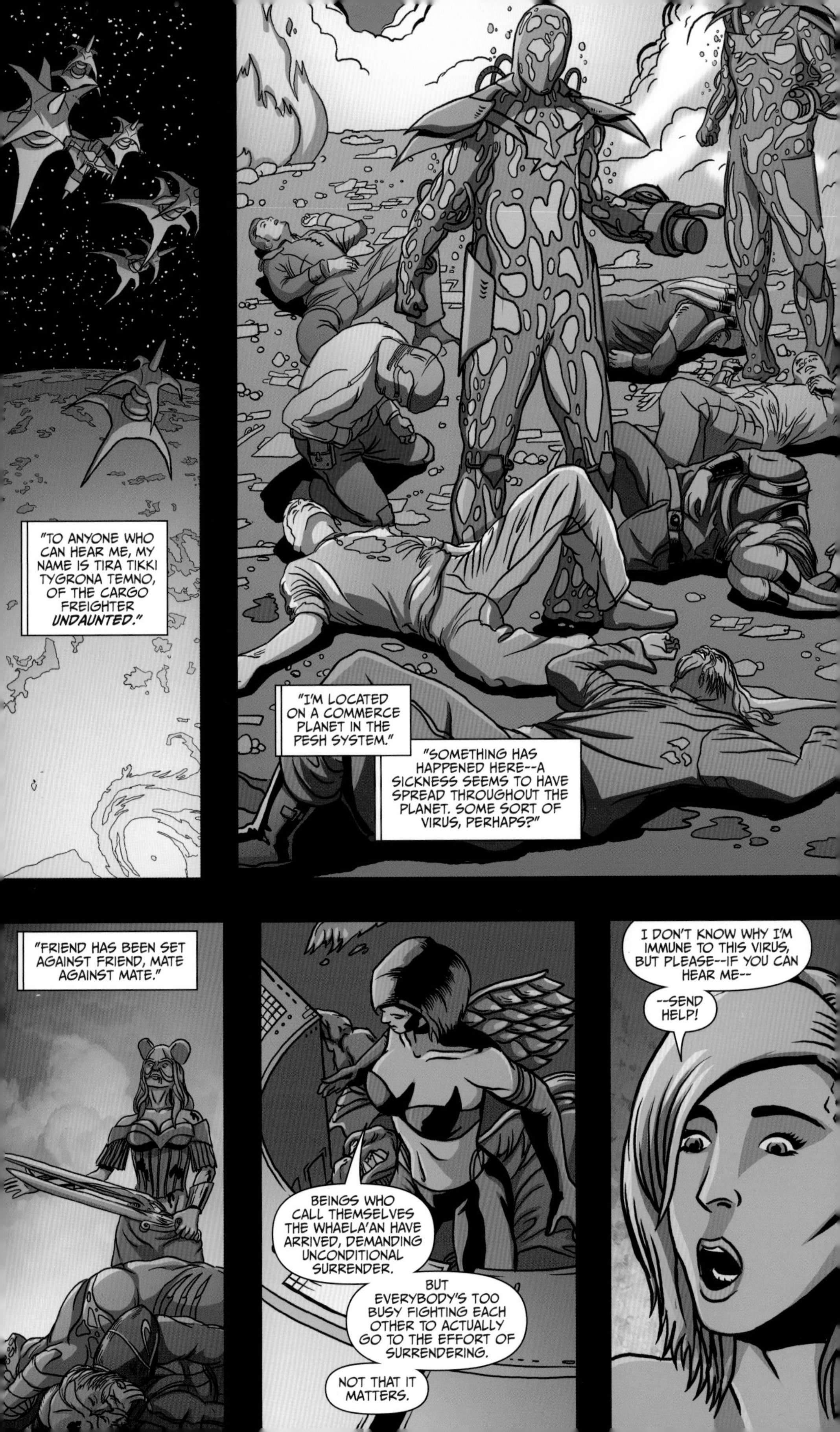
"TO ANYONE WHO CAN HEAR ME, MY NAME IS TIRA TIKKI TYGRONA TEMNO, OF THE CARGO FREIGHTER *UNDAUNTED.*"
"I'M LOCATED ON A COMMERCE PLANET IN THE PESH SYSTEM."
"SOMETHING HAS HAPPENED HERE--A SICKNESS SEEMS TO HAVE SPREAD THROUGHOUT THE PLANET. SOME SORT OF VIRUS, PERHAPS?"
"FRIEND HAS BEEN SET AGAINST FRIEND, MATE AGAINST MATE."
BEINGS WHO CALL THEMSELVES THE WHAELA'AN HAVE ARRIVED, DEMANDING UNCONDITIONAL SURRENDER.
BUT EVERYBODY'S TOO BUSY FIGHTING EACH OTHER TO ACTUALLY GO TO THE EFFORT OF SURRENDERING.
NOT THAT IT MATTERS.
I DON'T KNOW WHY I'M IMMUNE TO THIS VIRUS, BUT PLEASE--IF YOU CAN HEAR ME--
--SEND HELP!

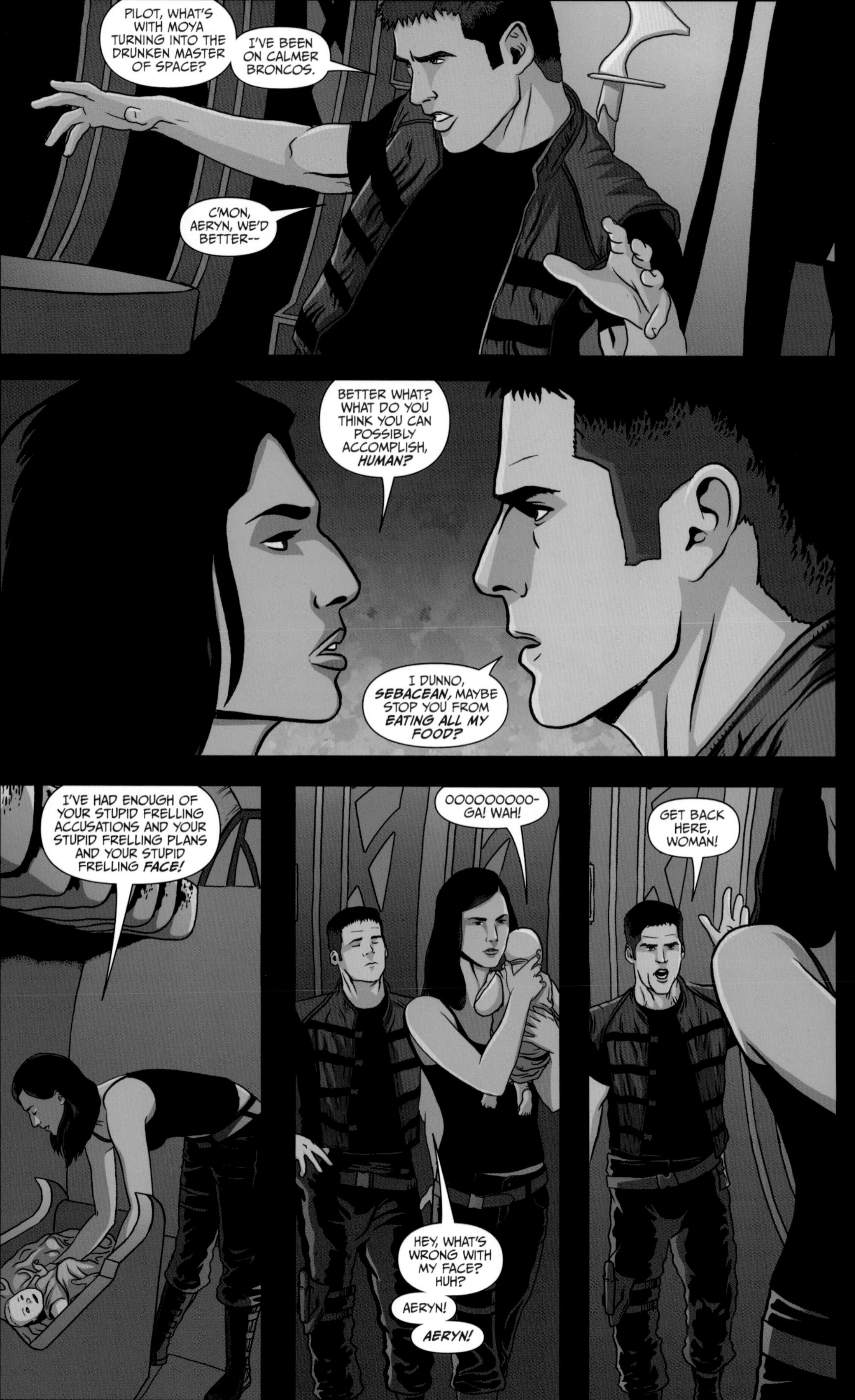
PILOT, WHAT'S WITH MOYA TURNING INTO THE DRUNKEN MASTER OF SPACE?
I'VE BEEN ON CALMER BRONCOS.
C'MON, AERYN, WE'D BETTER--
BETTER WHAT? WHAT DO YOU THINK YOU CAN POSSIBLY ACCOMPLISH, *HUMAN?*
I DUNNO, *SEBACEAN,* MAYBE STOP YOU FROM *EATING ALL MY FOOD?*
I'VE HAD ENOUGH OF YOUR STUPID FRELLING ACCUSATIONS AND YOUR STUPID FRELLING PLANS AND YOUR STUPID FRELLING *FACE!*
OOOOOOOOO-GA! WAH!
HEY, WHAT'S WRONG WITH MY FACE? HUH?
AERYN!
AERYN!
GET BACK HERE, WOMAN!

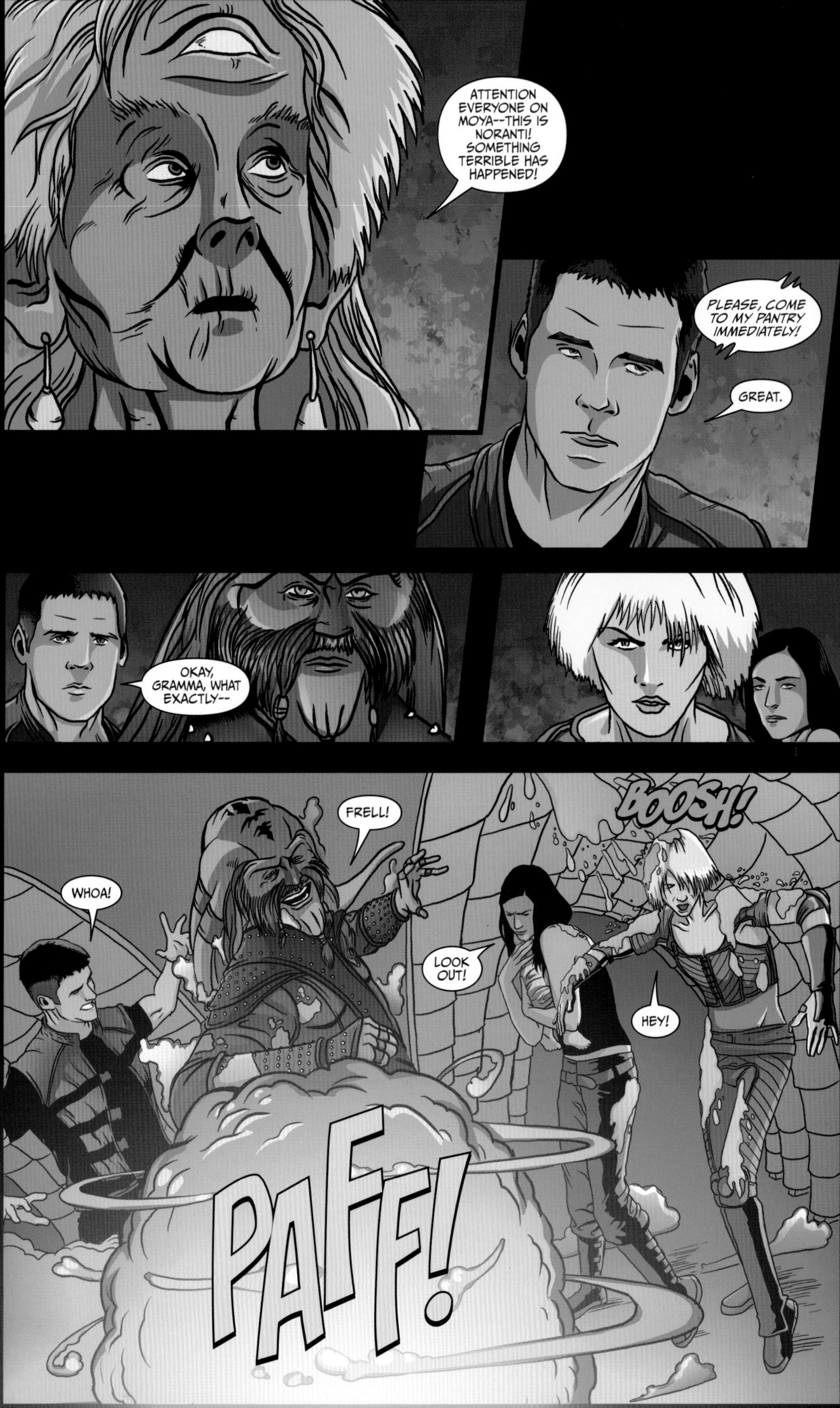
ATTENTION EVERYONE ON MOYA--THIS IS NORANTI! SOMETHING TERRIBLE HAS HAPPENED!
PLEASE, COME TO MY PANTRY IMMEDIATELY!
GREAT.
OKAY, GRAMMA, WHAT EXACTLY--
BOOSH!
FRELL!
WHOA!
LOOK OUT!
HEY!
PAFF!

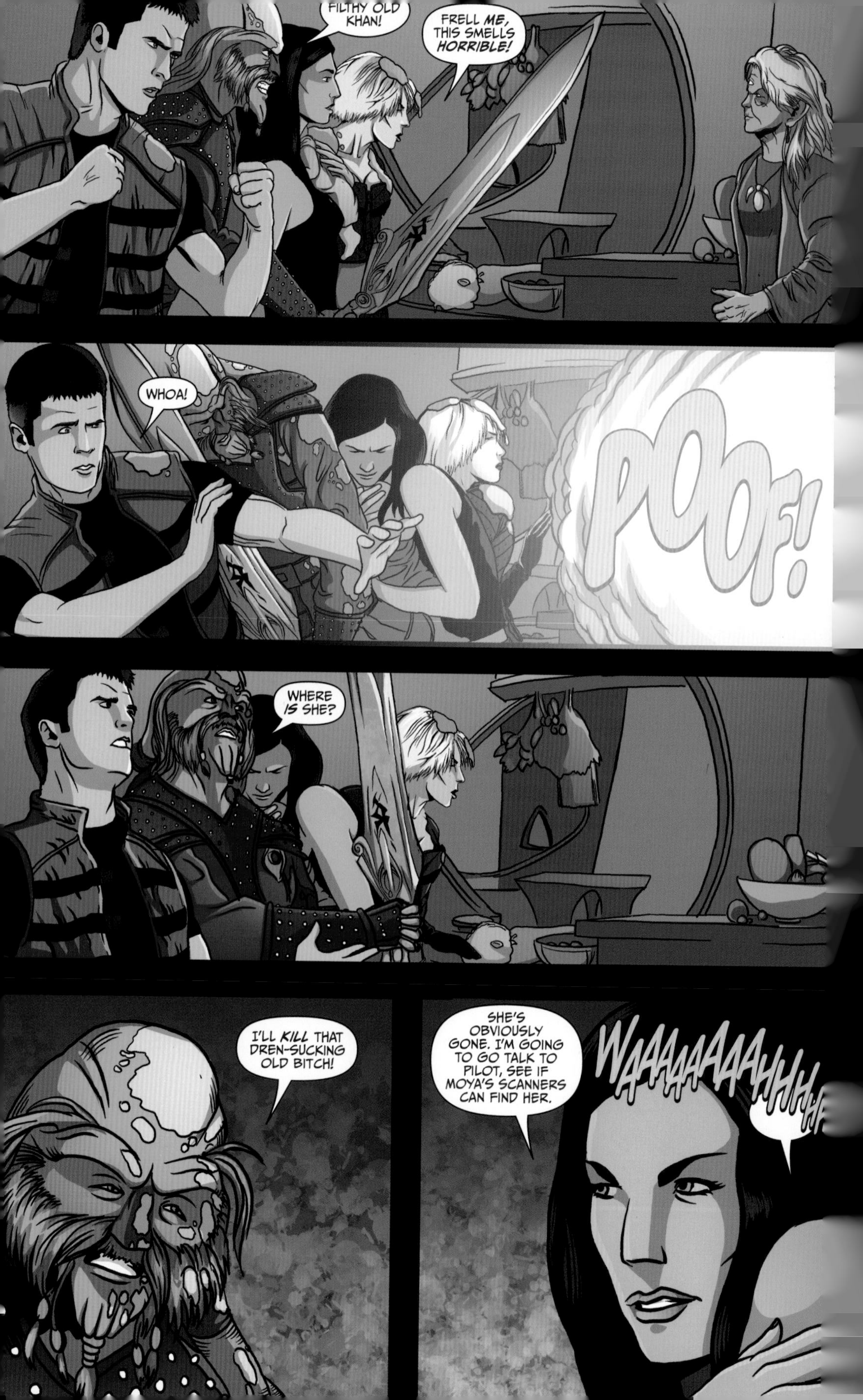
FILTHY OLD KHAN!
FRELL *ME*, THIS SMELLS *HORRIBLE!*
WHOA!
POOF!
WHERE *IS* SHE?
I'LL *KILL* THAT DREN-SUCKING OLD BITCH!
SHE'S OBVIOUSLY GONE. I'M GOING TO GO TALK TO PILOT, SEE IF MOYA'S SCANNERS CAN FIND HER.
WAAAAAAAAHHHH

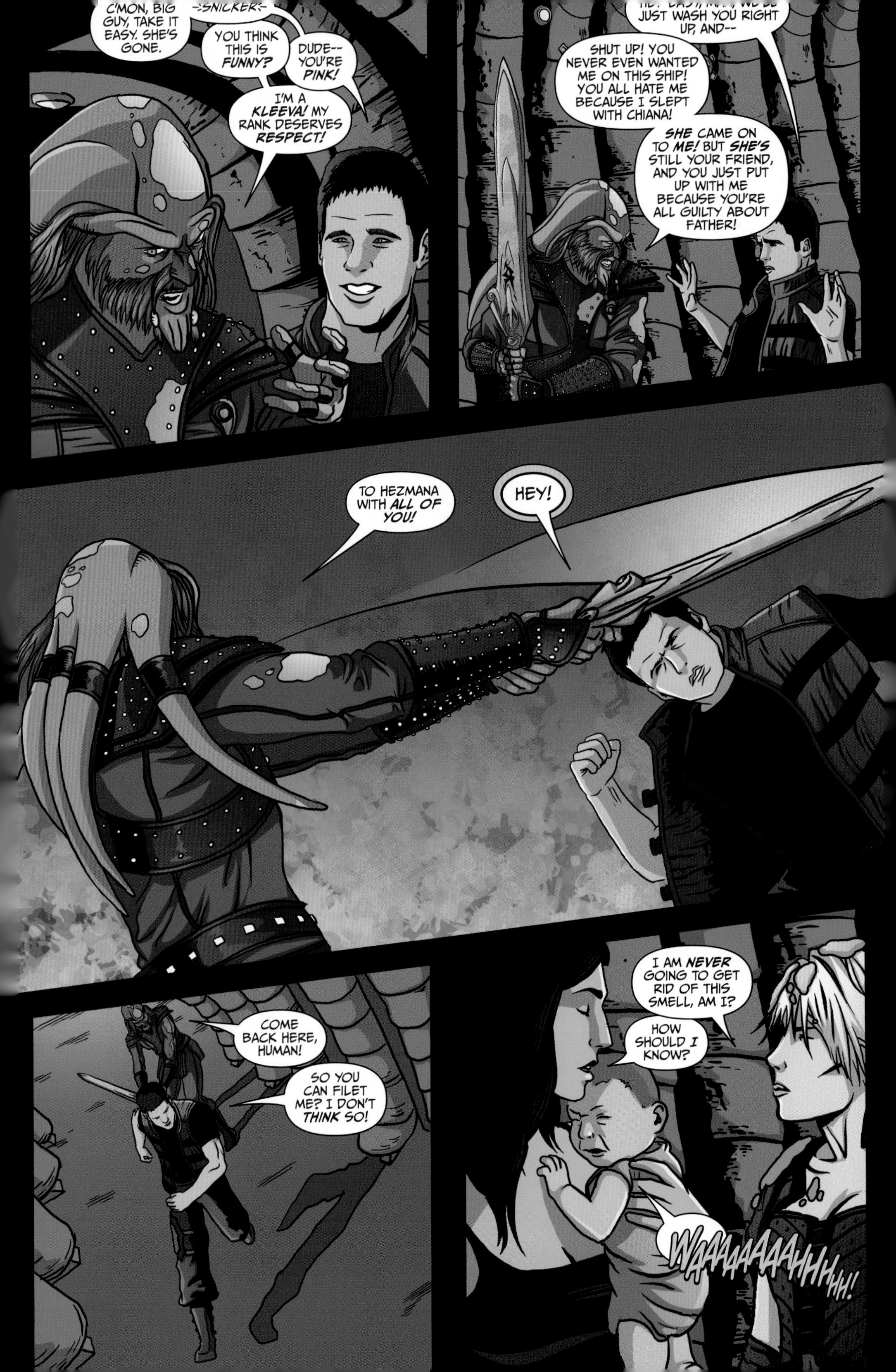
C'MON, BIG GUY, TAKE IT EASY. SHE'S GONE.
-SNICKER-
YOU THINK THIS IS *FUNNY?*
DUDE-- YOU'RE *PINK!*
I'M A *KLEEVA!* MY RANK DESERVES *RESPECT!*
JUST WASH YOU RIGHT UP, AND--
SHUT UP! YOU NEVER EVEN WANTED ME ON THIS SHIP! YOU ALL HATE ME BECAUSE I SLEPT WITH CHIANA!
SHE CAME ON TO *ME!* BUT *SHE'S* STILL YOUR FRIEND, AND YOU JUST PUT UP WITH ME BECAUSE YOU'RE ALL GUILTY ABOUT FATHER!
TO HEZMANA WITH *ALL OF YOU!*
HEY!
COME BACK HERE, HUMAN!
SO YOU CAN FILET ME? I DON'T *THINK* SO!
I AM *NEVER* GOING TO GET RID OF THIS SMELL, AM I?
HOW SHOULD *I* KNOW?
WAAAAAAAAHHHHH!

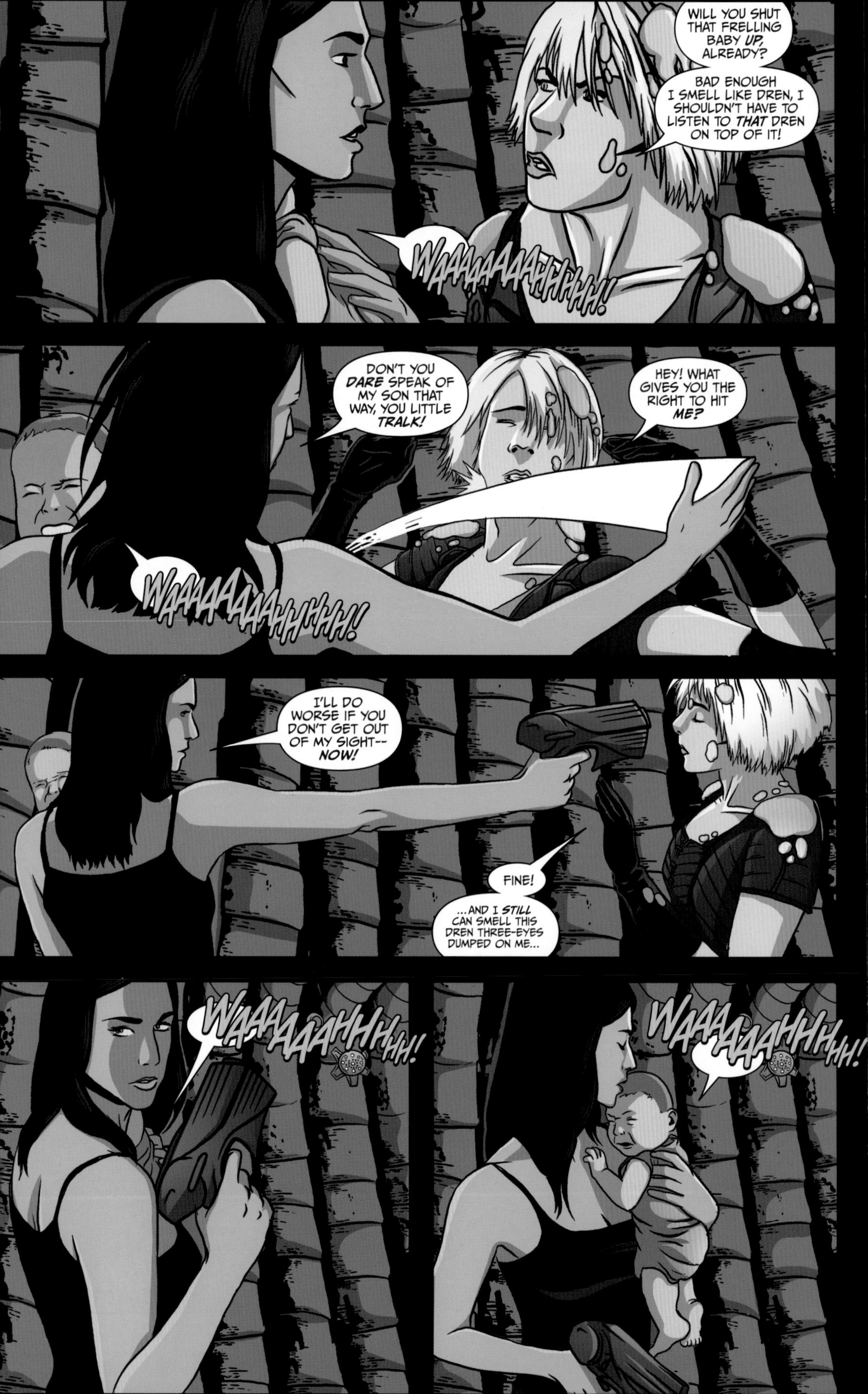
WILL YOU SHUT THAT FRELLING BABY *UP*, ALREADY?
BAD ENOUGH I SMELL LIKE DREN, I SHOULDN'T HAVE TO LISTEN TO *THAT* DREN ON TOP OF IT!
WAAAAAAAAAHHHHHH!
DON'T YOU *DARE* SPEAK OF MY SON THAT WAY, YOU LITTLE *TRALK!*
HEY! WHAT GIVES YOU THE RIGHT TO HIT *ME?*
WAAAAAAAAAHHHHH!
I'LL DO WORSE IF YOU DON'T GET OUT OF MY SIGHT-- *NOW!*
FINE!
...AND I *STILL* CAN SMELL THIS DREN THREE-EYES DUMPED ON ME...
WAAAAAAAHHHHHH!
WAAAAAAAHHHHHH!

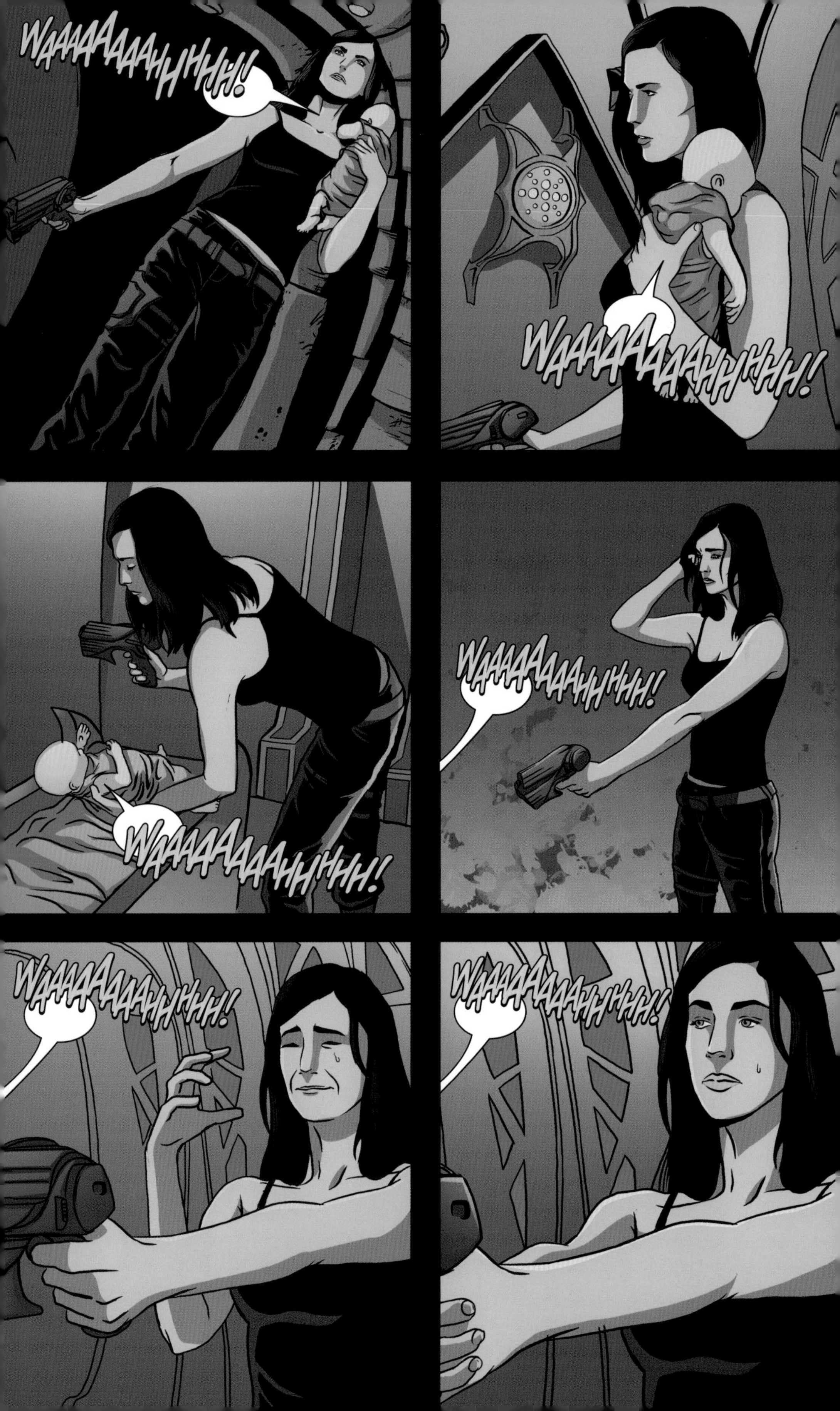

WAAAAAAAAHHHHH!
WAAAAAAAAAHHHHH!
WAAAAAAAAHHHHH!
WAAAAAAAAHHHHH!
WAAAAAAAAHHHHH!
WAAAAAAAAHHHHH!

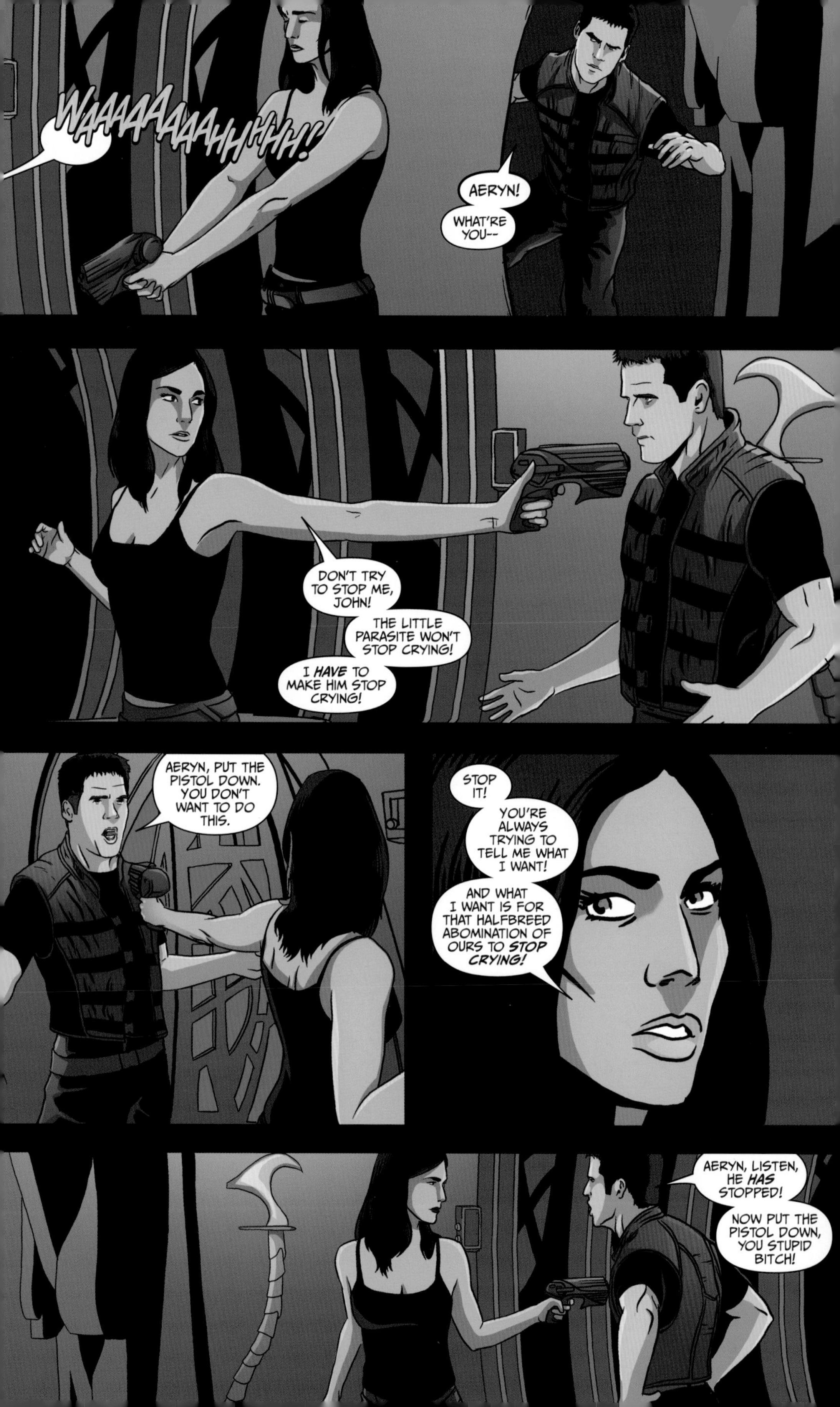
WAAAAAAAAAHHHHH!
AERYN!
WHAT'RE YOU--
DON'T TRY TO STOP ME, JOHN!
THE LITTLE PARASITE WON'T STOP CRYING!
I *HAVE* TO MAKE HIM STOP CRYING!
AERYN, PUT THE PISTOL DOWN. YOU DON'T WANT TO DO THIS.
STOP IT!
YOU'RE ALWAYS TRYING TO TELL ME WHAT I WANT!
AND WHAT I WANT IS FOR THAT HALFBREED ABOMINATION OF OURS TO *STOP CRYING!*
AERYN, LISTEN, HE *HAS* STOPPED!
NOW PUT THE PISTOL DOWN, YOU STUPID BITCH!

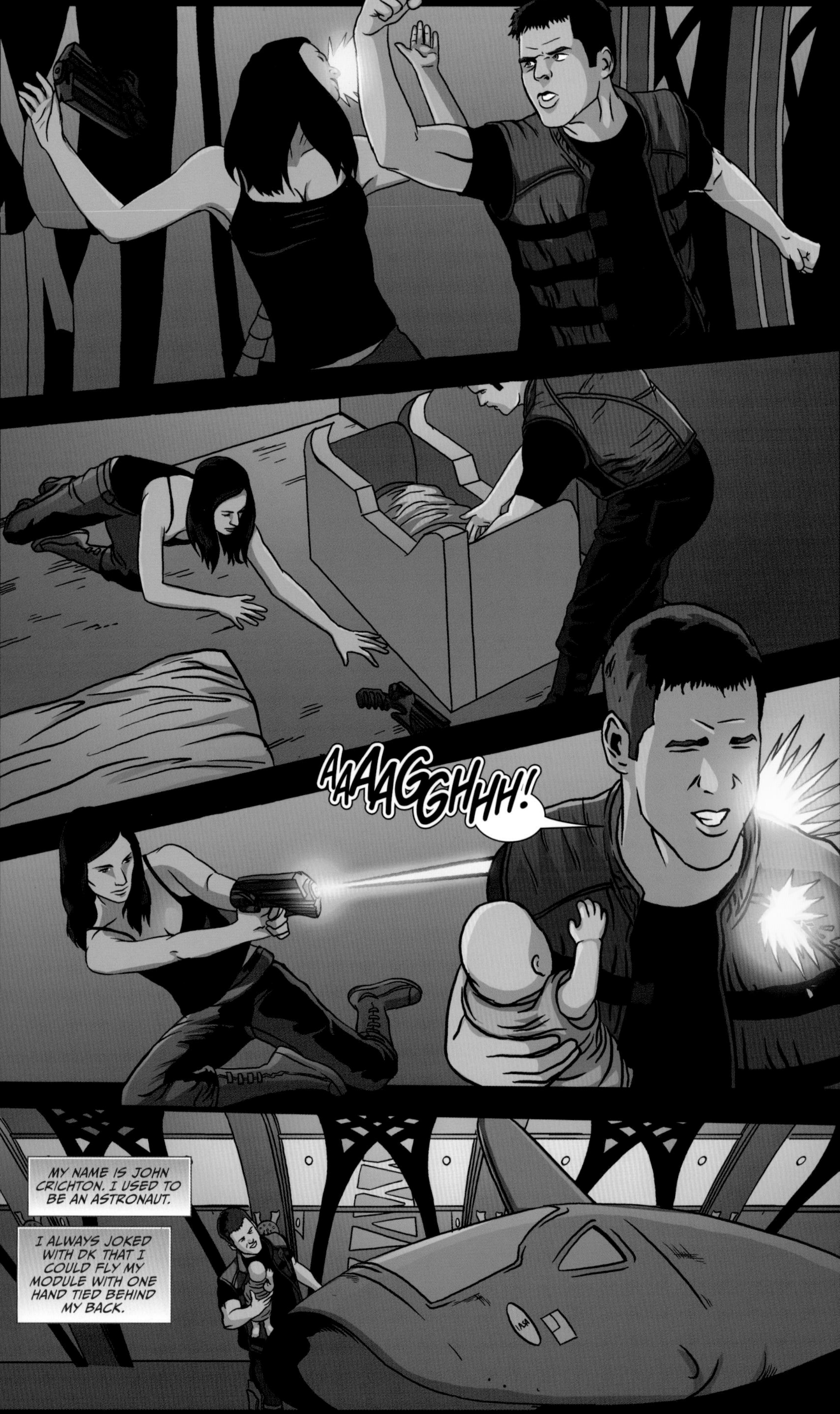
AAAAGGHHH!
MY NAME IS JOHN CRICHTON. I USED TO BE AN ASTRONAUT.
I ALWAYS JOKED WITH DK THAT I COULD FLY MY MODULE WITH ONE HAND TIED BEHIND MY BACK.

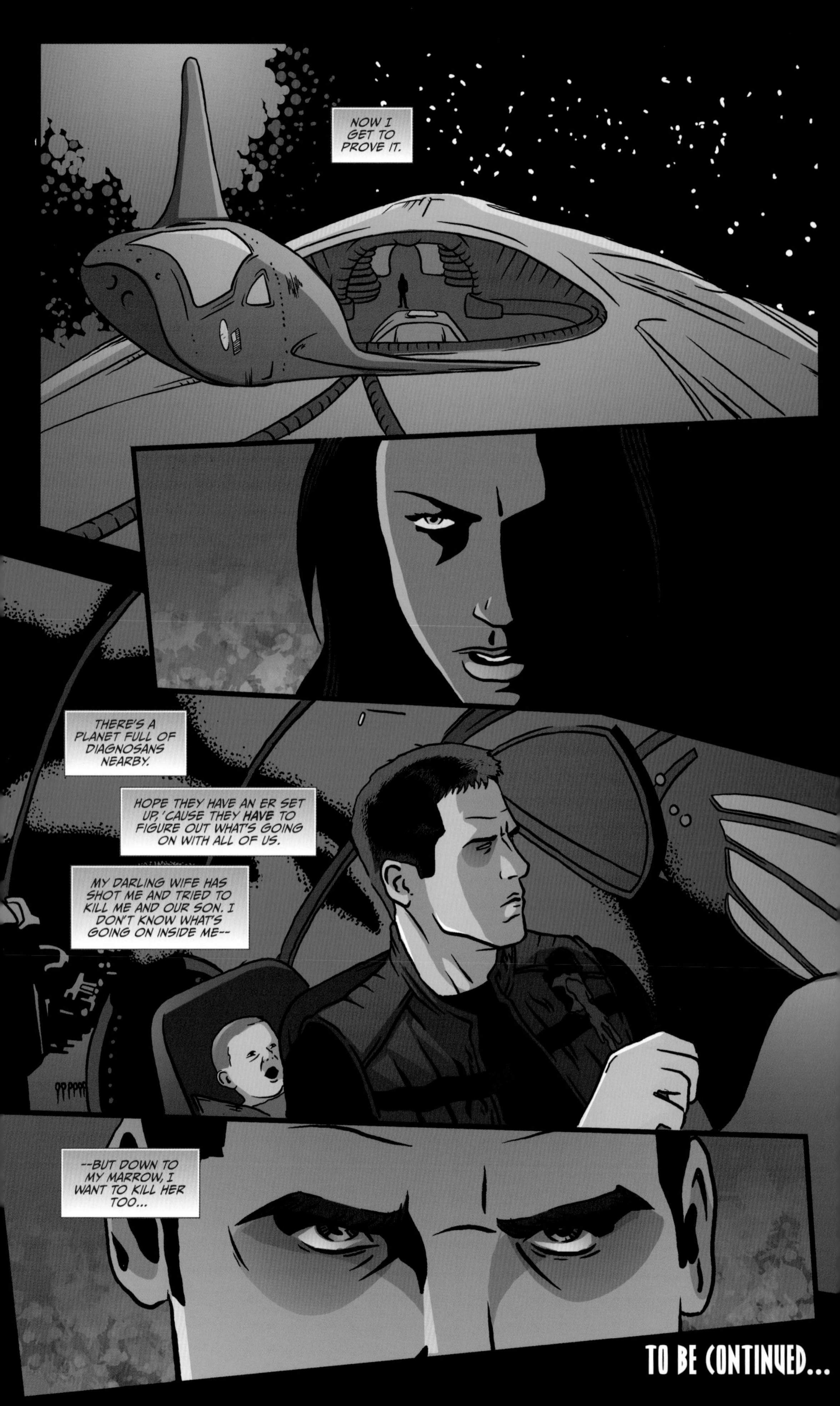
NOW I GET TO PROVE IT.
THERE'S A PLANET FULL OF DIAGNOSANS NEARBY.
HOPE THEY HAVE AN ER SET UP, 'CAUSE THEY HAVE TO FIGURE OUT WHAT'S GOING ON WITH ALL OF US.
MY DARLING WIFE HAS SHOT ME AND TRIED TO KILL ME AND OUR SON. I DON'T KNOW WHAT'S GOING ON INSIDE ME--
--BUT DOWN TO MY MARROW, I WANT TO KILL HER TOO...
TO BE CONTINUED...

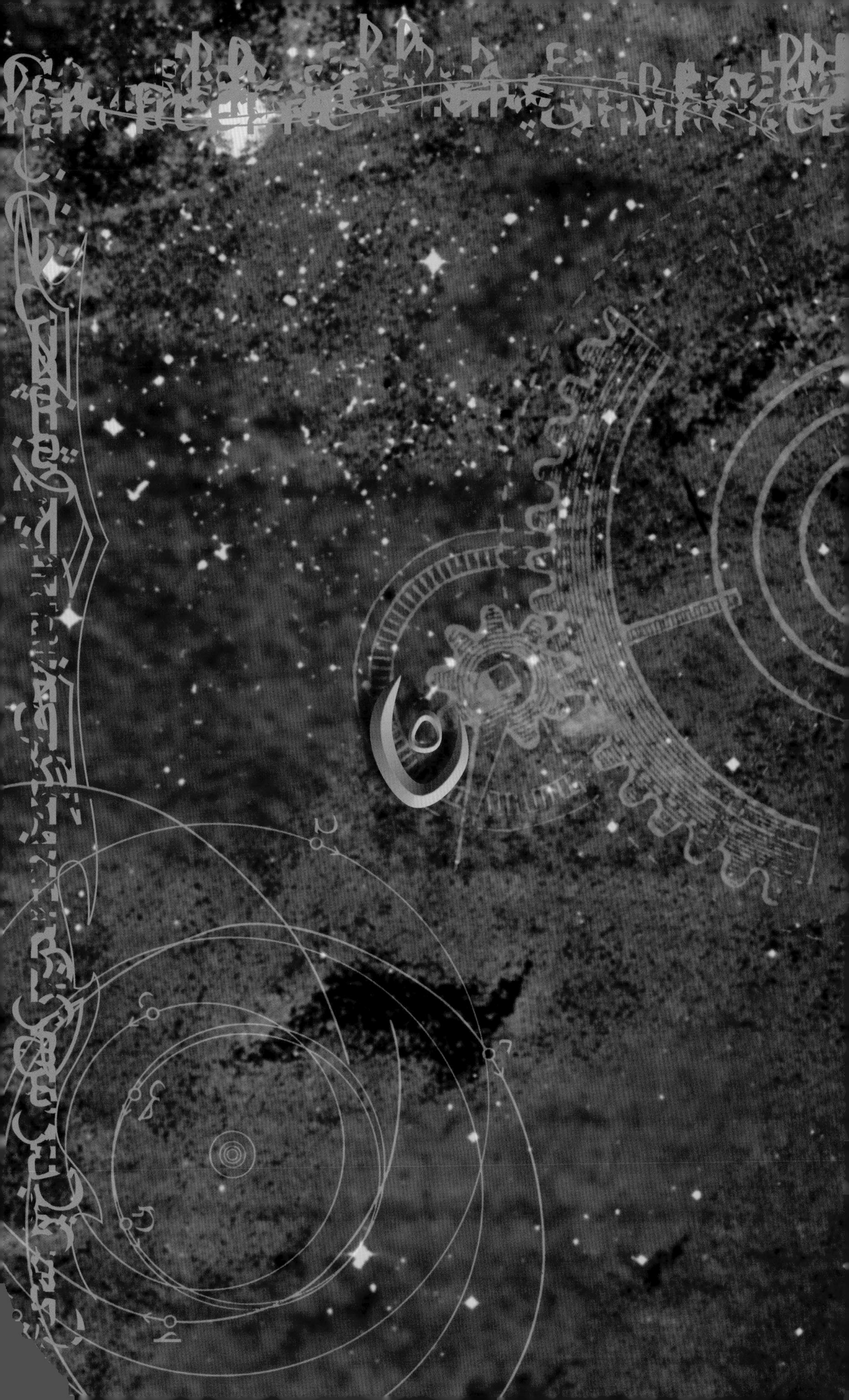

BOOK THREE

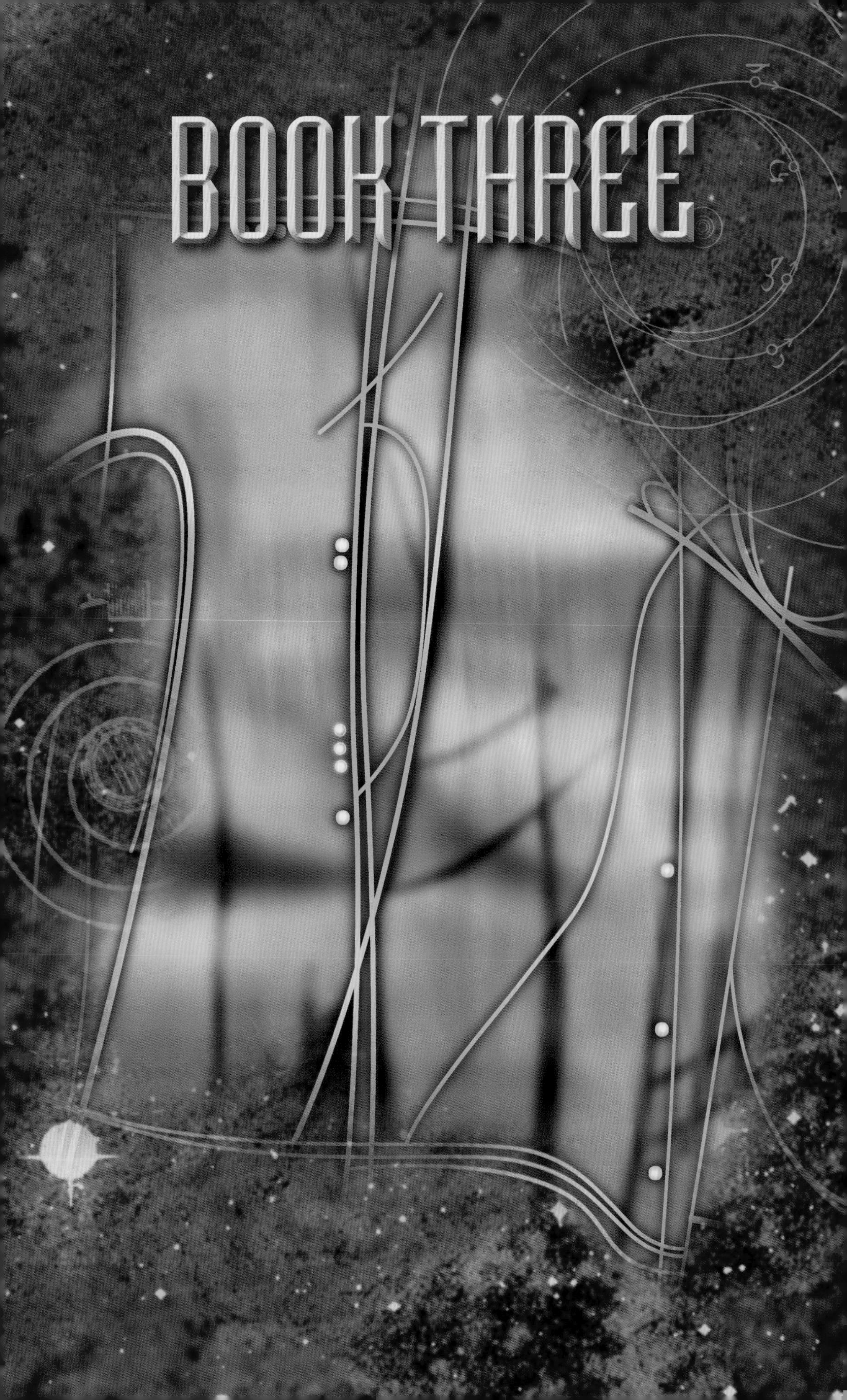

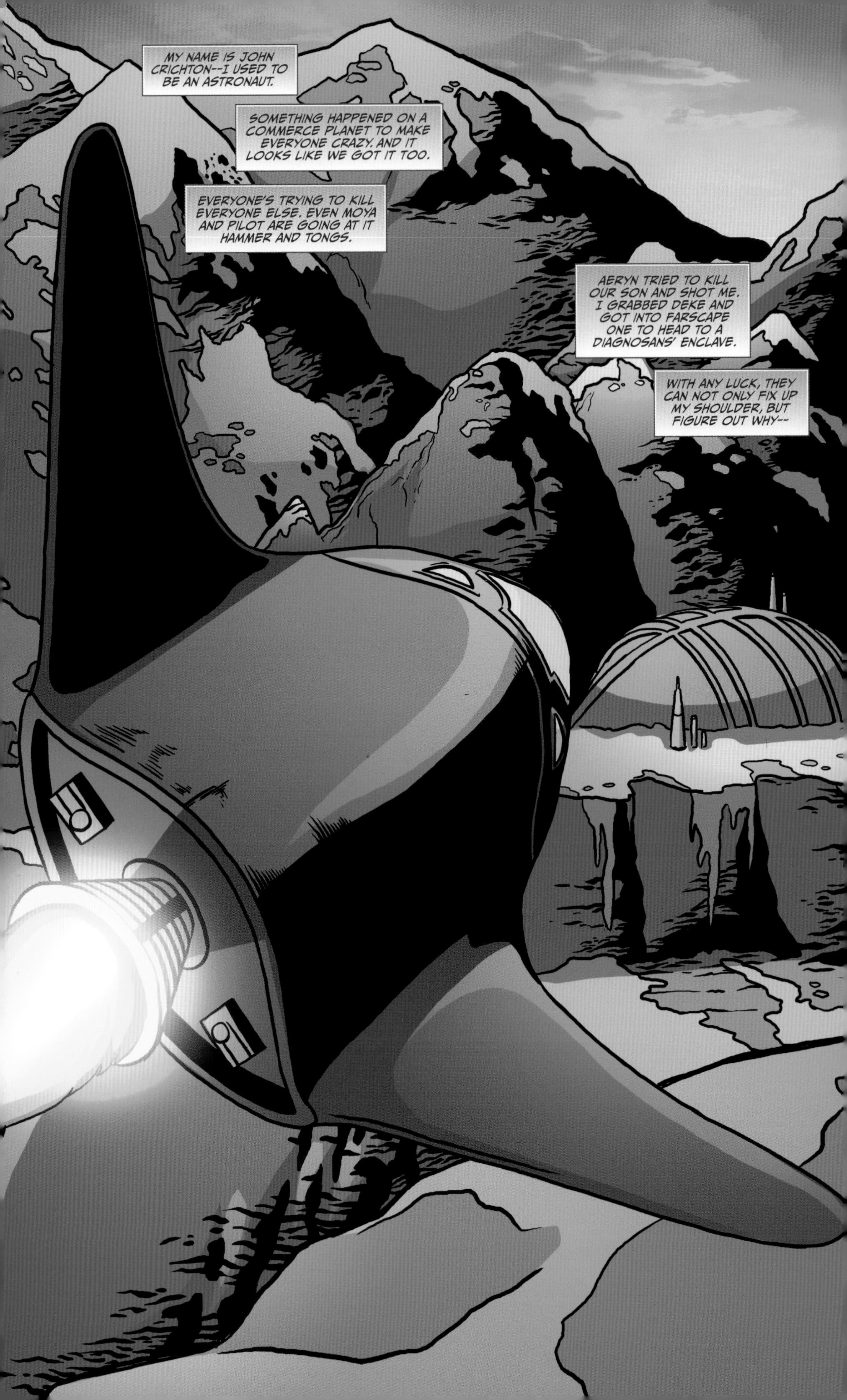
MY NAME IS JOHN CRICHTON--I USED TO BE AN ASTRONAUT.
SOMETHING HAPPENED ON A COMMERCE PLANET TO MAKE EVERYONE CRAZY. AND IT LOOKS LIKE WE GOT IT TOO.
EVERYONE'S TRYING TO KILL EVERYONE ELSE. EVEN MOYA AND PILOT ARE GOING AT IT HAMMER AND TONGS.
AERYN TRIED TO KILL OUR SON AND SHOT ME. I GRABBED DEKE AND GOT INTO FARSCAPE ONE TO HEAD TO A DIAGNOSANS' ENCLAVE.
WITH ANY LUCK, THEY CAN NOT ONLY FIX UP MY SHOULDER, BUT FIGURE OUT WHY--

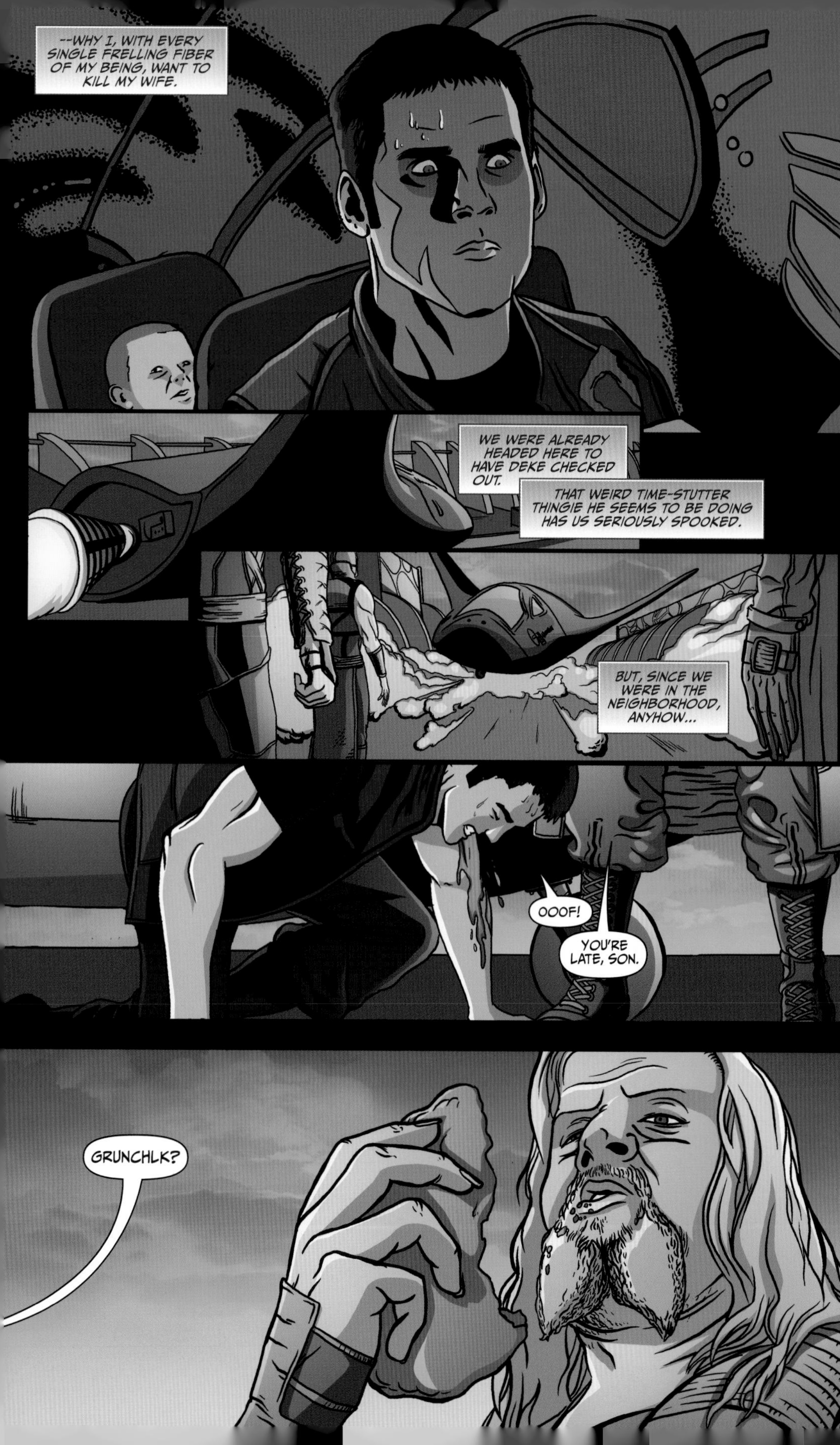
--WHY I, WITH EVERY SINGLE FRELLING FIBER OF MY BEING, WANT TO KILL MY WIFE.
WE WERE ALREADY HEADED HERE TO HAVE DEKE CHECKED OUT.
THAT WEIRD TIME-STUTTER THINGIE HE SEEMS TO BE DOING HAS US SERIOUSLY SPOOKED.
BUT, SINCE WE WERE IN THE NEIGHBORHOOD, ANYHOW...
OOOF!
YOU'RE LATE, SON.
GRUNCHLK?

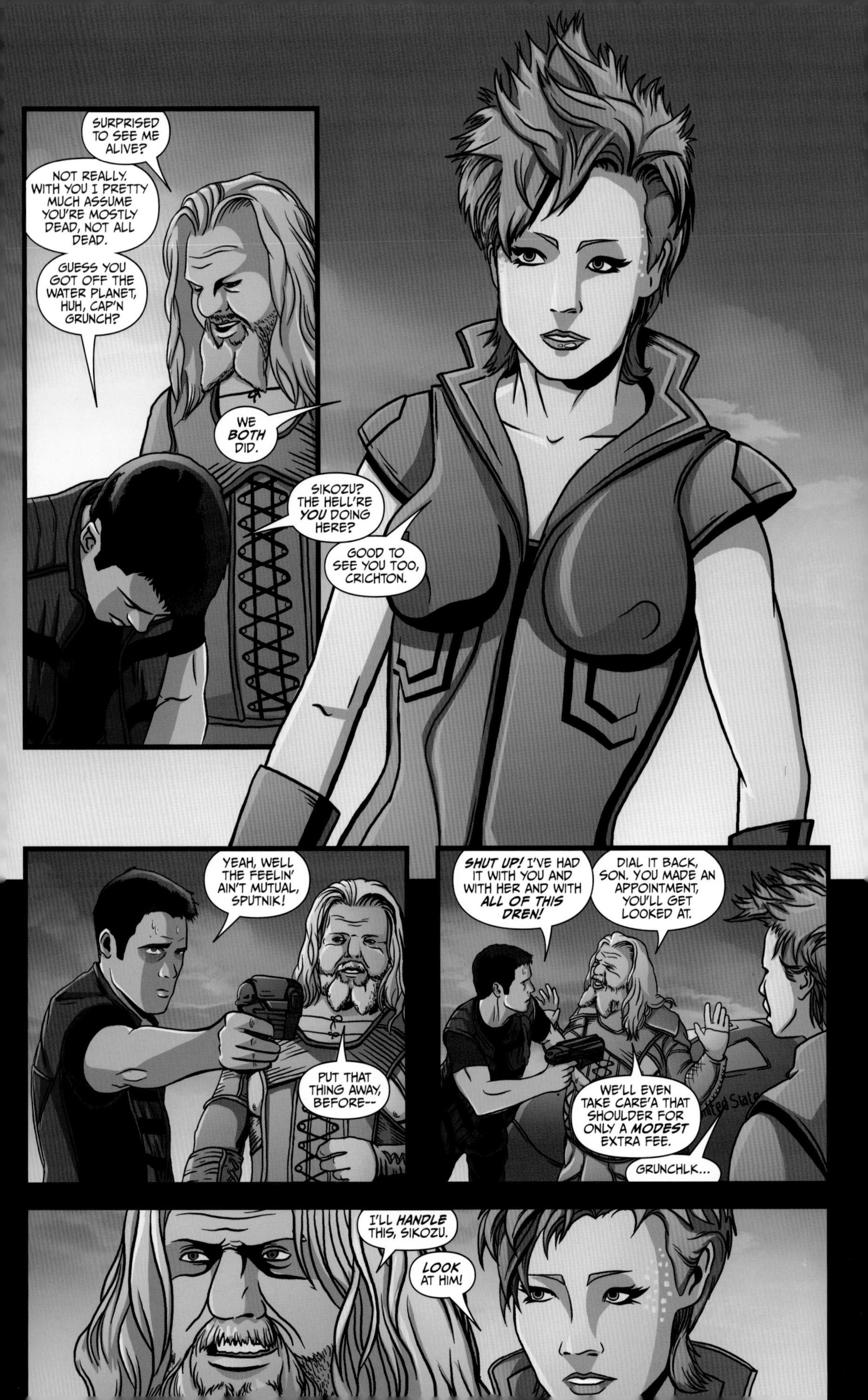
SURPRISED TO SEE ME ALIVE?
NOT REALLY. WITH YOU I PRETTY MUCH ASSUME YOU'RE MOSTLY DEAD, NOT ALL DEAD.
GUESS YOU GOT OFF THE WATER PLANET, HUH, CAP'N GRUNCH?
WE *BOTH* DID.
SIKOZU? THE HELL'RE *YOU* DOING HERE?
GOOD TO SEE YOU TOO, CRICHTON.
YEAH, WELL THE FEELIN' AIN'T MUTUAL, SPUTNIK!
PUT THAT THING AWAY, BEFORE--
SHUT UP! I'VE HAD IT WITH YOU AND WITH HER AND WITH *ALL OF THIS DREN!*
DIAL IT BACK, SON. YOU MADE AN APPOINTMENT, YOU'LL GET LOOKED AT.
WE'LL EVEN TAKE CARE'A THAT SHOULDER FOR ONLY A *MODEST* EXTRA FEE.
GRUNCHLK...
I'LL *HANDLE* THIS, SIKOZU.
LOOK AT HIM!

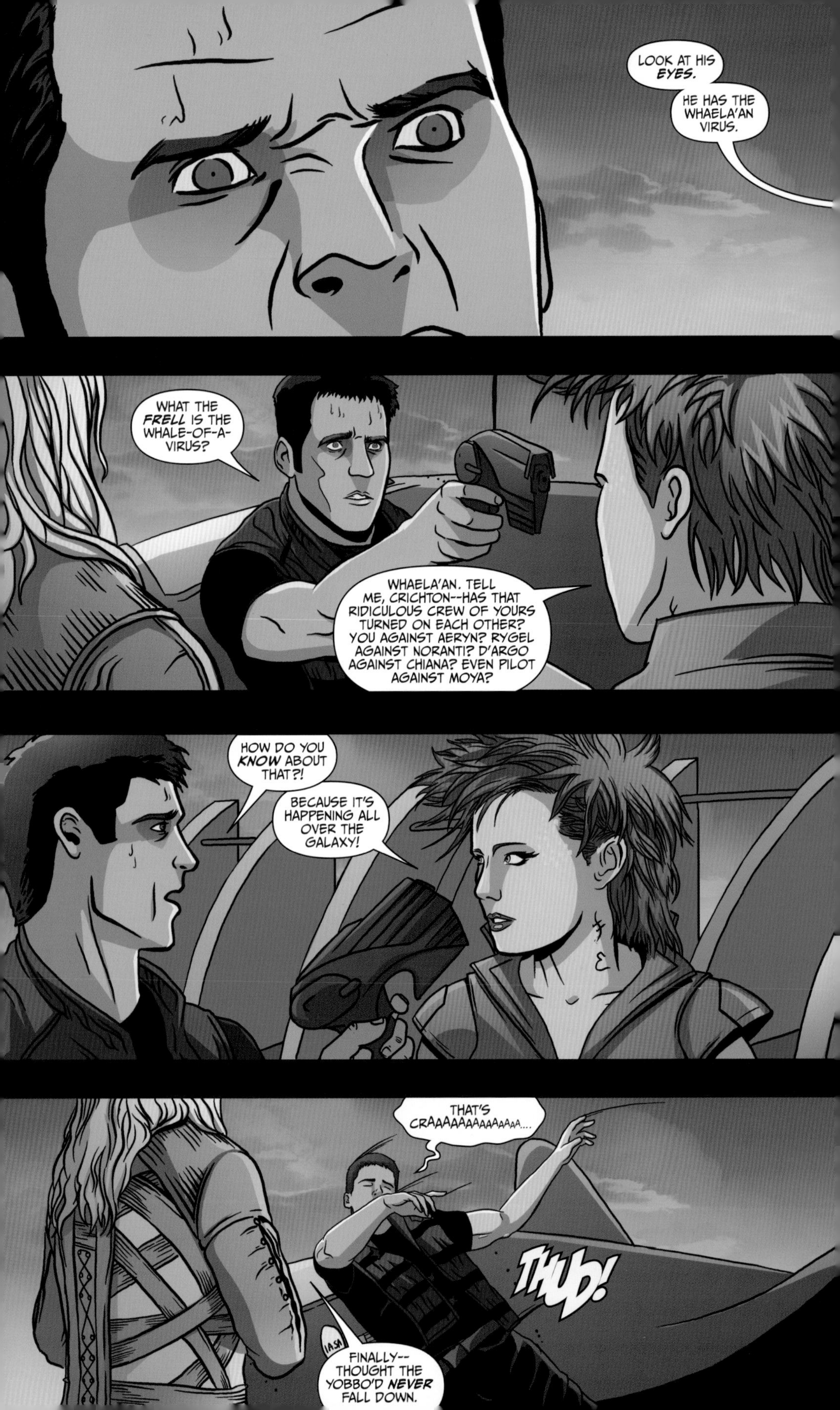
LOOK AT HIS *EYES.*
HE HAS THE WHAELA'AN VIRUS.
WHAT THE *FRELL* IS THE WHALE-OF-A-VIRUS?
WHAELA'AN. TELL ME, CRICHTON--HAS THAT RIDICULOUS CREW OF YOURS TURNED ON EACH OTHER? YOU AGAINST AERYN? RYGEL AGAINST NORANTI? D'ARGO AGAINST CHIANA? EVEN PILOT AGAINST MOYA?
HOW DO YOU *KNOW* ABOUT THAT?!
BECAUSE IT'S HAPPENING ALL OVER THE GALAXY!
THAT'S CRAAAAAAAAAAAAA....
THUD!
FINALLY-- THOUGHT THE YOBBO'D *NEVER* FALL DOWN.

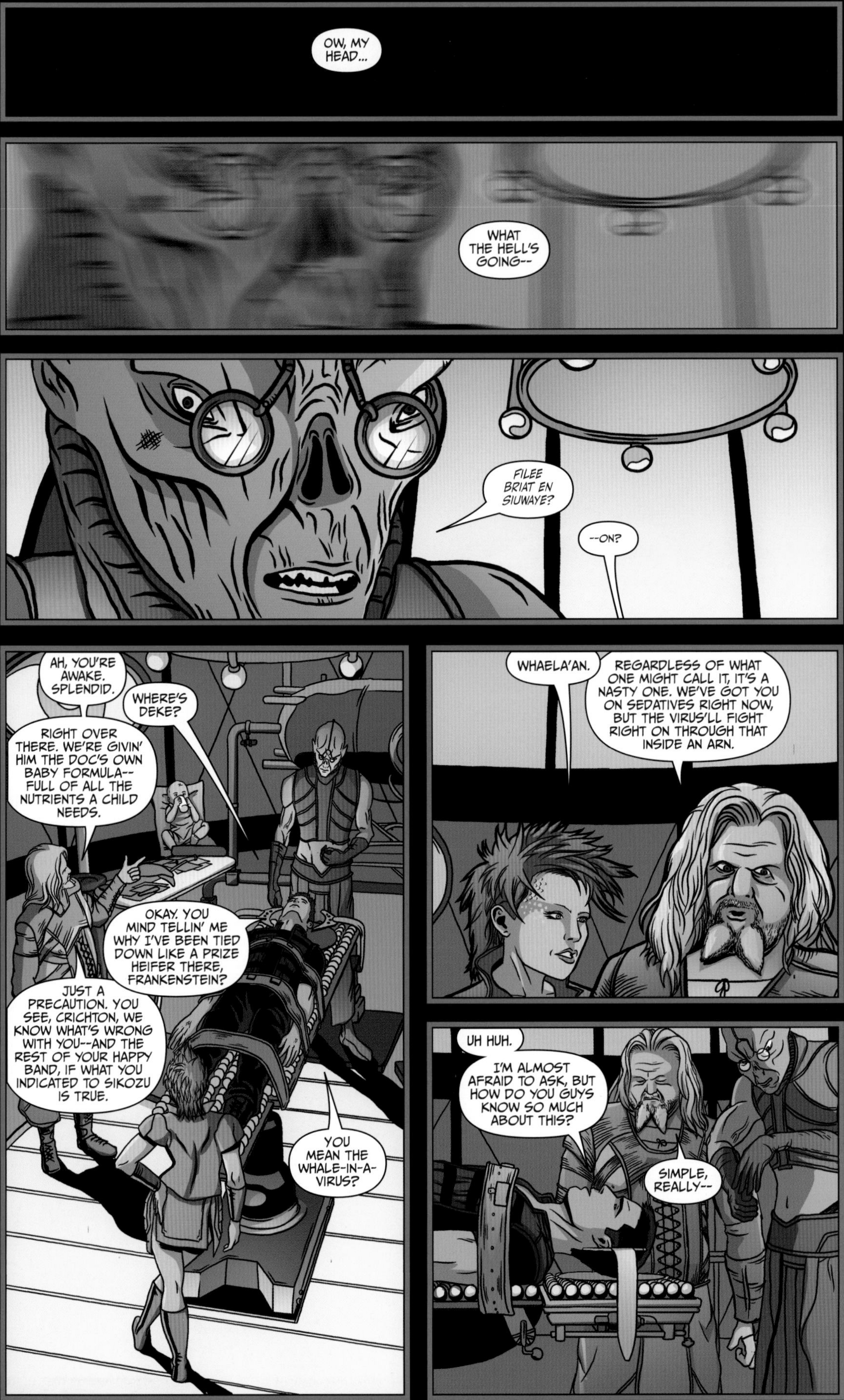
OW, MY HEAD...
WHAT THE HELL'S GOING--
FILEE BRIAT EN SIUWAYE?
--ON?
AH, YOU'RE AWAKE. SPLENDID.
WHERE'S DEKE?
RIGHT OVER THERE. WE'RE GIVIN' HIM THE DOC'S OWN BABY FORMULA-- FULL OF ALL THE NUTRIENTS A CHILD NEEDS.
OKAY. YOU MIND TELLIN' ME WHY I'VE BEEN TIED DOWN LIKE A PRIZE HEIFER THERE, FRANKENSTEIN?
JUST A PRECAUTION. YOU SEE, CRICHTON, WE KNOW WHAT'S WRONG WITH YOU--AND THE REST OF YOUR HAPPY BAND, IF WHAT YOU INDICATED TO SIKOZU IS TRUE.
YOU MEAN THE WHALE-IN-A-VIRUS?
WHAELA'AN.
REGARDLESS OF WHAT ONE MIGHT CALL IT, IT'S A NASTY ONE. WE'VE GOT YOU ON SEDATIVES RIGHT NOW, BUT THE VIRUS'LL FIGHT RIGHT ON THROUGH THAT INSIDE AN ARN.
UH HUH.
I'M ALMOST AFRAID TO ASK, BUT HOW DO YOU GUYS KNOW SO MUCH ABOUT THIS?
SIMPLE, REALLY--

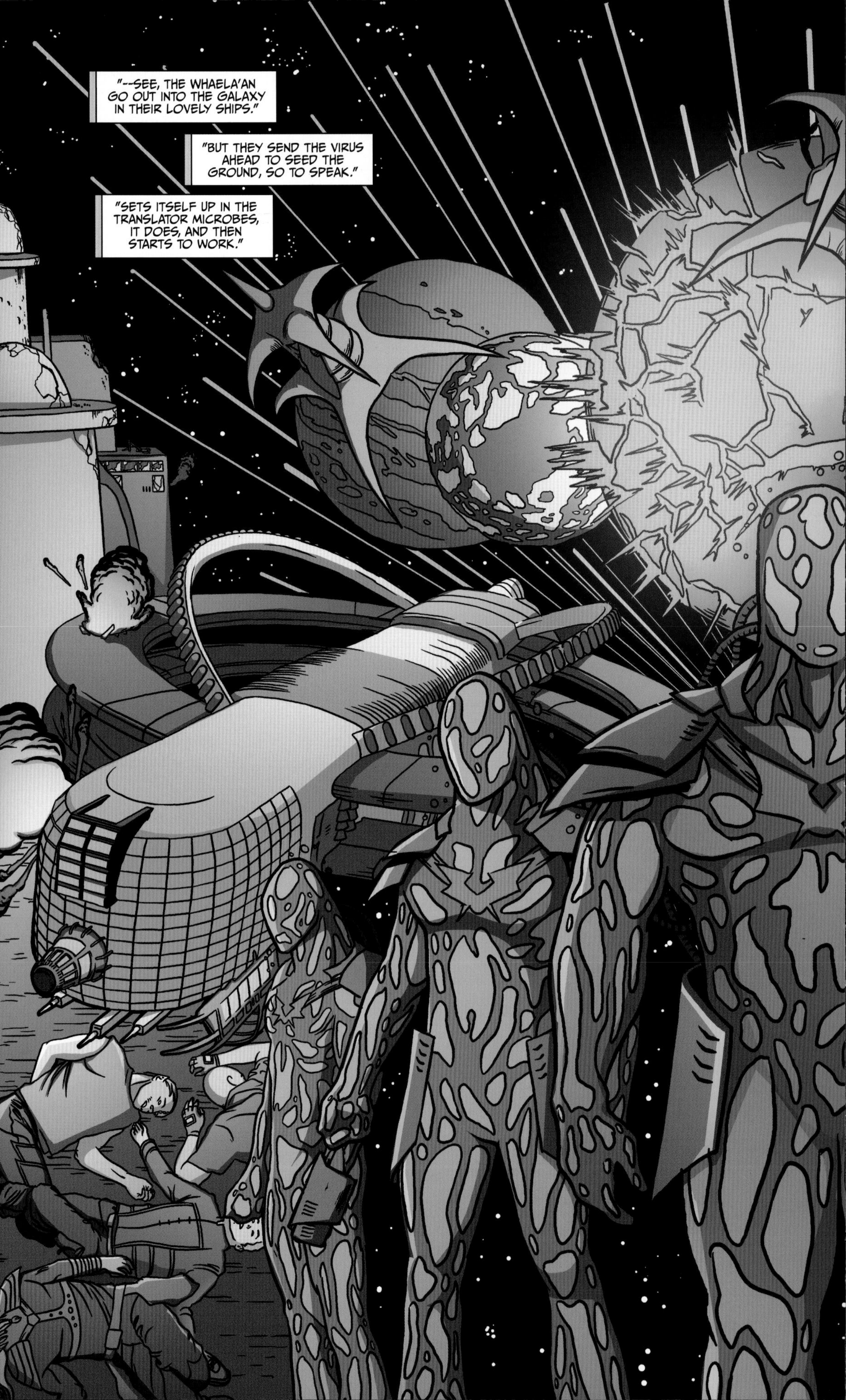
"--SEE, THE WHAELA'AN GO OUT INTO THE GALAXY IN THEIR LOVELY SHIPS."
"BUT THEY SEND THE VIRUS AHEAD TO SEED THE GROUND, SO TO SPEAK."
"SETS ITSELF UP IN THE TRANSLATOR MICROBES, IT DOES, AND THEN STARTS TO WORK."

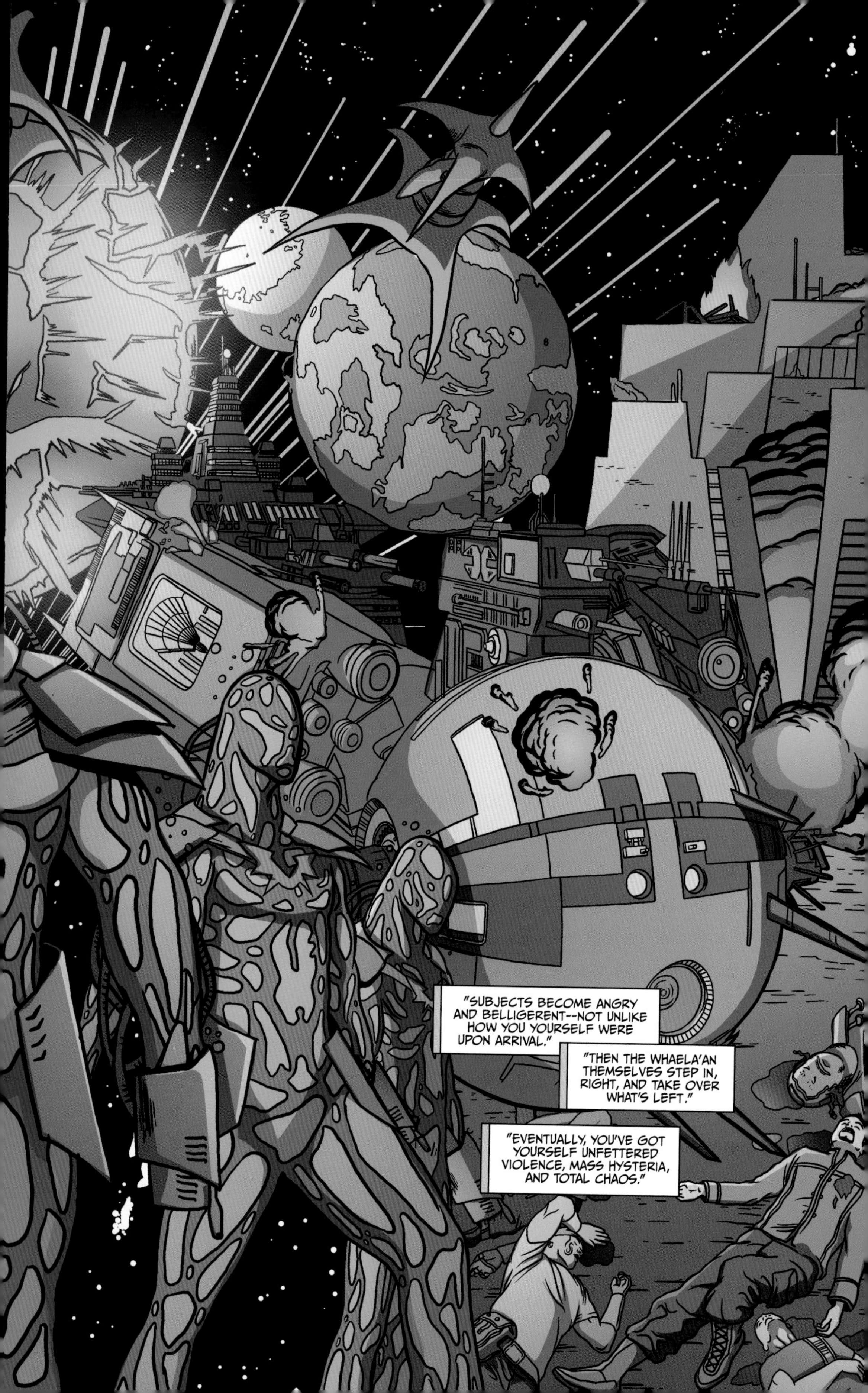
"SUBJECTS BECOME ANGRY AND BELLIGERENT--NOT UNLIKE HOW YOU YOURSELF WERE UPON ARRIVAL."
"THEN THE WHAELA'AN THEMSELVES STEP IN, RIGHT, AND TAKE OVER WHAT'S LEFT."
"EVENTUALLY, YOU'VE GOT YOURSELF UNFETTERED VIOLENCE, MASS HYSTERIA, AND TOTAL CHAOS."

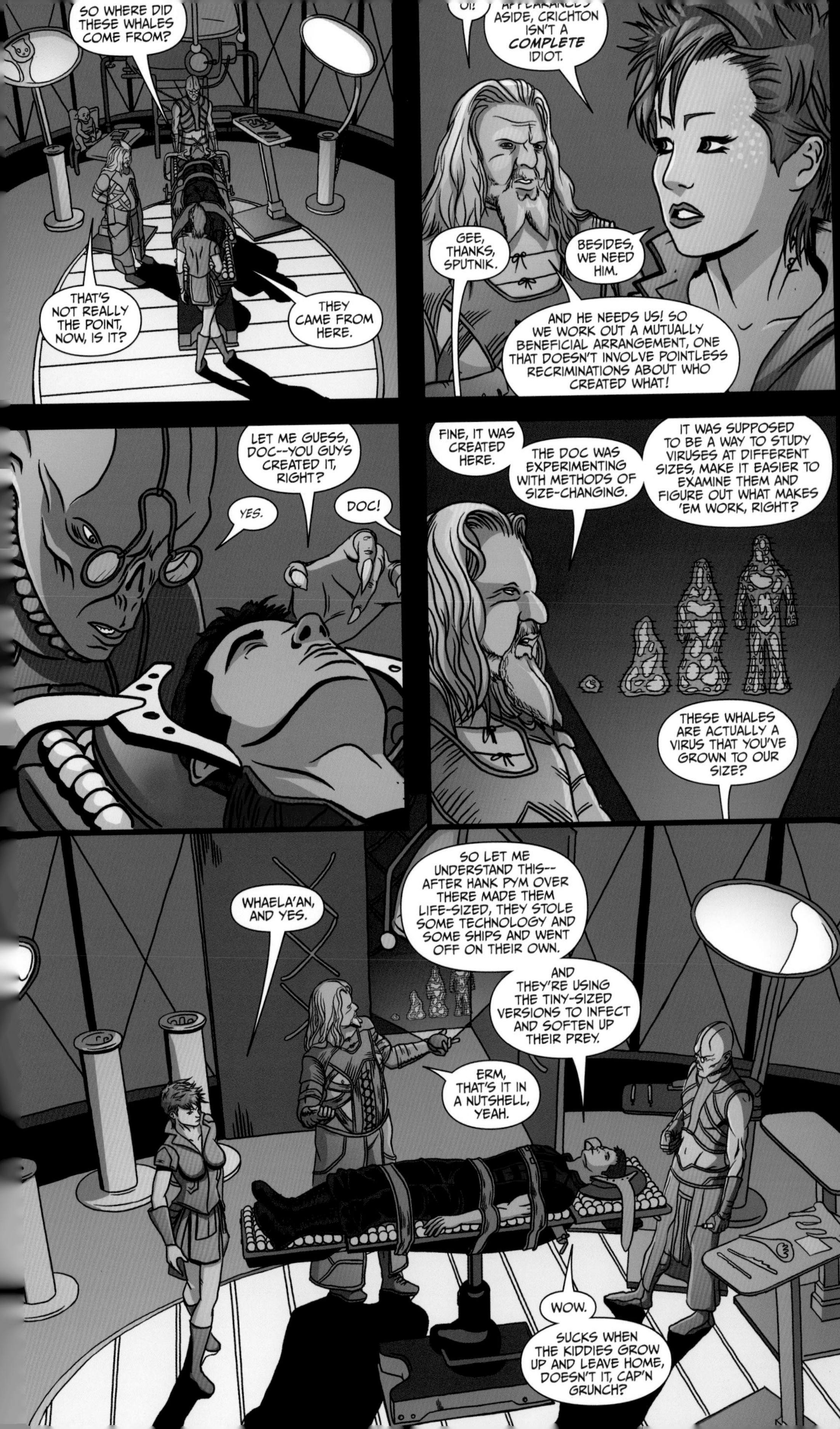
SO WHERE DID THESE WHALES COME FROM?
THAT'S NOT REALLY THE POINT, NOW, IS IT?
THEY CAME FROM HERE.
OI!
ASIDE, CRICHTON ISN'T A *COMPLETE* IDIOT.
GEE, THANKS, SPUTNIK.
BESIDES, WE NEED HIM.
AND HE NEEDS US! SO WE WORK OUT A MUTUALLY BENEFICIAL ARRANGEMENT, ONE THAT DOESN'T INVOLVE POINTLESS RECRIMINATIONS ABOUT WHO CREATED WHAT!
LET ME GUESS, DOC--YOU GUYS CREATED IT, RIGHT?
YES.
DOC!
FINE, IT WAS CREATED HERE.
THE DOC WAS EXPERIMENTING WITH METHODS OF SIZE-CHANGING.
IT WAS SUPPOSED TO BE A WAY TO STUDY VIRUSES AT DIFFERENT SIZES, MAKE IT EASIER TO EXAMINE THEM AND FIGURE OUT WHAT MAKES 'EM WORK, RIGHT?
THESE WHALES ARE ACTUALLY A VIRUS THAT YOU'VE GROWN TO OUR SIZE?
SO LET ME UNDERSTAND THIS-- AFTER HANK PYM OVER THERE MADE THEM LIFE-SIZED, THEY STOLE SOME TECHNOLOGY AND SOME SHIPS AND WENT OFF ON THEIR OWN.
WHAELA'AN, AND YES.
AND THEY'RE USING THE TINY-SIZED VERSIONS TO INFECT AND SOFTEN UP THEIR PREY.
ERM, THAT'S IT IN A NUTSHELL, YEAH.
WOW.
SUCKS WHEN THE KIDDIES GROW UP AND LEAVE HOME, DOESN'T IT, CAP'N GRUNCH?

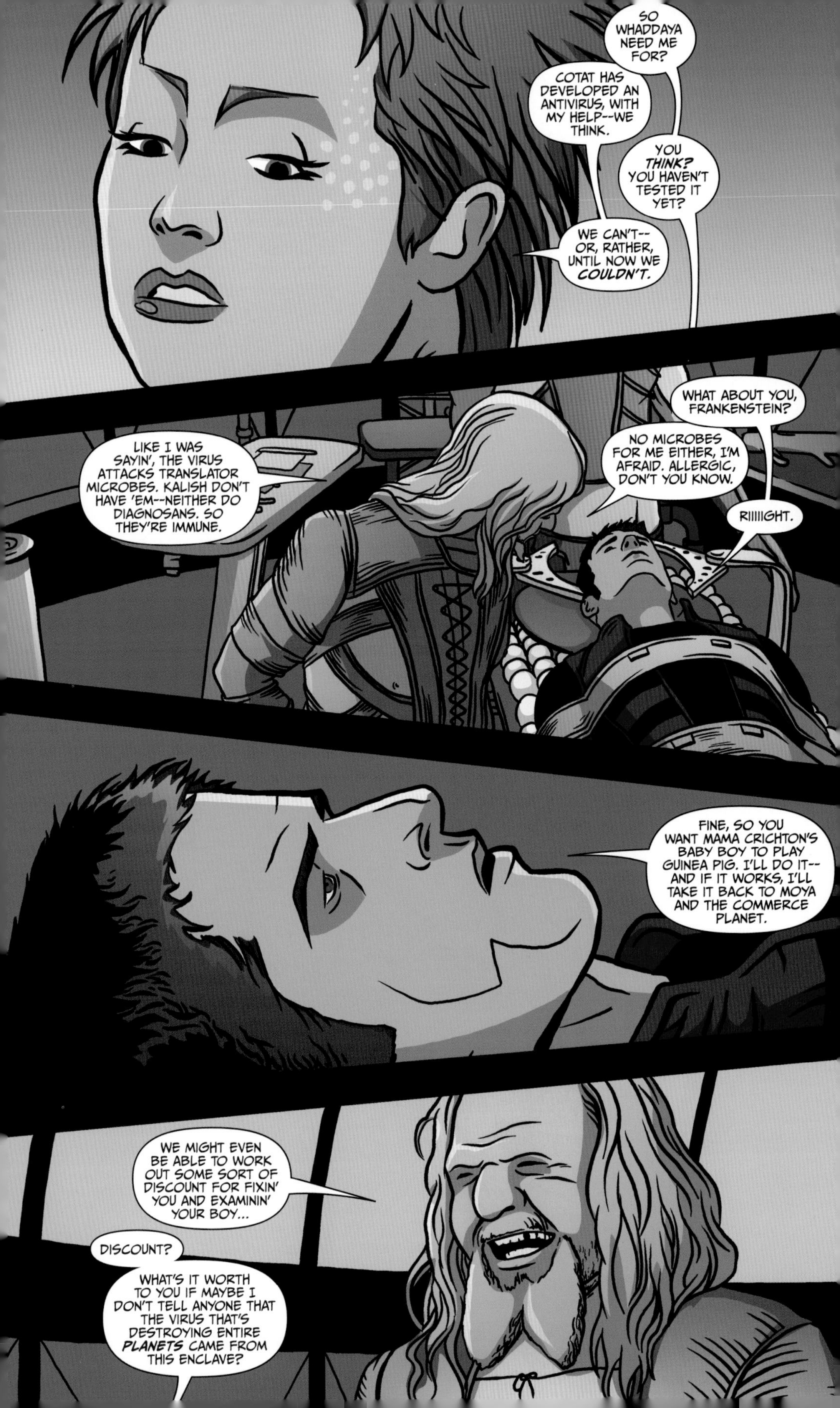
SO WHADDAYA NEED ME FOR?
COTAT HAS DEVELOPED AN ANTIVIRUS, WITH MY HELP--WE THINK.
YOU *THINK?* YOU HAVEN'T TESTED IT YET?
WE CAN'T--OR, RATHER, UNTIL NOW WE *COULDN'T.*
LIKE I WAS SAYIN', THE VIRUS ATTACKS TRANSLATOR MICROBES. KALISH DON'T HAVE 'EM--NEITHER DO DIAGNOSANS. SO THEY'RE IMMUNE.
WHAT ABOUT YOU, FRANKENSTEIN?
NO MICROBES FOR ME EITHER, I'M AFRAID. ALLERGIC, DON'T YOU KNOW.
RIIIIIGHT.
FINE, SO YOU WANT MAMA CRICHTON'S BABY BOY TO PLAY GUINEA PIG. I'LL DO IT--AND IF IT WORKS, I'LL TAKE IT BACK TO MOYA AND THE COMMERCE PLANET.
WE MIGHT EVEN BE ABLE TO WORK OUT SOME SORT OF DISCOUNT FOR FIXIN' YOU AND EXAMININ' YOUR BOY...
DISCOUNT?
WHAT'S IT WORTH TO YOU IF MAYBE I DON'T TELL ANYONE THAT THE VIRUS THAT'S DESTROYING ENTIRE *PLANETS* CAME FROM THIS ENCLAVE?

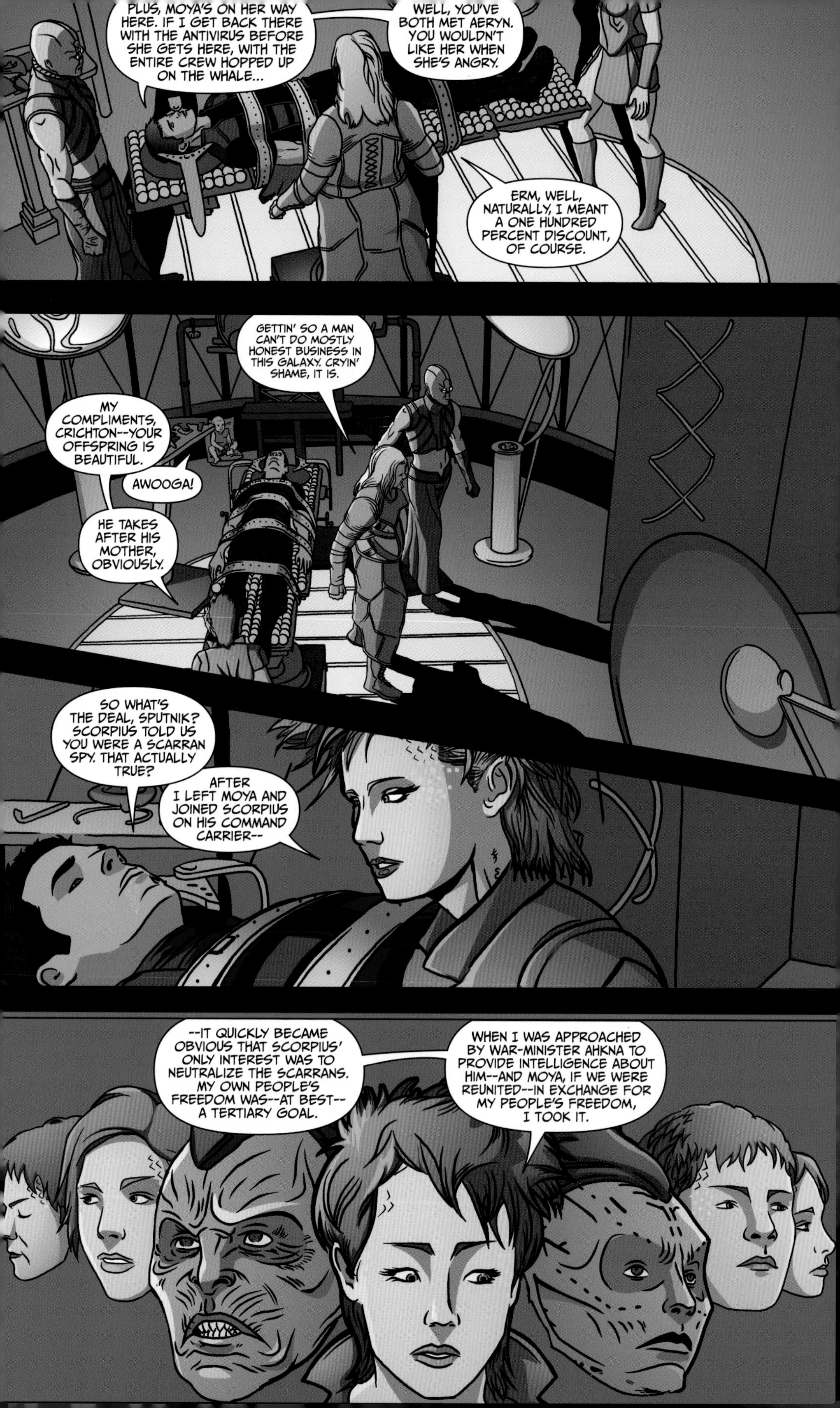
PLUS, MOYA'S ON HER WAY HERE. IF I GET BACK THERE WITH THE ANTIVIRUS BEFORE SHE GETS HERE, WITH THE ENTIRE CREW HOPPED UP ON THE WHALE...
WELL, YOU'VE BOTH MET AERYN. YOU WOULDN'T LIKE HER WHEN SHE'S ANGRY.
ERM, WELL, NATURALLY, I MEANT A ONE HUNDRED PERCENT DISCOUNT, OF COURSE.
GETTIN' SO A MAN CAN'T DO MOSTLY HONEST BUSINESS IN THIS GALAXY. CRYIN' SHAME, IT IS.
MY COMPLIMENTS, CRICHTON--YOUR OFFSPRING IS BEAUTIFUL.
AWOOGA!
HE TAKES AFTER HIS MOTHER, OBVIOUSLY.
SO WHAT'S THE DEAL, SPUTNIK? SCORPIUS TOLD US YOU WERE A SCARRAN SPY. THAT ACTUALLY TRUE?
AFTER I LEFT MOYA AND JOINED SCORPIUS ON HIS COMMAND CARRIER--
--IT QUICKLY BECAME OBVIOUS THAT SCORPIUS' ONLY INTEREST WAS TO NEUTRALIZE THE SCARRANS. MY OWN PEOPLE'S FREEDOM WAS--AT BEST--A TERTIARY GOAL.
WHEN I WAS APPROACHED BY WAR-MINISTER AHKNA TO PROVIDE INTELLIGENCE ABOUT HIM--AND MOYA, IF WE WERE REUNITED--IN EXCHANGE FOR MY PEOPLE'S FREEDOM, I TOOK IT.

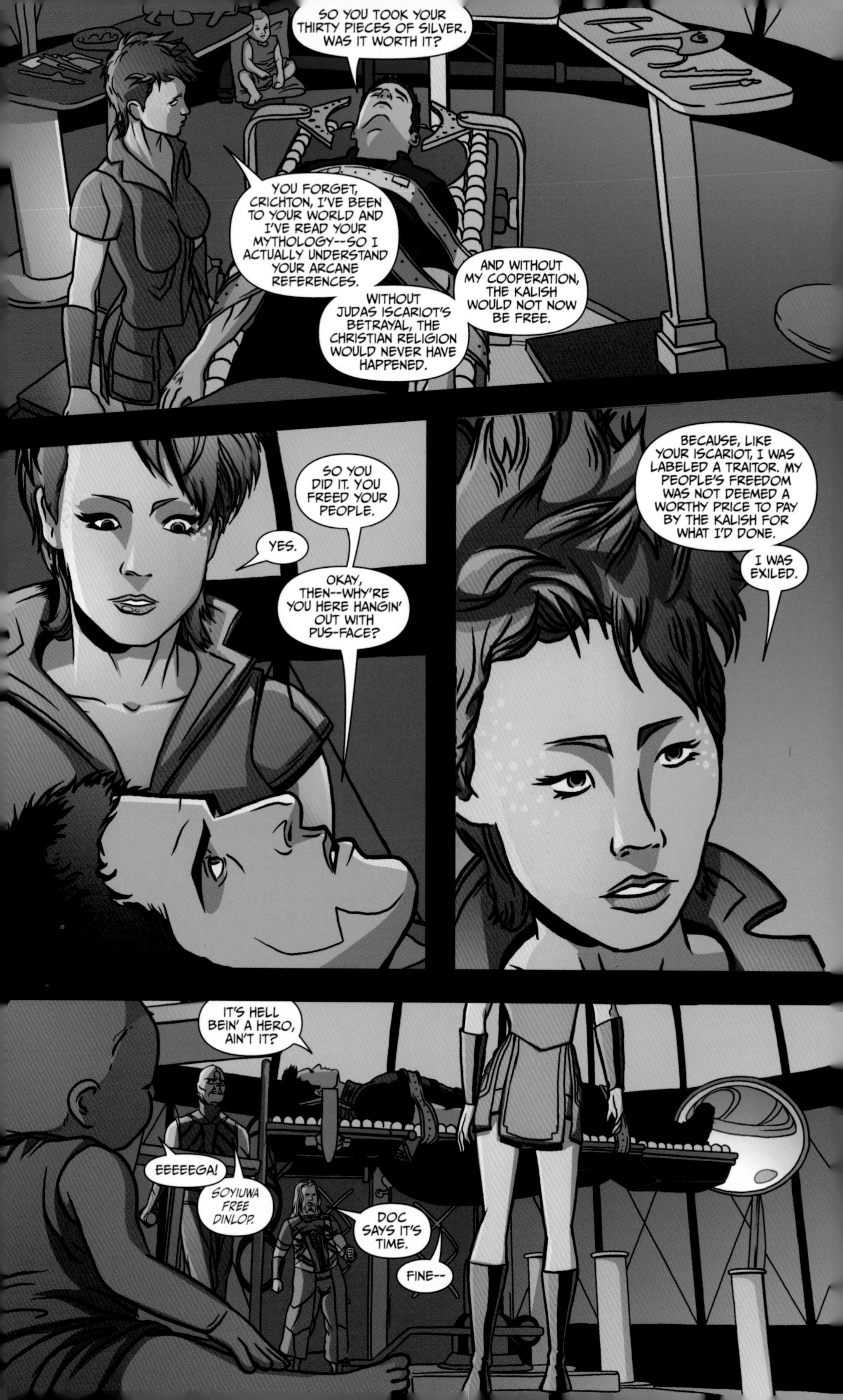
SO YOU TOOK YOUR THIRTY PIECES OF SILVER. WAS IT WORTH IT?
YOU FORGET, CRICHTON, I'VE BEEN TO YOUR WORLD AND I'VE READ YOUR MYTHOLOGY--SO I ACTUALLY UNDERSTAND YOUR ARCANE REFERENCES.
WITHOUT JUDAS ISCARIOT'S BETRAYAL, THE CHRISTIAN RELIGION WOULD NEVER HAVE HAPPENED.
AND WITHOUT MY COOPERATION, THE KALISH WOULD NOT NOW BE FREE.
SO YOU DID IT. YOU FREED YOUR PEOPLE.
YES.
OKAY, THEN--WHY'RE YOU HERE HANGIN' OUT WITH PUS-FACE?
BECAUSE, LIKE YOUR ISCARIOT, I WAS LABELED A TRAITOR. MY PEOPLE'S FREEDOM WAS NOT DEEMED A WORTHY PRICE TO PAY BY THE KALISH FOR WHAT I'D DONE.
I WAS EXILED.
IT'S HELL BEIN' A HERO, AIN'T IT?
EEEEEGA!
SOYIUWA FREE DINLOP.
DOC SAYS IT'S TIME.
FINE--

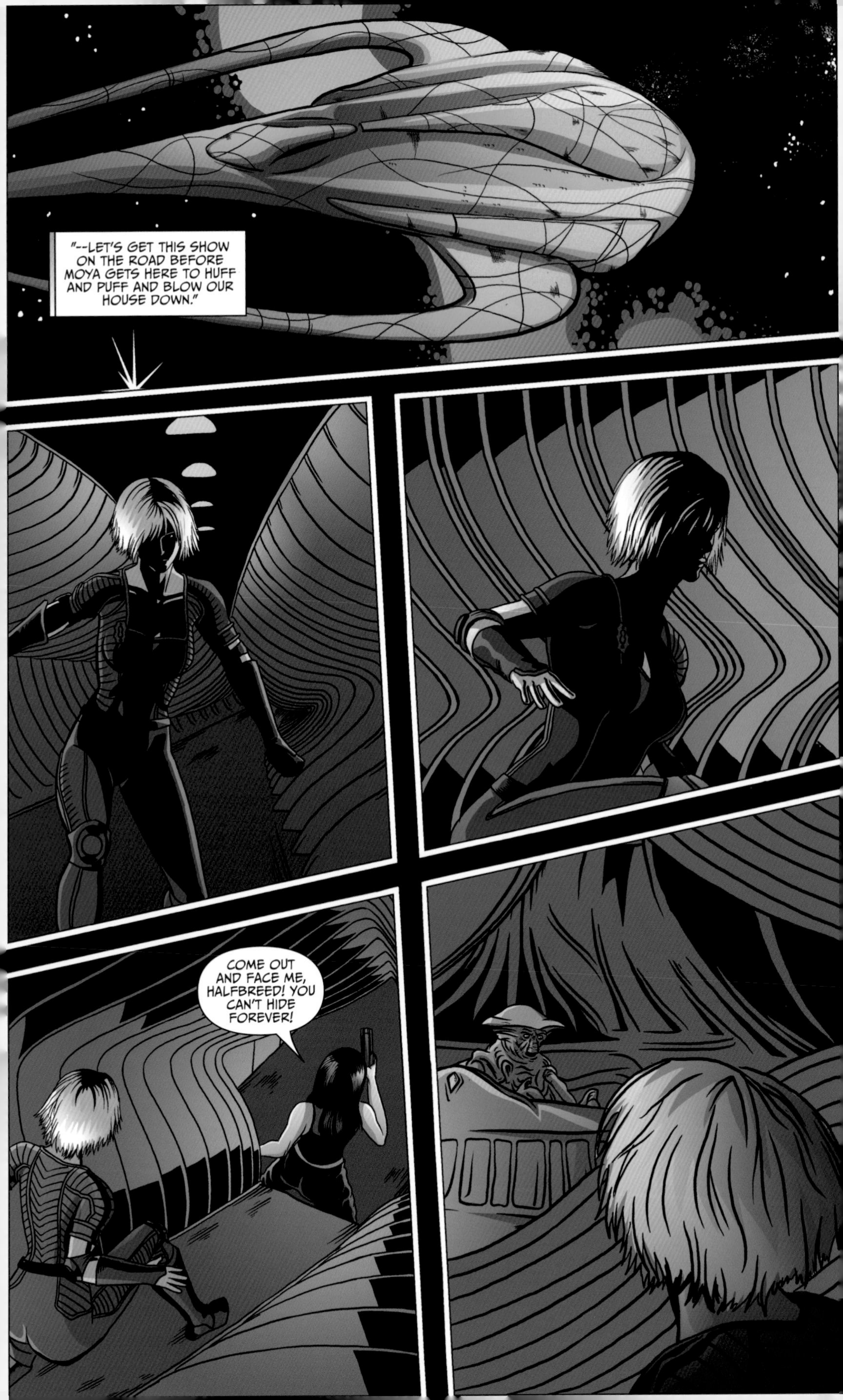
"--LET'S GET THIS SHOW ON THE ROAD BEFORE MOYA GETS HERE TO HUFF AND PUFF AND BLOW OUR HOUSE DOWN."
COME OUT AND FACE ME, HALFBREED! YOU CAN'T HIDE FOREVER!

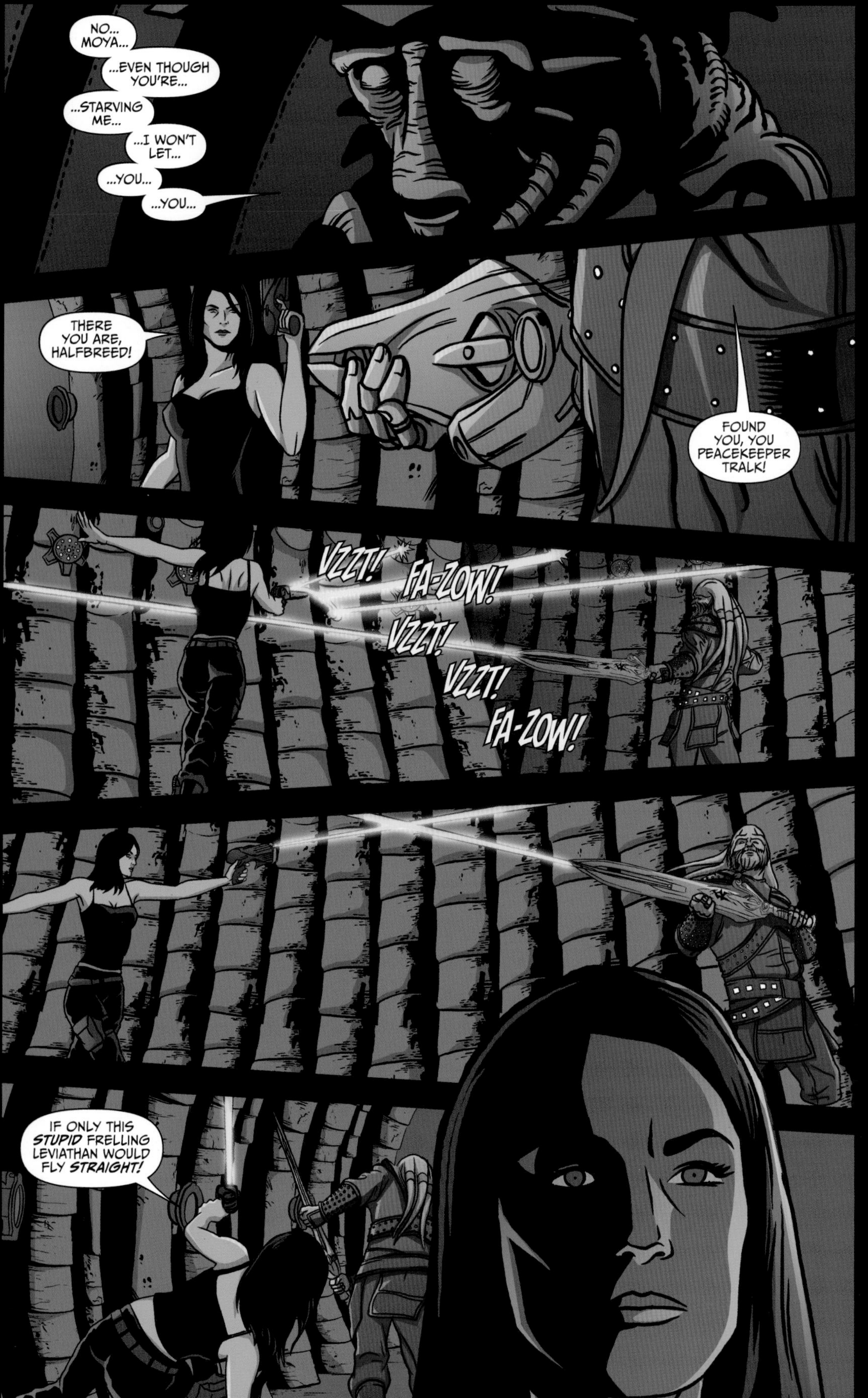
NO... MOYA...
...EVEN THOUGH YOU'RE...
...STARVING ME...
...I WON'T LET...
...YOU...
...YOU...
THERE YOU ARE, HALFBREED!
FOUND YOU, YOU PEACEKEEPER TRALK!
VZZT!
FA-ZOW!
VZZT!
VZZT!
FA-ZOW!
IF ONLY THIS *STUPID* FRELLING LEVIATHAN WOULD FLY *STRAIGHT!*

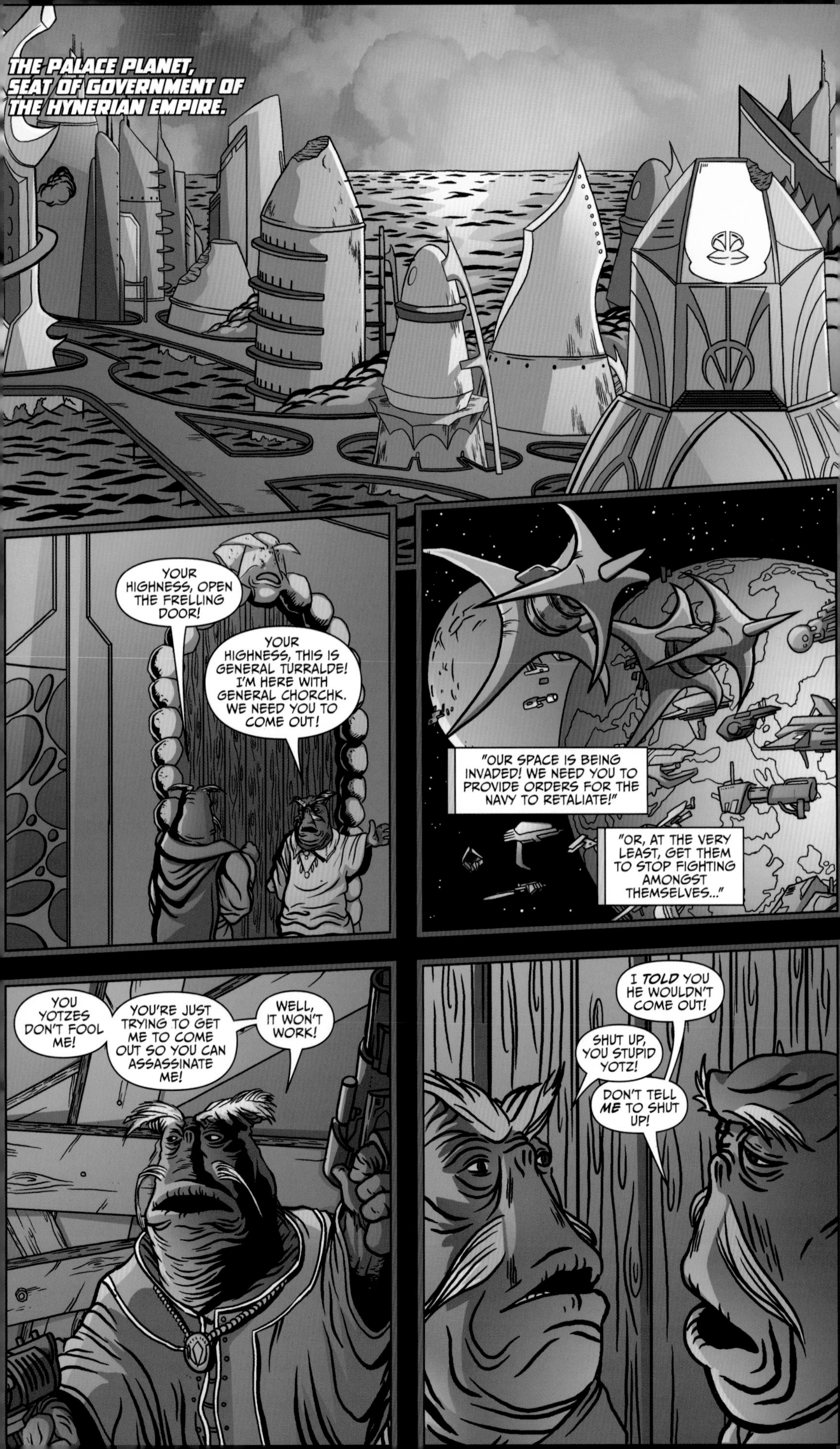
THE PALACE PLANET, SEAT OF GOVERNMENT OF THE HYNERIAN EMPIRE.
YOUR HIGHNESS, OPEN THE FRELLING DOOR!
YOUR HIGHNESS, THIS IS GENERAL TURRALDE! I'M HERE WITH GENERAL CHORCHK. WE NEED YOU TO COME OUT!
"OUR SPACE IS BEING INVADED! WE NEED YOU TO PROVIDE ORDERS FOR THE NAVY TO RETALIATE!"
"OR, AT THE VERY LEAST, GET THEM TO STOP FIGHTING AMONGST THEMSELVES..."
YOU YOTZES DON'T FOOL ME!
YOU'RE JUST TRYING TO GET ME TO COME OUT SO YOU CAN ASSASSINATE ME!
WELL, IT WON'T WORK!
I ***TOLD*** YOU HE WOULDN'T COME OUT!
SHUT UP, YOU STUPID YOTZ!
DON'T TELL ***ME*** TO SHUT UP!

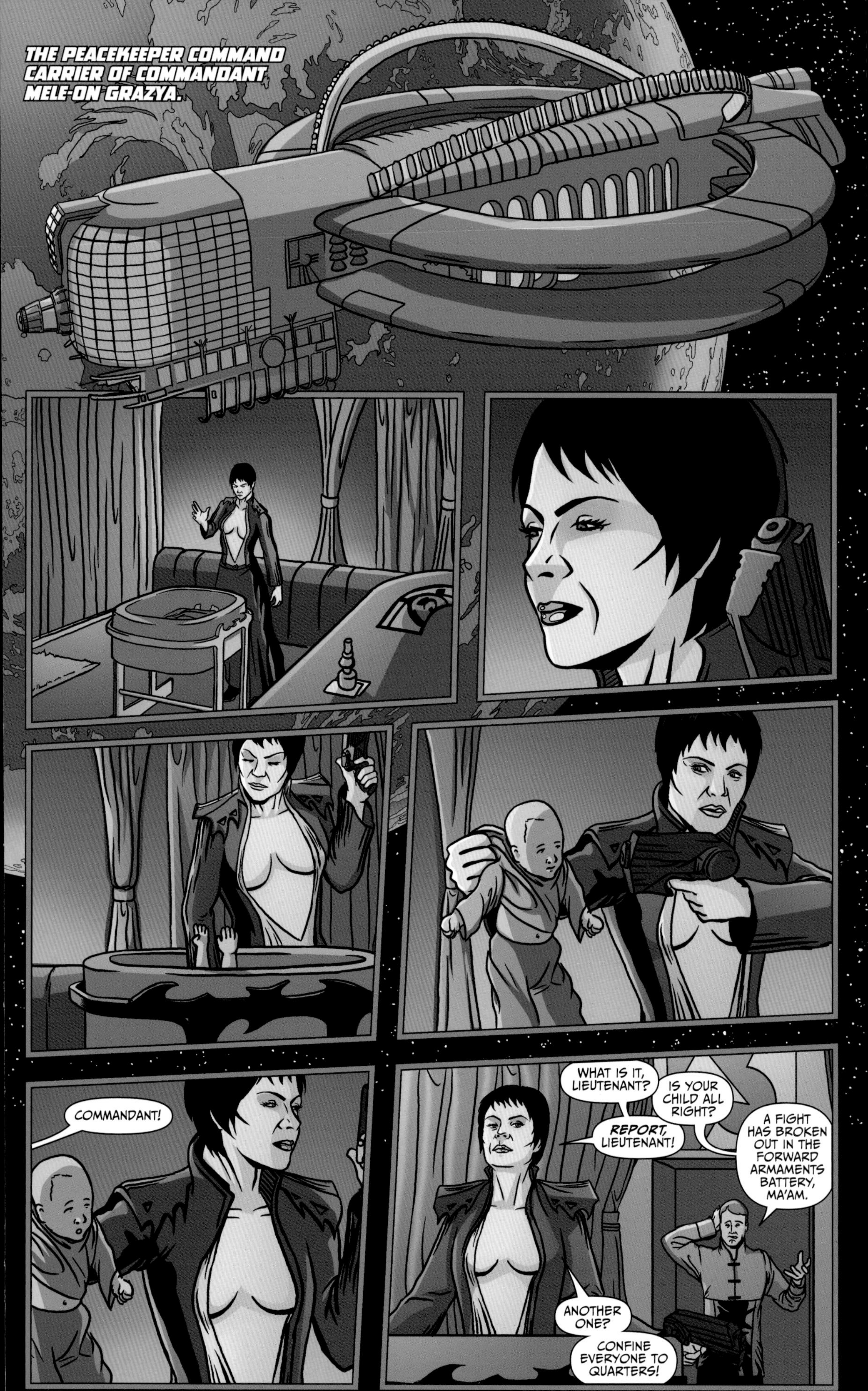
THE PEACEKEEPER COMMAND CARRIER OF COMMANDANT MELE-ON GRAZYA.
COMMANDANT!
WHAT IS IT, LIEUTENANT?
IS YOUR CHILD ALL RIGHT?
REPORT, LIEUTENANT!
A FIGHT HAS BROKEN OUT IN THE FORWARD ARMAMENTS BATTERY, MA'AM.
ANOTHER ONE?
CONFINE EVERYONE TO QUARTERS!

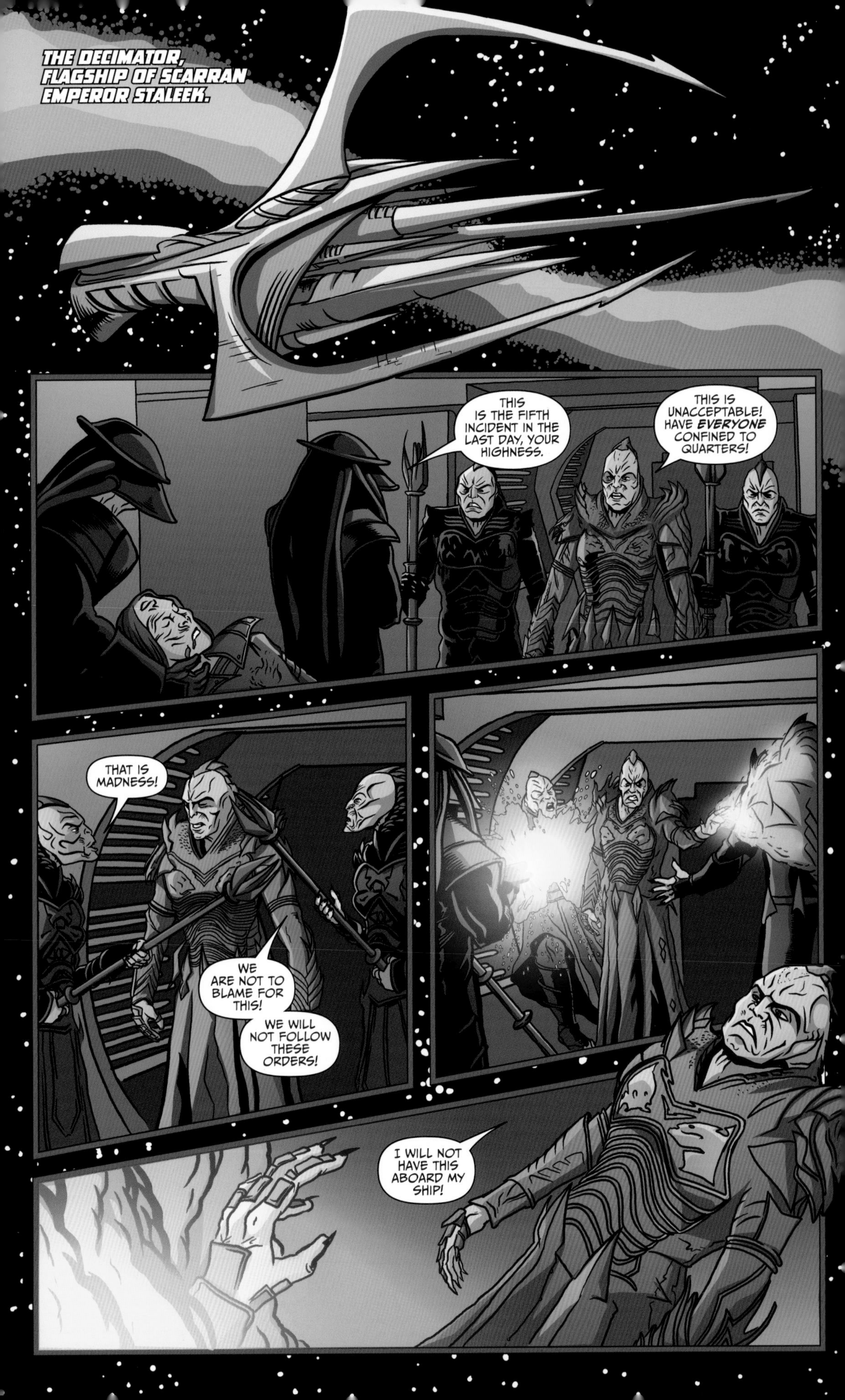
THE DECIMATOR, FLAGSHIP OF SCARRAN EMPEROR STALEEK.
THIS IS THE FIFTH INCIDENT IN THE LAST DAY, YOUR HIGHNESS.
THIS IS UNACCEPTABLE! HAVE *EVERYONE* CONFINED TO QUARTERS!
THAT IS MADNESS!
WE ARE NOT TO BLAME FOR THIS!
WE WILL NOT FOLLOW THESE ORDERS!
I WILL NOT HAVE THIS ABOARD MY SHIP!

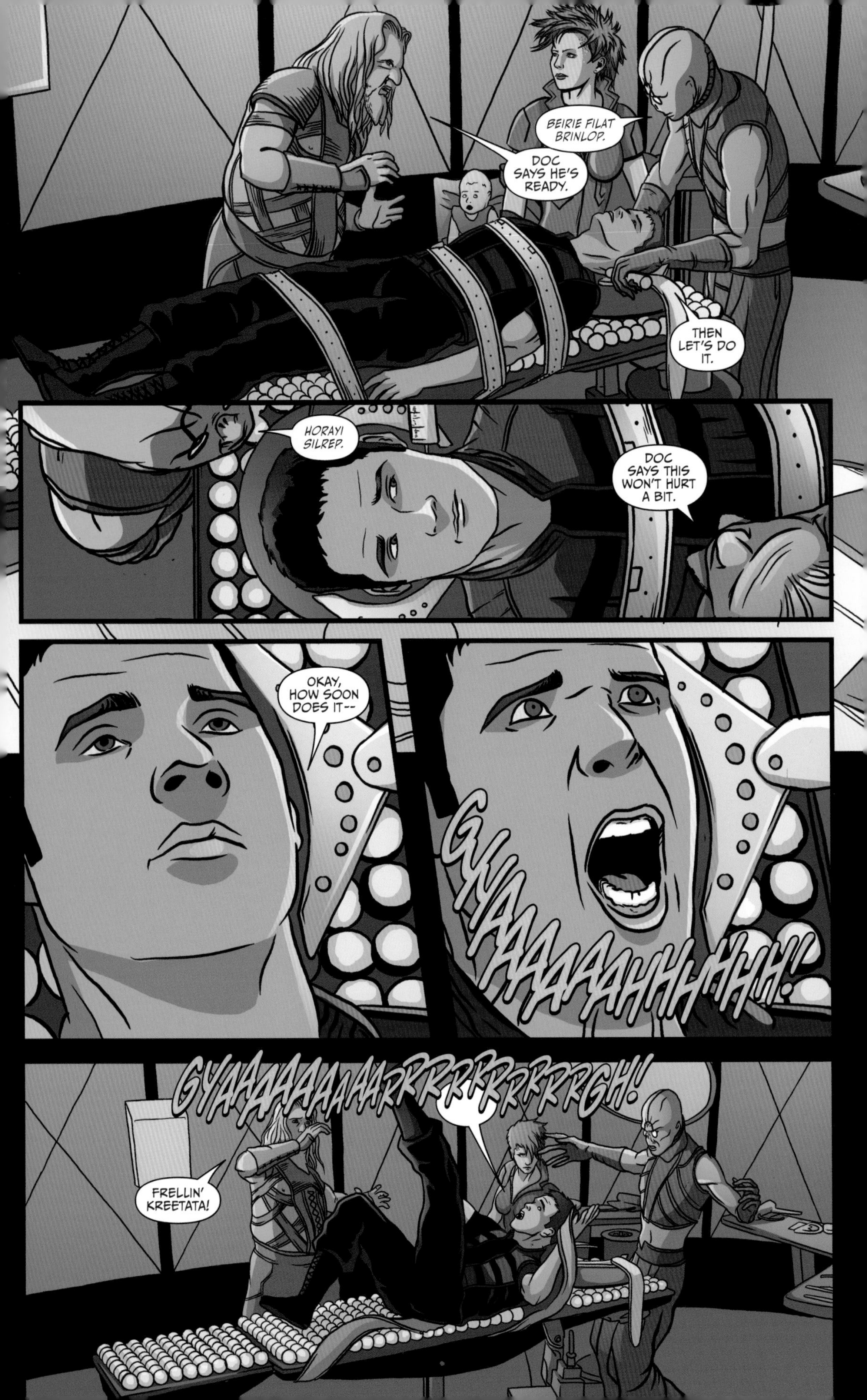
BEIRIE FILAT BRINLOP.
DOC SAYS HE'S READY.
THEN LET'S DO IT.
HORAY! SILREP.
DOC SAYS THIS WON'T HURT A BIT.
OKAY, HOW SOON DOES IT--
GYAAAAAAAAAHHHHHHH!
GYAAAAAAAAARRRRRRRRRRGH!
FRELLIN' KREETATA!

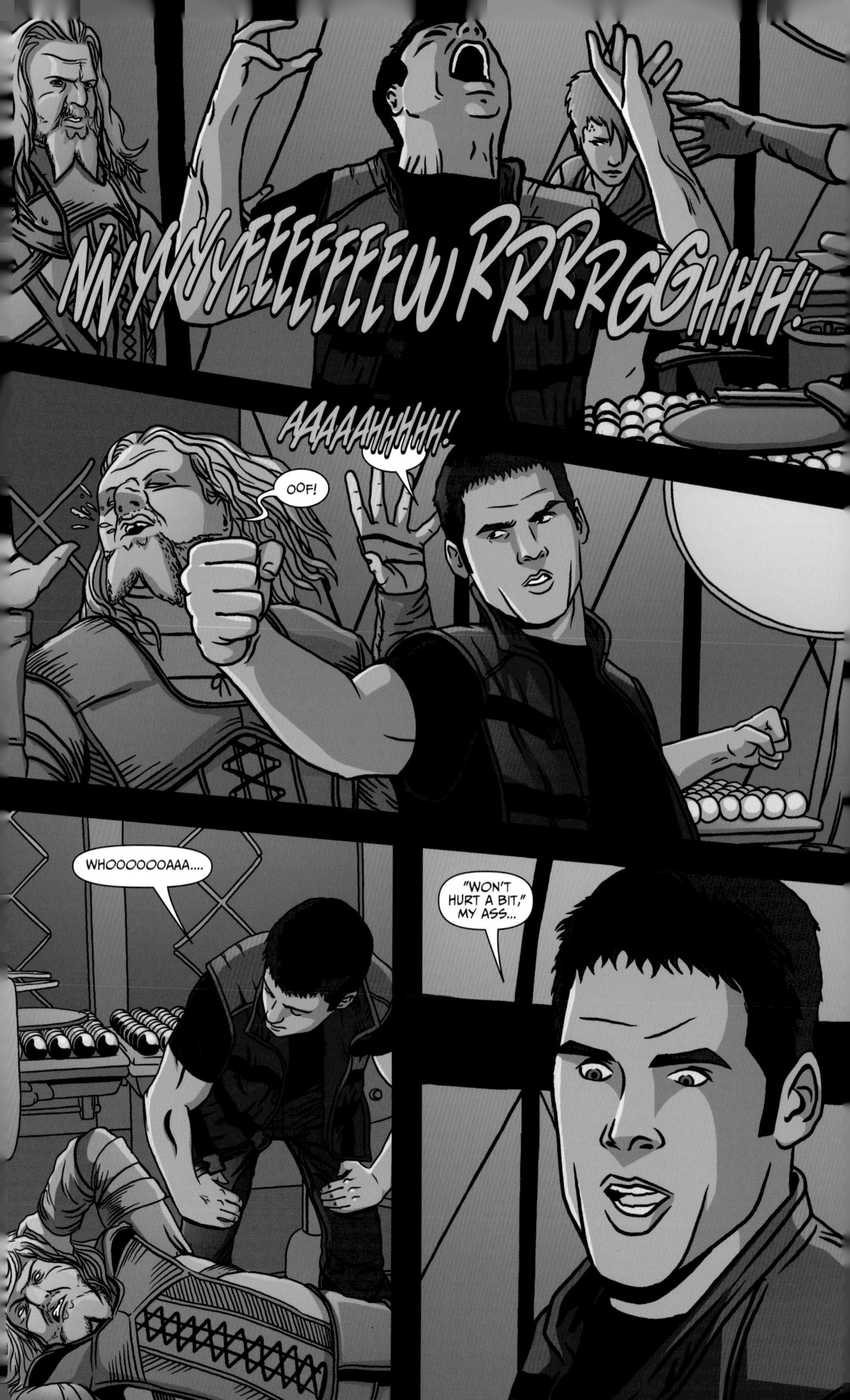
NNYYYYEEEEEEEEEUURRRRGGHHH!
AAAAAHHHHH!
OOF!
WHOOOOOOAAA....
"WON'T HURT A BIT," MY ASS...

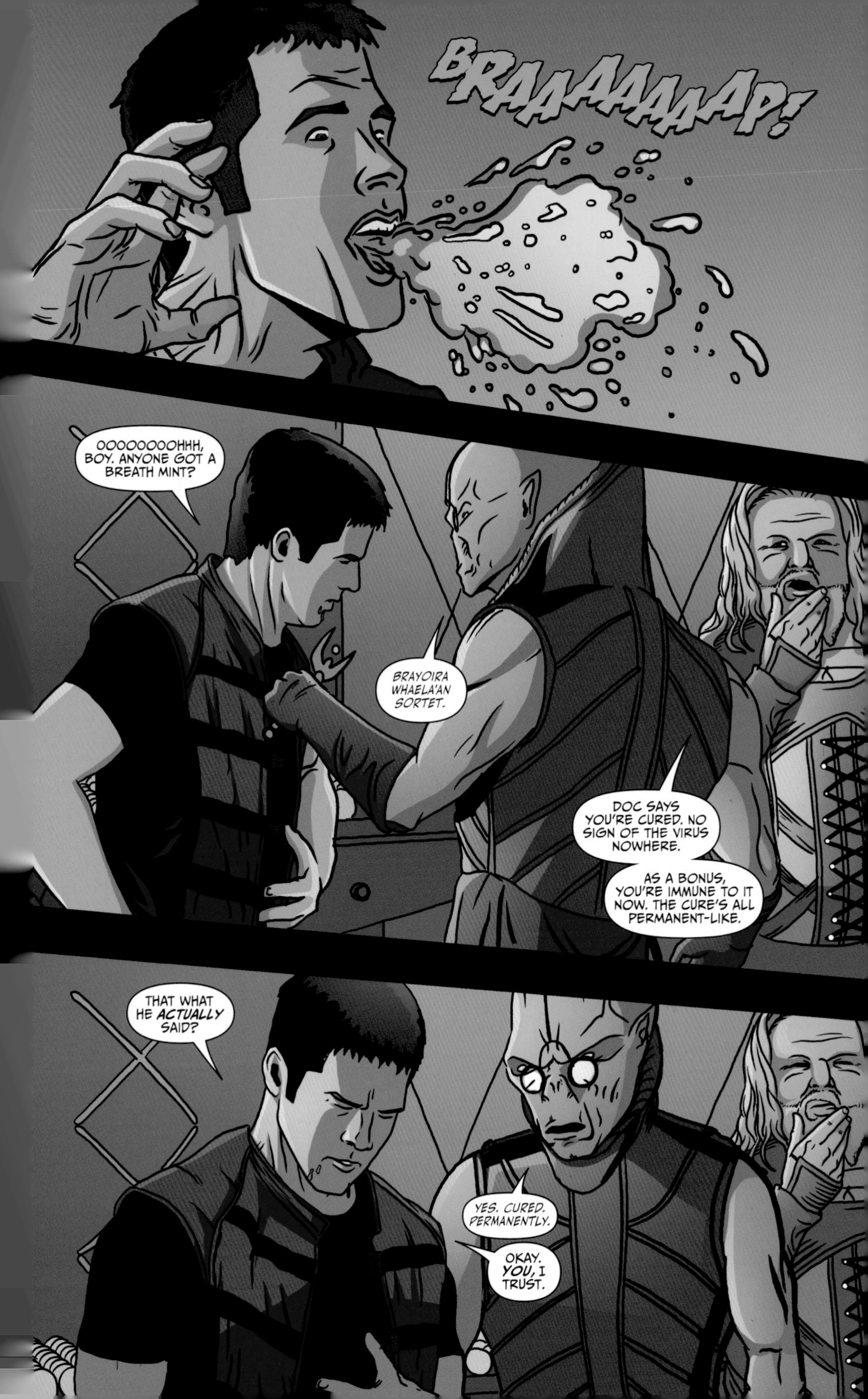
BRAAAAAAAP!
OOOOOOOOHHH, BOY. ANYONE GOT A BREATH MINT?
BRAYOIRA WHAELA'AN SORTET.
DOC SAYS YOU'RE CURED. NO SIGN OF THE VIRUS NOWHERE.
AS A BONUS, YOU'RE IMMUNE TO IT NOW. THE CURE'S ALL PERMANENT-LIKE.
THAT WHAT HE *ACTUALLY* SAID?
YES. CURED. PERMANENTLY.
OKAY. *YOU*, I TRUST.

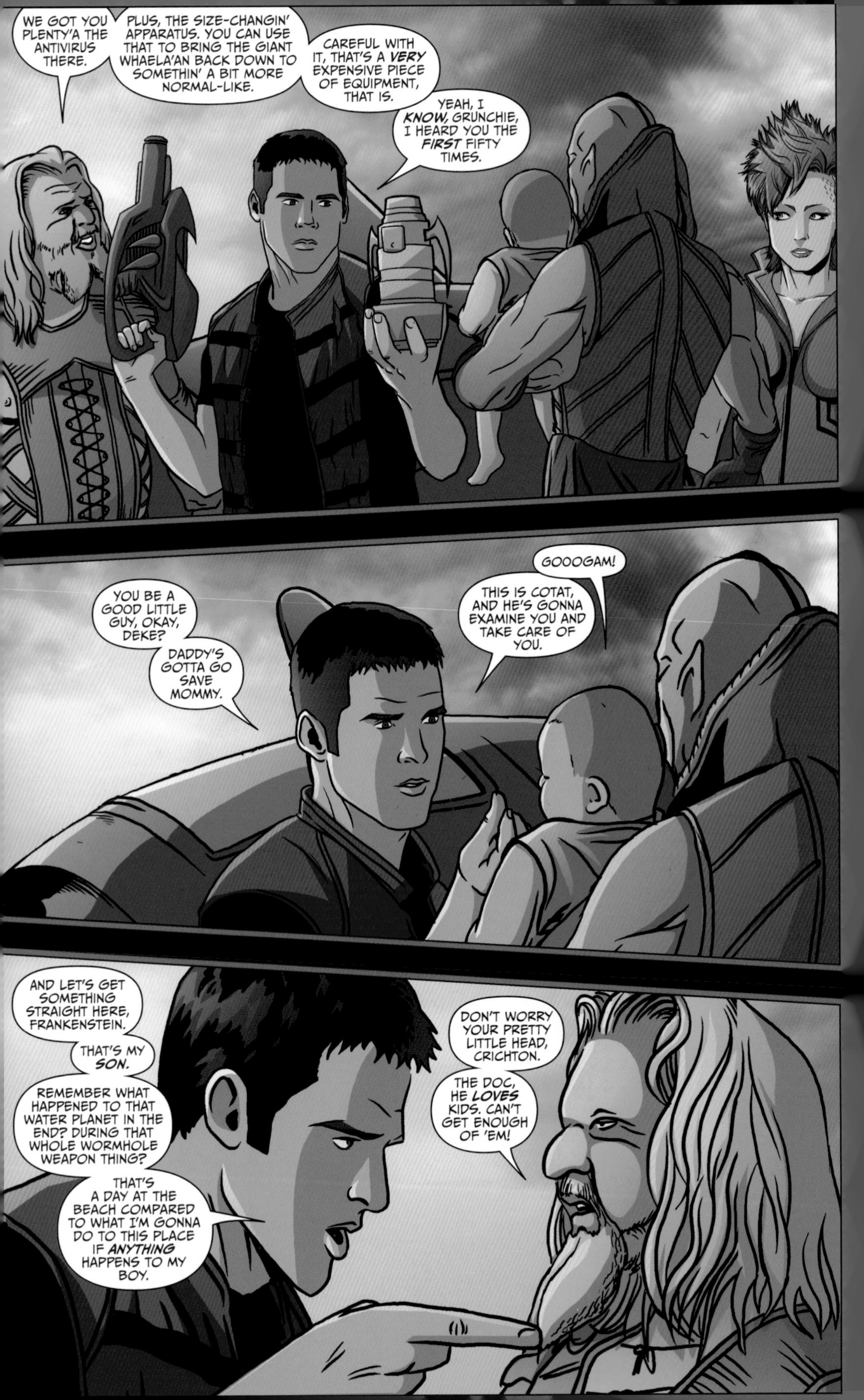
WE GOT YOU PLENTY'A THE ANTIVIRUS THERE.
PLUS, THE SIZE-CHANGIN' APPARATUS. YOU CAN USE THAT TO BRING THE GIANT WHAELA'AN BACK DOWN TO SOMETHIN' A BIT MORE NORMAL-LIKE.
CAREFUL WITH IT, THAT'S A **VERY** EXPENSIVE PIECE OF EQUIPMENT, THAT IS.
YEAH, I **KNOW,** GRUNCHIE, I HEARD YOU THE **FIRST** FIFTY TIMES.
YOU BE A GOOD LITTLE GUY, OKAY, DEKE?
DADDY'S GOTTA GO SAVE MOMMY.
THIS IS COTAT, AND HE'S GONNA EXAMINE YOU AND TAKE CARE OF YOU.
GOOOGAM!
AND LET'S GET SOMETHING STRAIGHT HERE, FRANKENSTEIN.
THAT'S MY **SON.**
REMEMBER WHAT HAPPENED TO THAT WATER PLANET IN THE END? DURING THAT WHOLE WORMHOLE WEAPON THING?
THAT'S A DAY AT THE BEACH COMPARED TO WHAT I'M GONNA DO TO THIS PLACE IF **ANYTHING** HAPPENS TO MY BOY.
DON'T WORRY YOUR PRETTY LITTLE HEAD, CRICHTON.
THE DOC, HE **LOVES** KIDS. CAN'T GET ENOUGH OF 'EM!

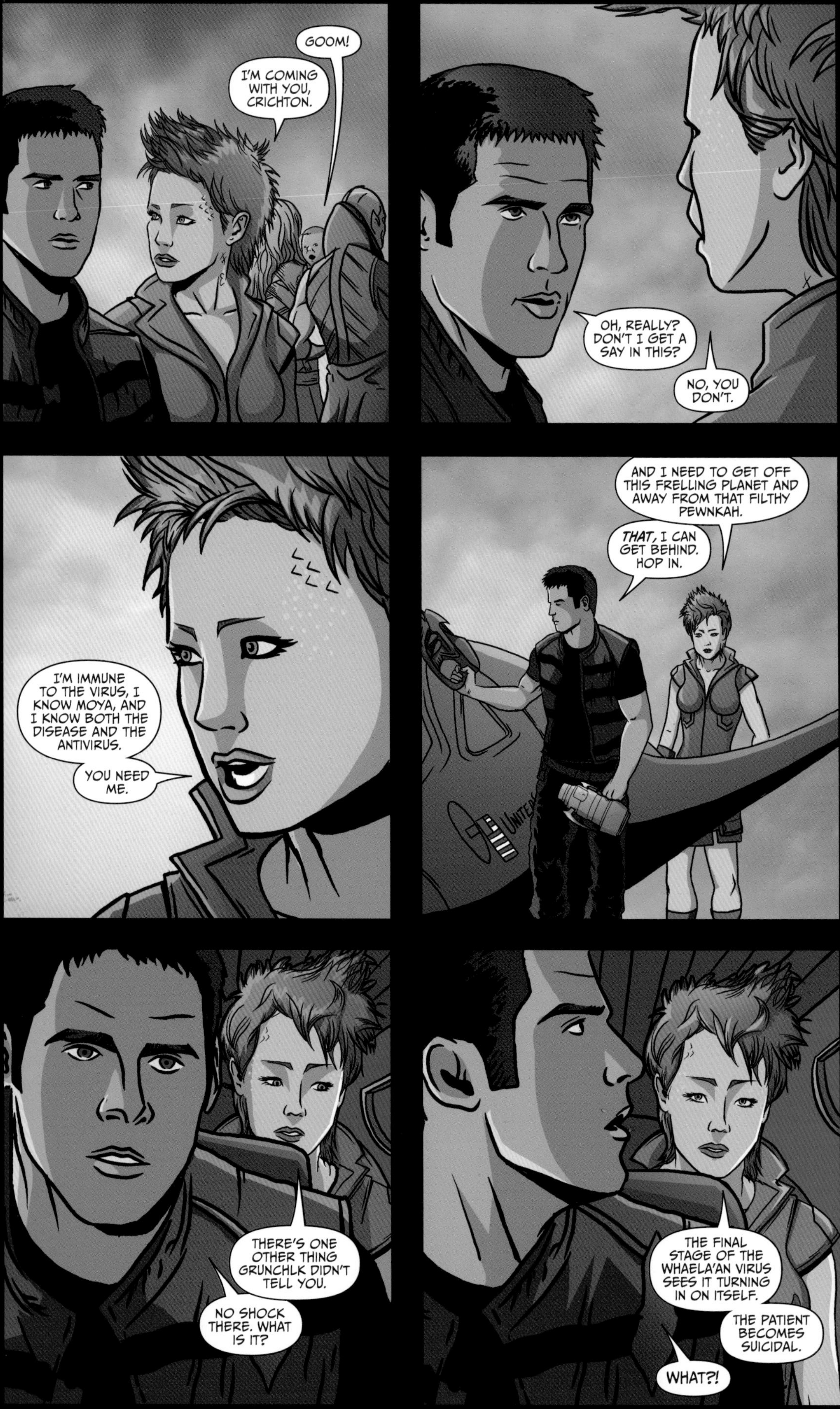
GOOM!
I'M COMING WITH YOU, CRICHTON.
OH, REALLY? DON'T I GET A SAY IN THIS?
NO, YOU DON'T.
I'M IMMUNE TO THE VIRUS, I KNOW MOYA, AND I KNOW BOTH THE DISEASE AND THE ANTIVIRUS.
YOU NEED ME.
AND I NEED TO GET OFF THIS FRELLING PLANET AND AWAY FROM THAT FILTHY PEWNKAH.
THAT, I CAN GET BEHIND. HOP IN.
UNITED
THERE'S ONE OTHER THING GRUNCHLK DIDN'T TELL YOU.
NO SHOCK THERE. WHAT IS IT?
THE FINAL STAGE OF THE WHAELA'AN VIRUS SEES IT TURNING IN ON ITSELF.
THE PATIENT BECOMES SUICIDAL.
WHAT?!

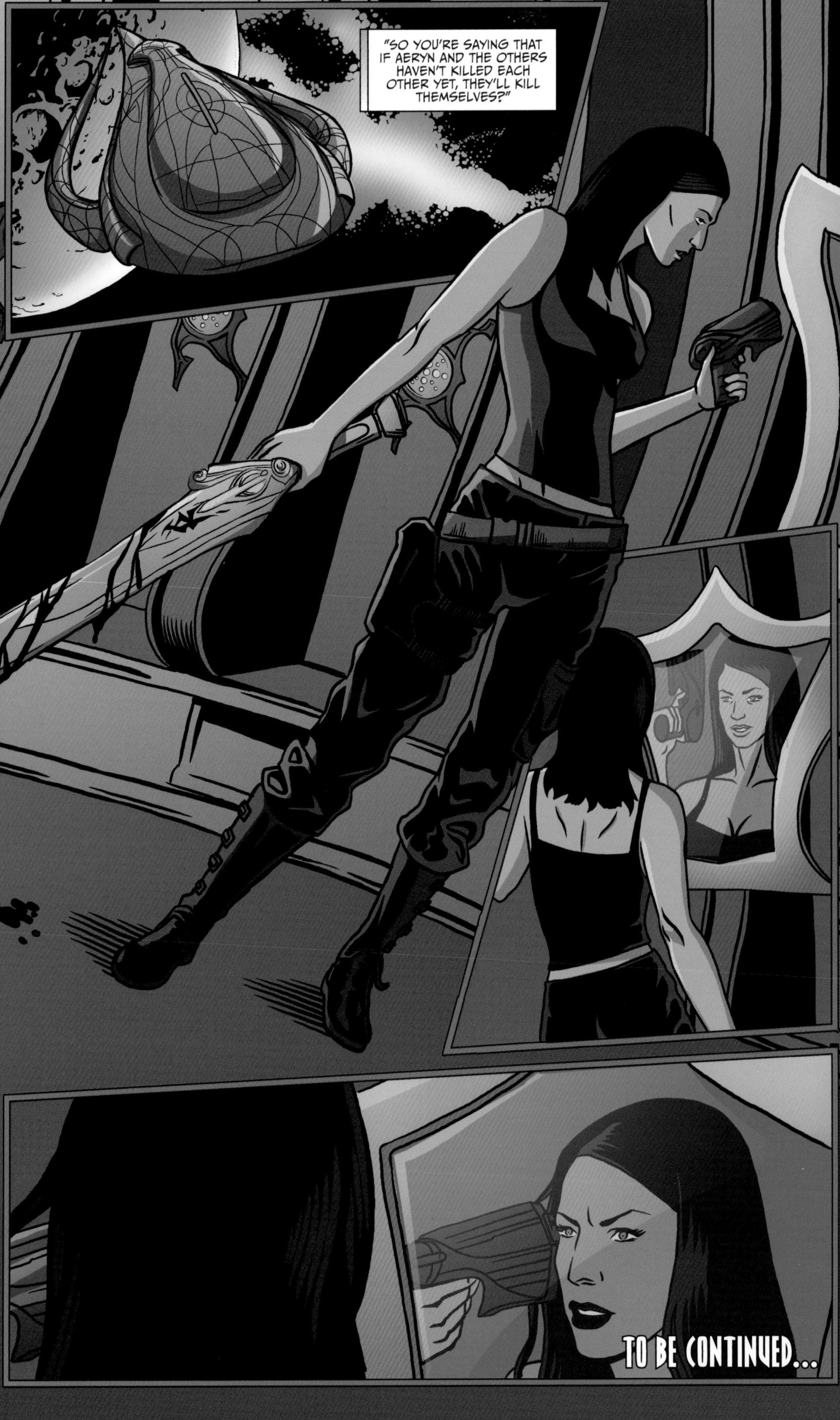
"SO YOU'RE SAYING THAT IF AERYN AND THE OTHERS HAVEN'T KILLED EACH OTHER YET, THEY'LL KILL THEMSELVES?"
TO BE CONTINUED...

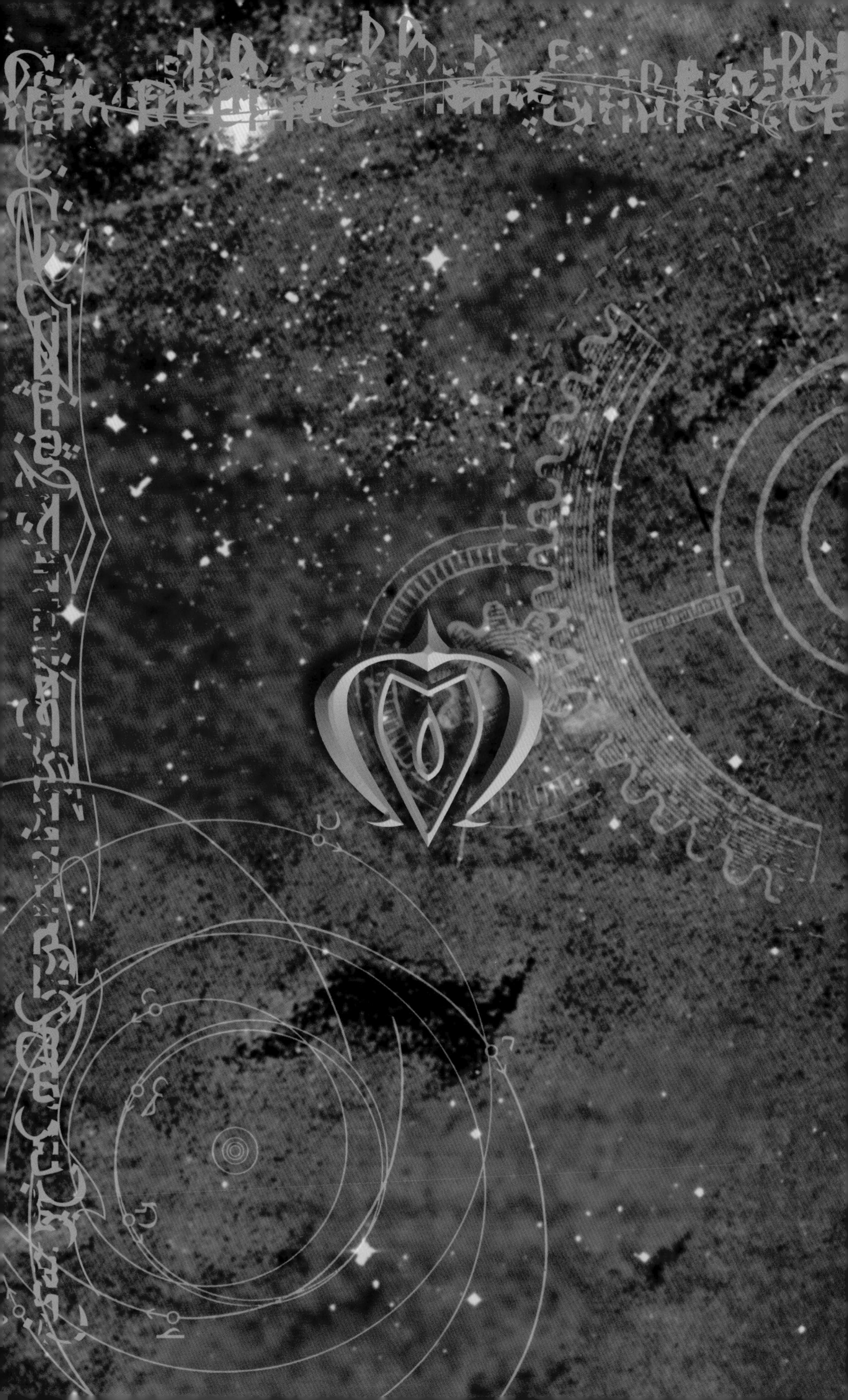

BOOK FOUR

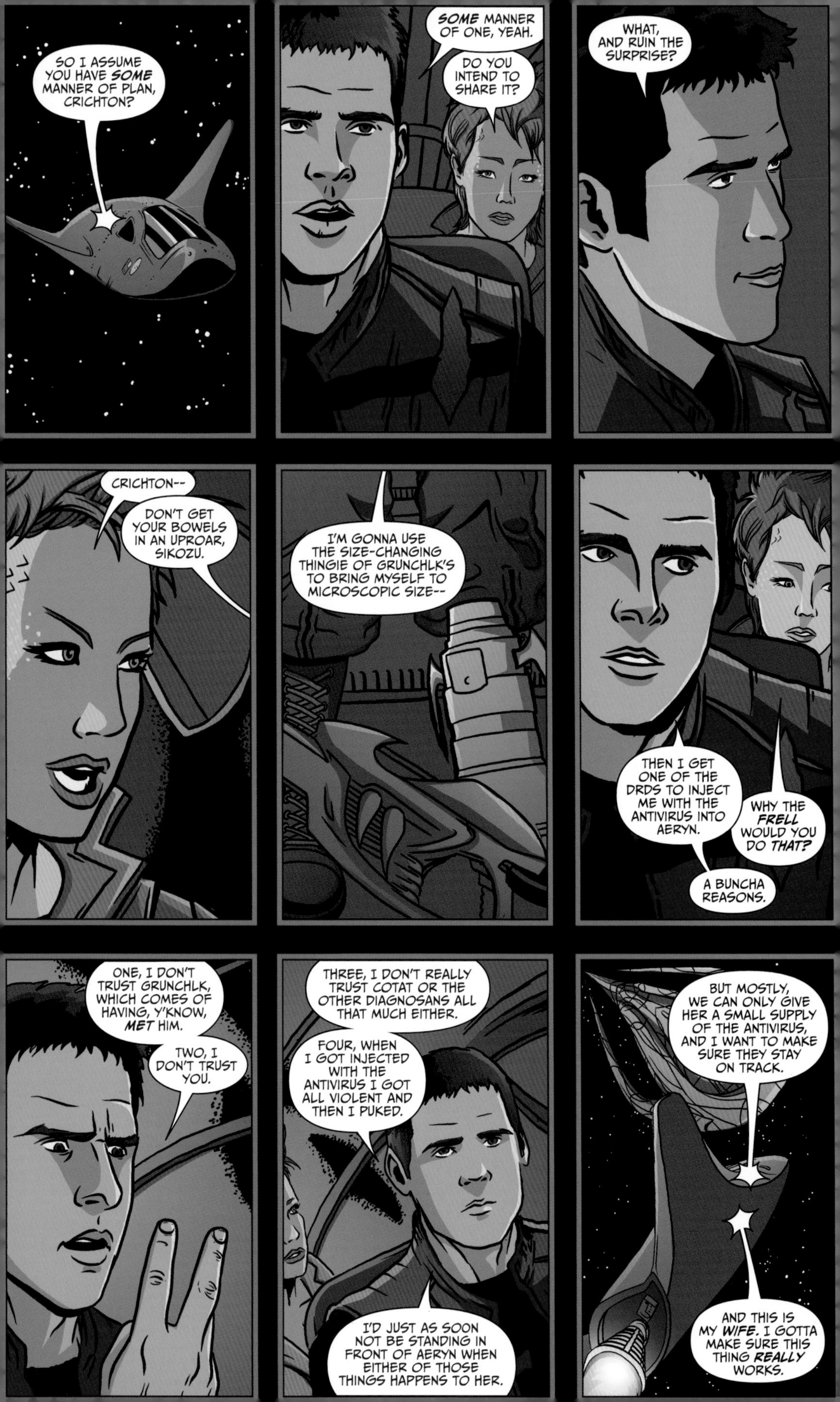
SO I ASSUME YOU HAVE **SOME** MANNER OF PLAN, CRICHTON?
SOME MANNER OF ONE, YEAH.
DO YOU INTEND TO SHARE IT?
WHAT, AND RUIN THE SURPRISE?
CRICHTON--
DON'T GET YOUR BOWELS IN AN UPROAR, SIKOZU.
I'M GONNA USE THE SIZE-CHANGING THINGIE OF GRUNCHLK'S TO BRING MYSELF TO MICROSCOPIC SIZE--
THEN I GET ONE OF THE DRDS TO INJECT ME WITH THE ANTIVIRUS INTO AERYN.
WHY THE **FRELL** WOULD YOU DO **THAT?**
A BUNCHA REASONS.
ONE, I DON'T TRUST GRUNCHLK, WHICH COMES OF HAVING, Y'KNOW, **MET** HIM.
TWO, I DON'T TRUST YOU.
THREE, I DON'T REALLY TRUST COTAT OR THE OTHER DIAGNOSANS ALL THAT MUCH EITHER.
FOUR, WHEN I GOT INJECTED WITH THE ANTIVIRUS I GOT ALL VIOLENT AND THEN I PUKED.
I'D JUST AS SOON NOT BE STANDING IN FRONT OF AERYN WHEN EITHER OF THOSE THINGS HAPPENS TO HER.
BUT MOSTLY, WE CAN ONLY GIVE HER A SMALL SUPPLY OF THE ANTIVIRUS, AND I WANT TO MAKE SURE THEY STAY ON TRACK.
AND THIS IS MY **WIFE**. I GOTTA MAKE SURE THIS THING **REALLY** WORKS.

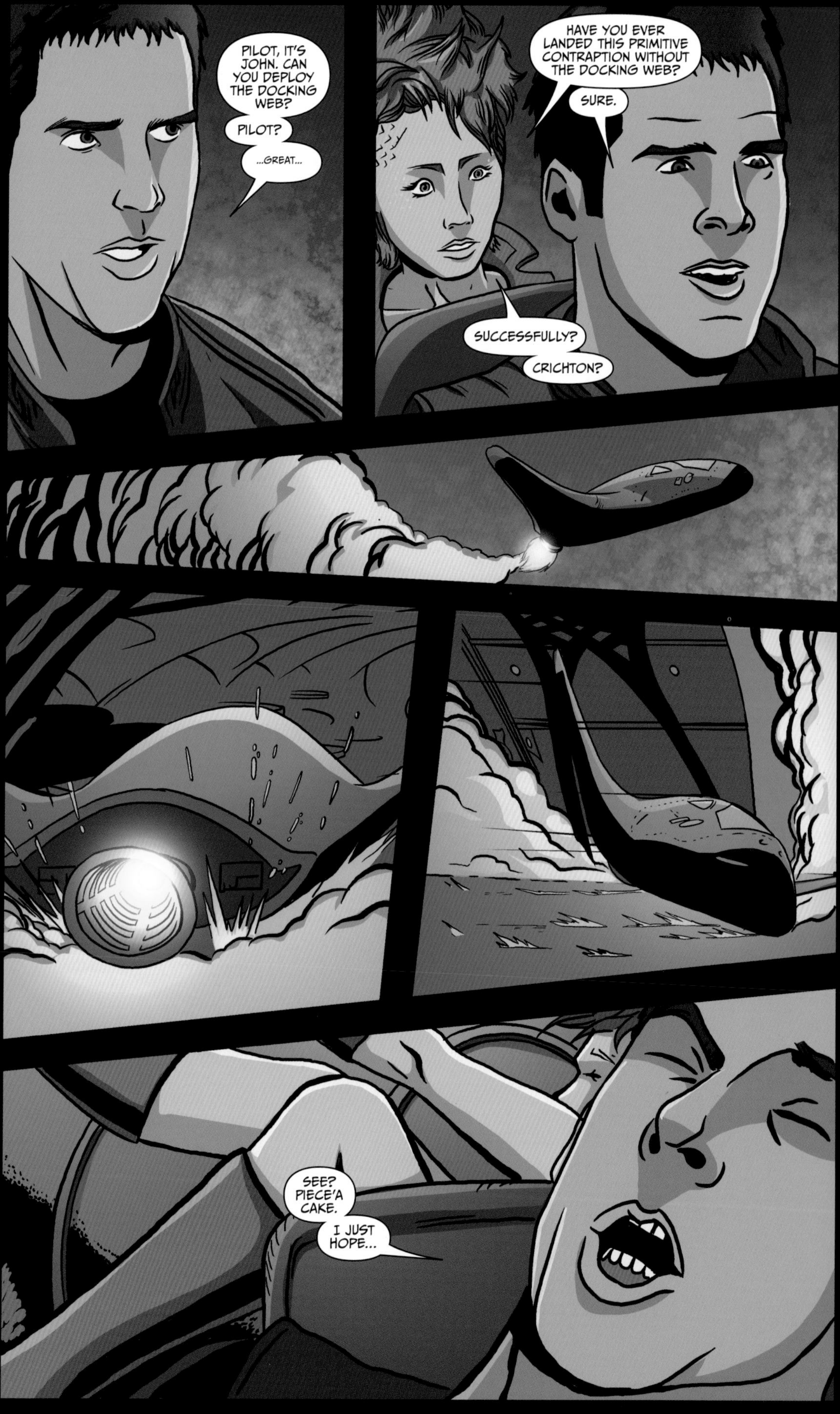
PILOT, IT'S JOHN. CAN YOU DEPLOY THE DOCKING WEB?
PILOT?
...GREAT...
HAVE YOU EVER LANDED THIS PRIMITIVE CONTRAPTION WITHOUT THE DOCKING WEB?
SURE.
SUCCESSFULLY?
CRICHTON?
SEE? PIECE'A CAKE.
I JUST HOPE...

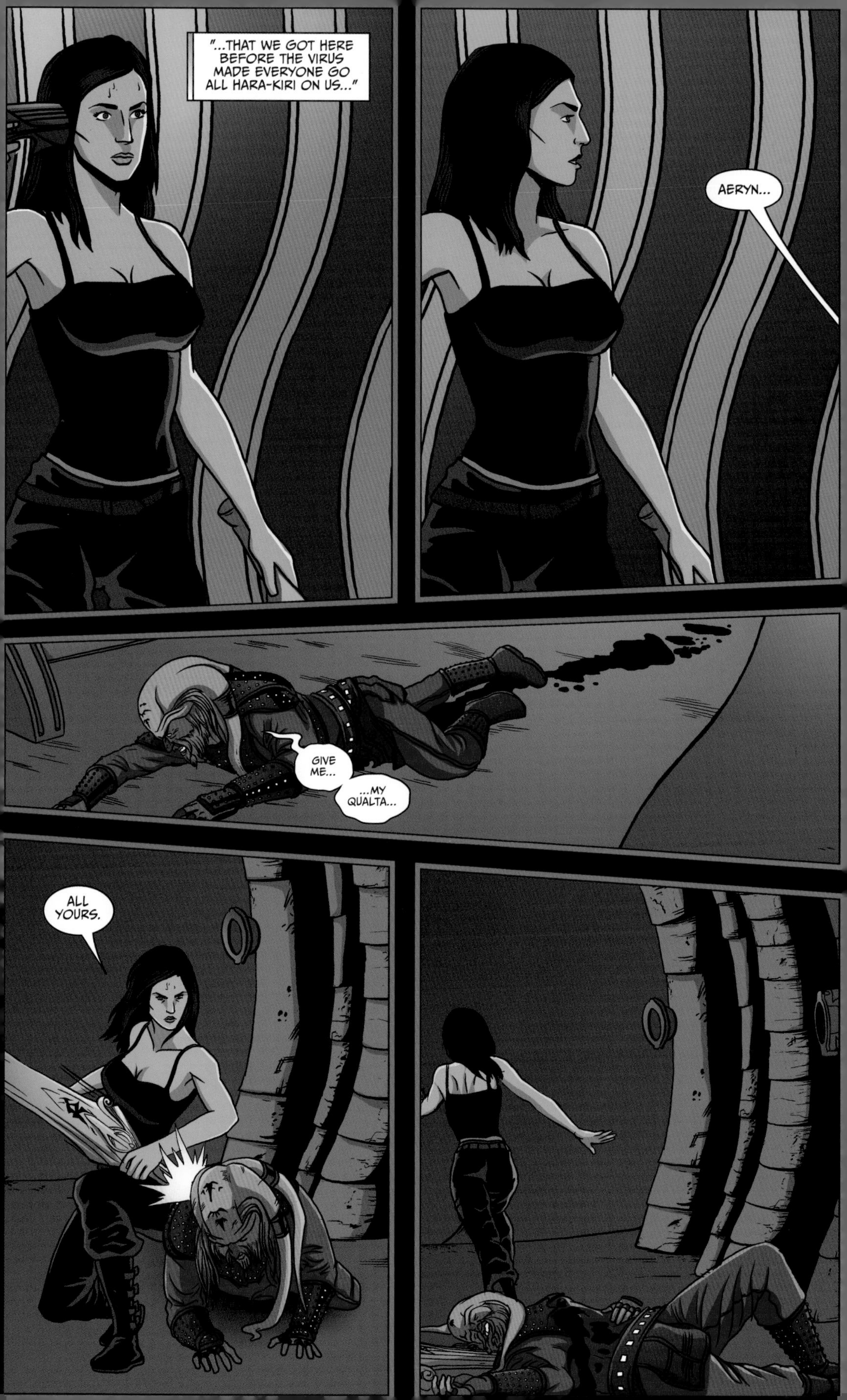
"...THAT WE GOT HERE BEFORE THE VIRUS MADE EVERYONE GO ALL HARA-KIRI ON US..."
AERYN...
GIVE ME...
...MY QUALTA...
ALL YOURS.

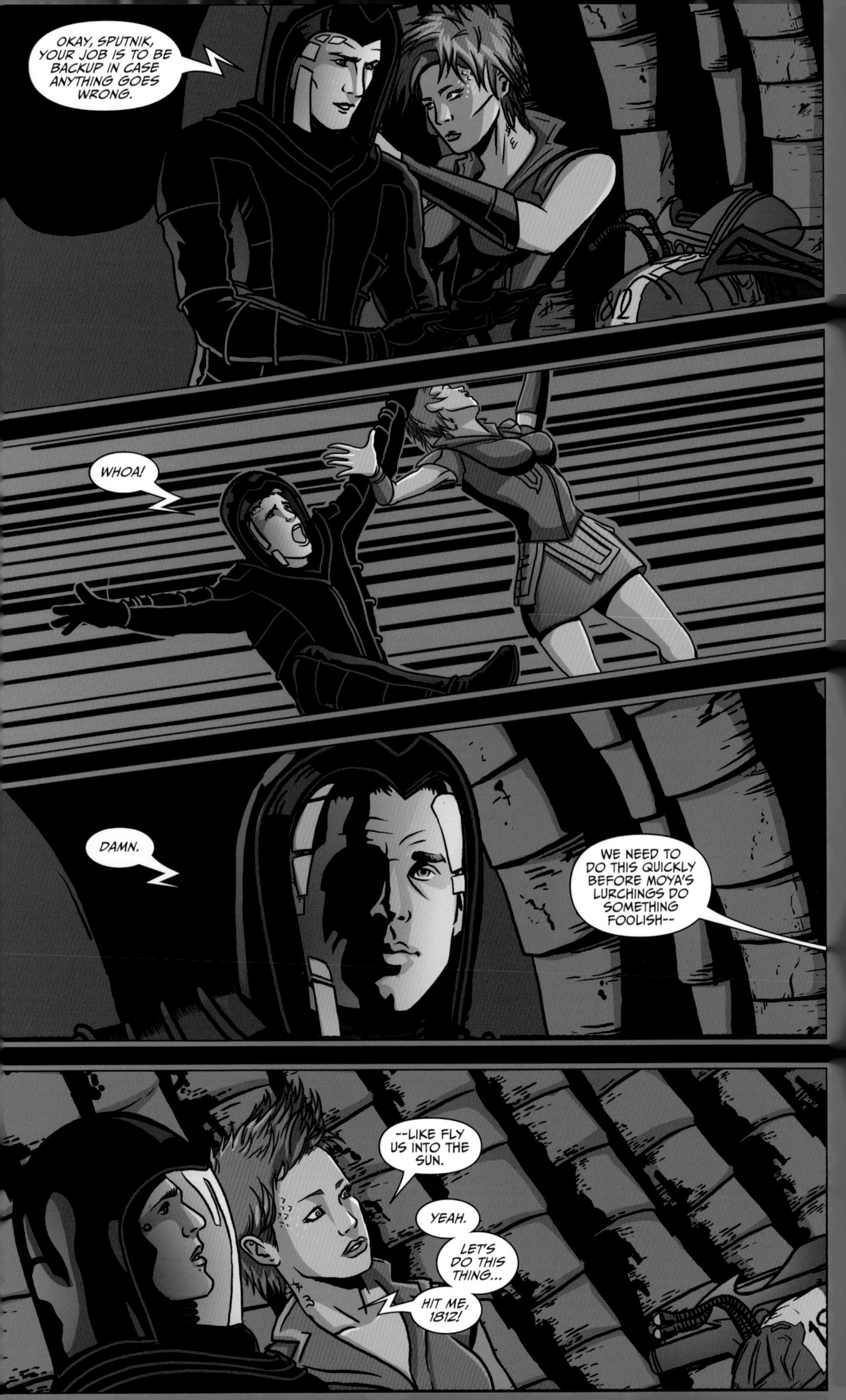
OKAY, SPUTNIK, YOUR JOB IS TO BE BACKUP IN CASE ANYTHING GOES WRONG.
WHOA!
DAMN.
WE NEED TO DO THIS QUICKLY BEFORE MOYA'S LURCHINGS DO SOMETHING FOOLISH--
--LIKE FLY US INTO THE SUN.
YEAH.
LET'S DO THIS THING...
HIT ME, 1812!

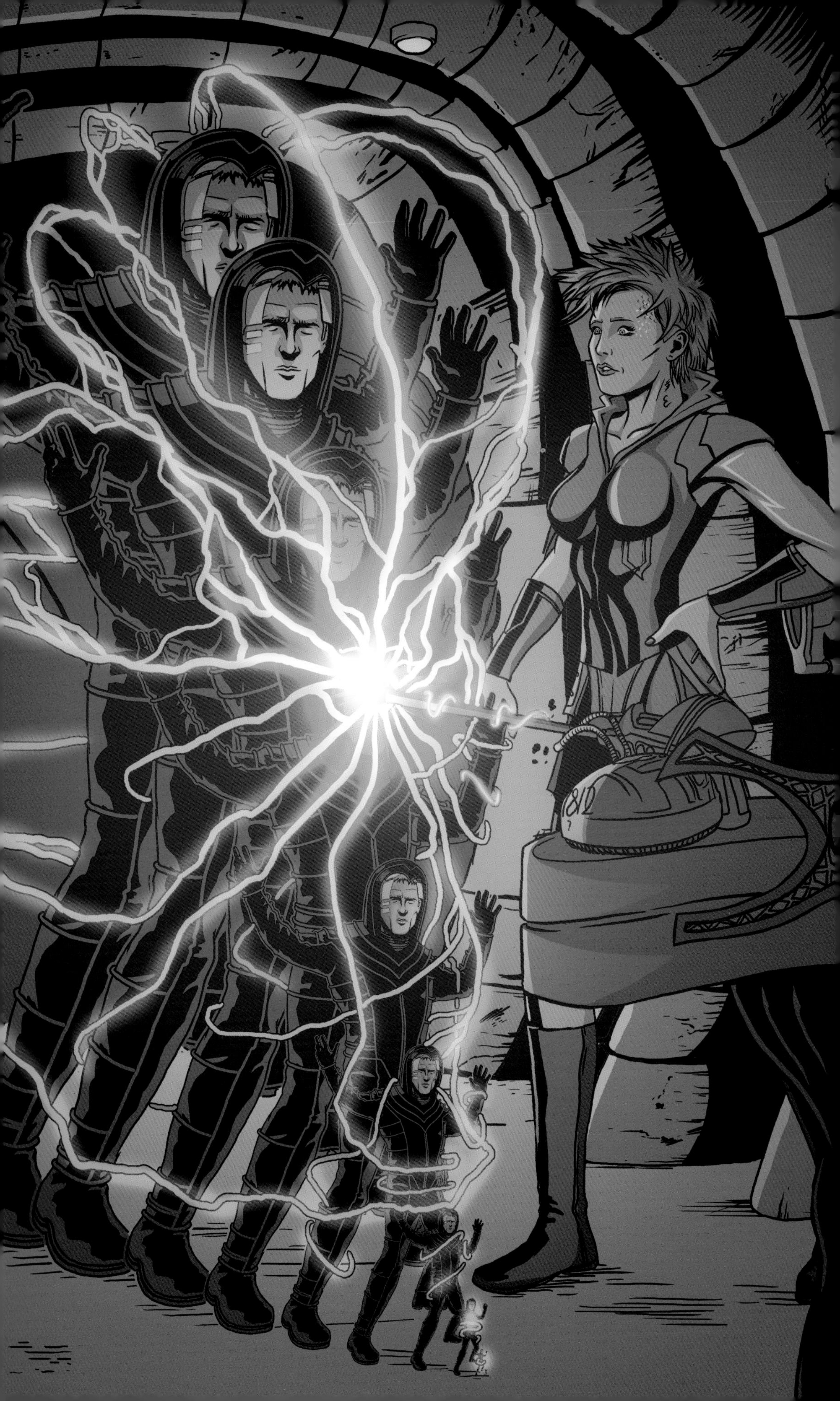

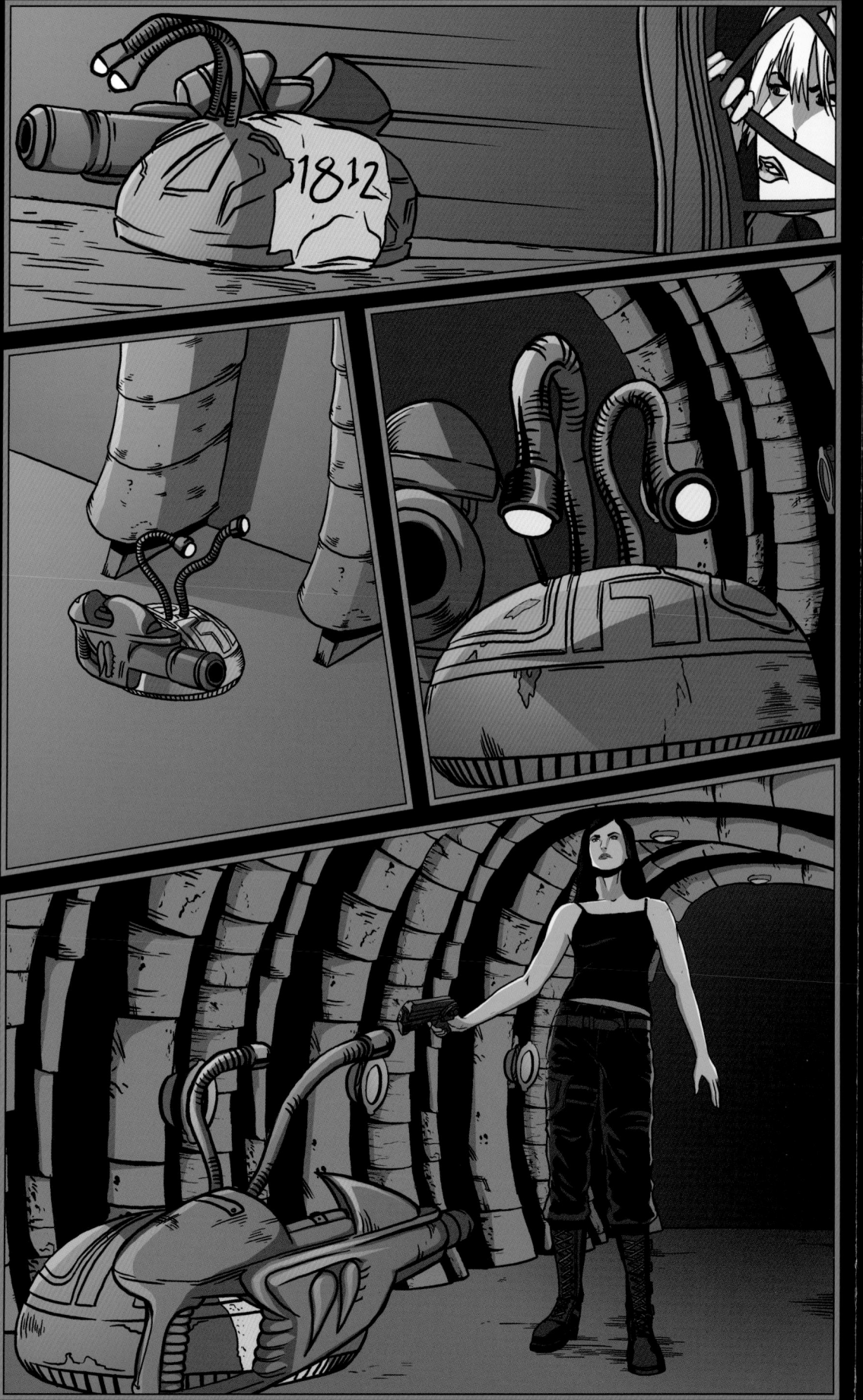

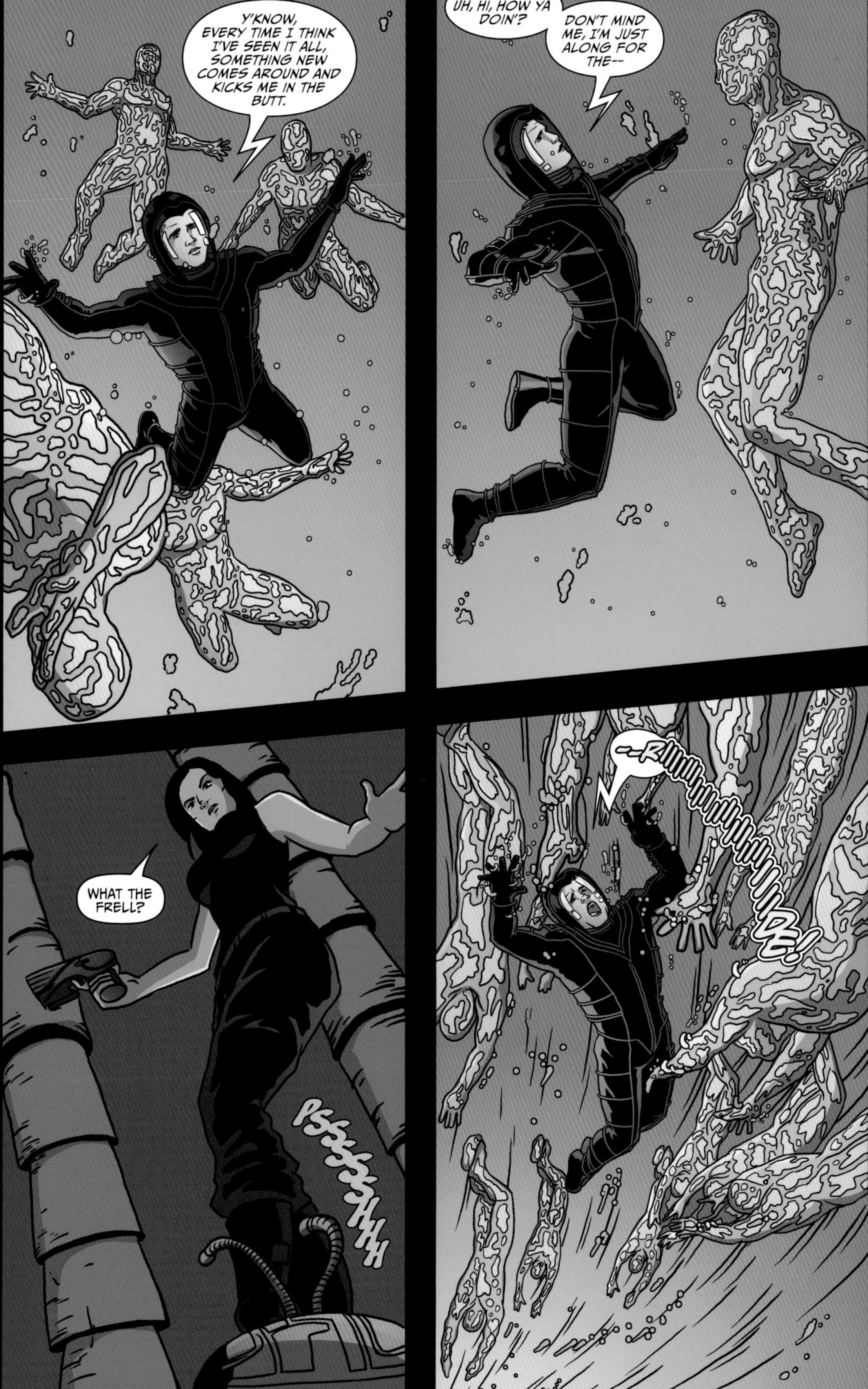
Y'KNOW, EVERY TIME I THINK I'VE SEEN IT ALL, SOMETHING NEW COMES AROUND AND KICKS ME IN THE BUTT.
UH, HI, HOW YA DOIN'?
DON'T MIND ME, I'M JUST ALONG FOR THE--
WHAT THE FRELL?
PSSSSSHHH
--RIIIIIIIIIIIIIIIIIDE!

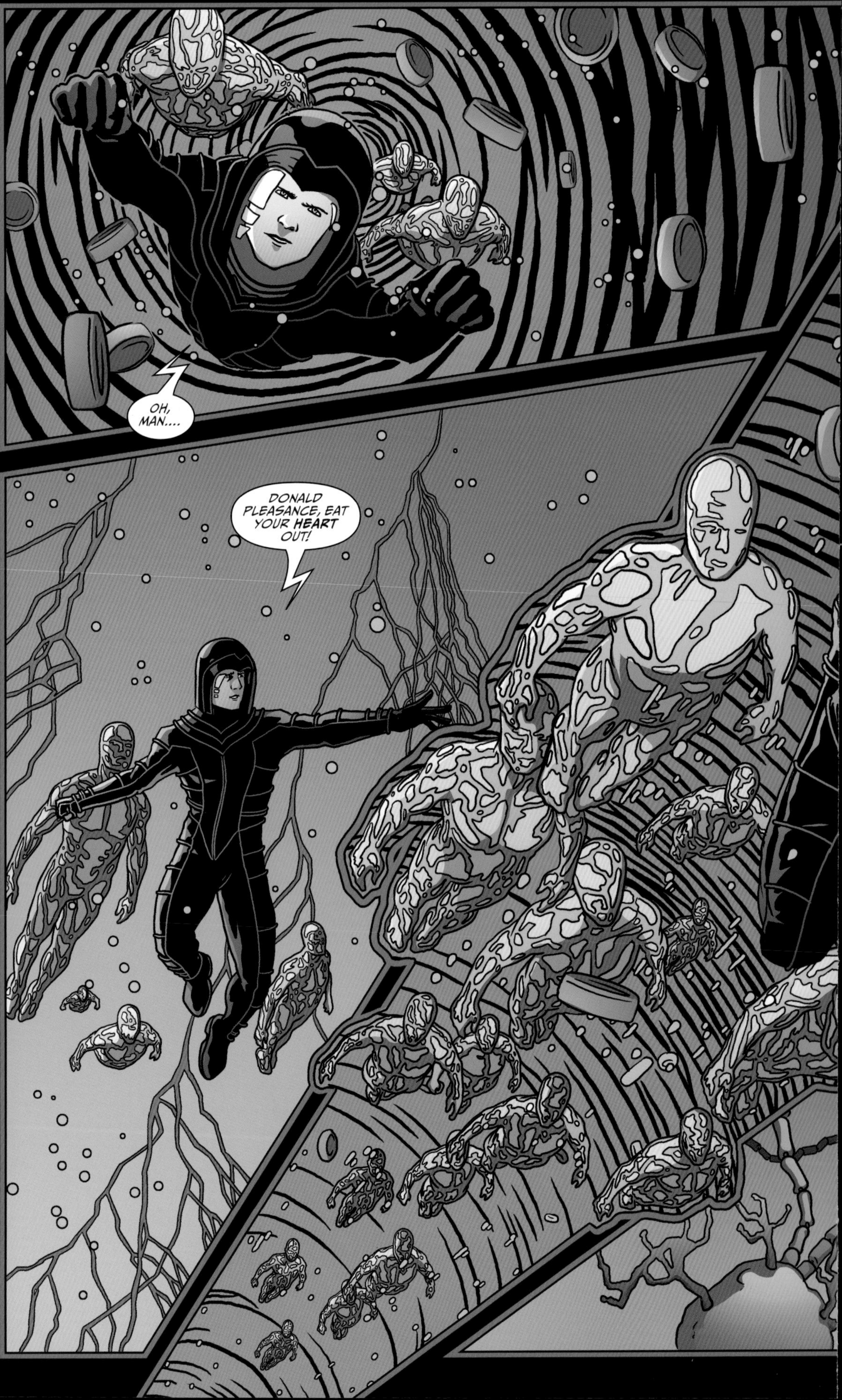
OH, MAN....
DONALD PLEASANCE, EAT YOUR **HEART** OUT!

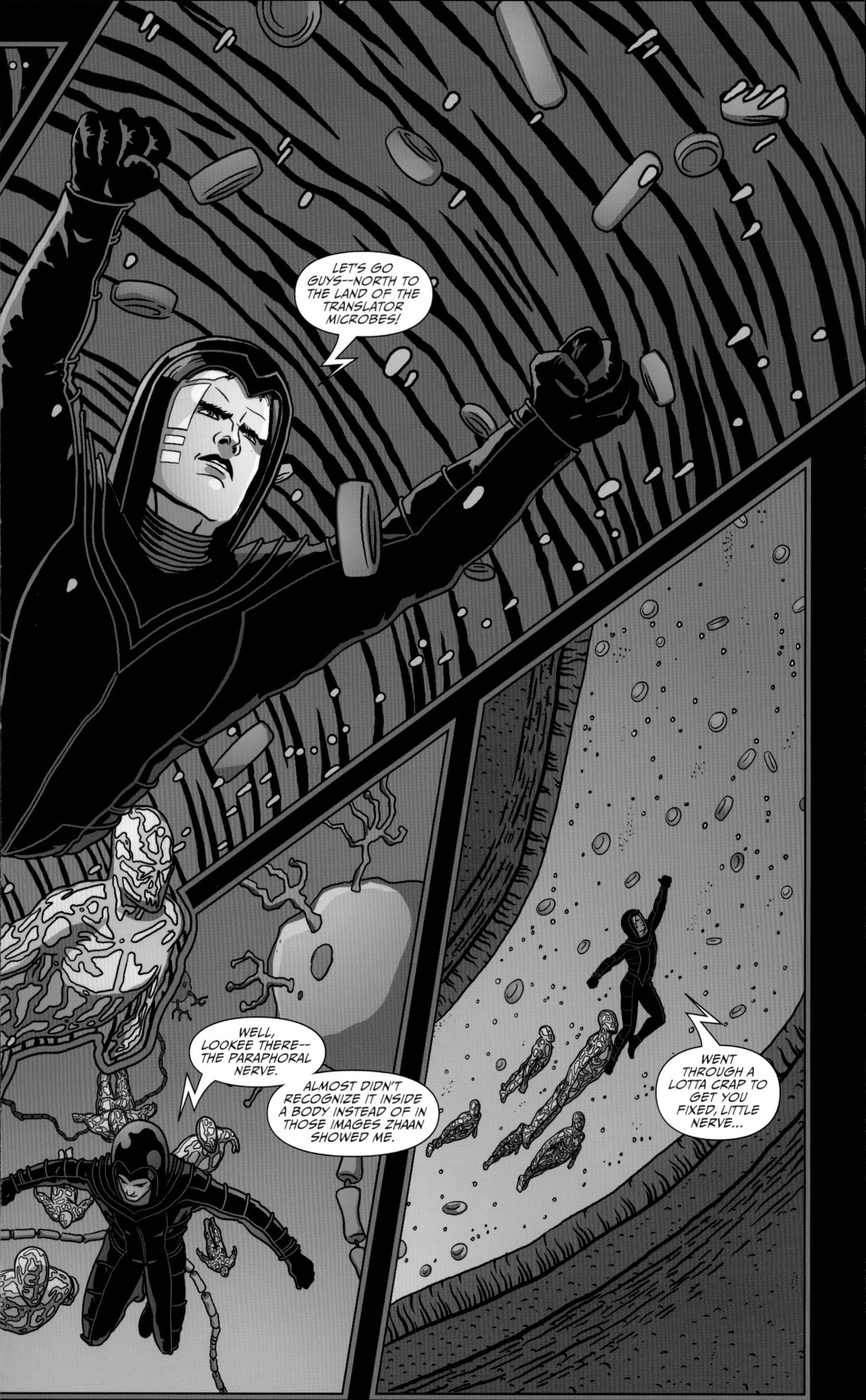
LET'S GO GUYS--NORTH TO THE LAND OF THE TRANSLATOR MICROBES!
WELL, LOOKEE THERE--THE PARAPHORAL NERVE.
ALMOST DIDN'T RECOGNIZE IT INSIDE A BODY INSTEAD OF IN THOSE IMAGES ZHAAN SHOWED ME.
WENT THROUGH A LOTTA CRAP TO GET YOU FIXED, LITTLE NERVE...

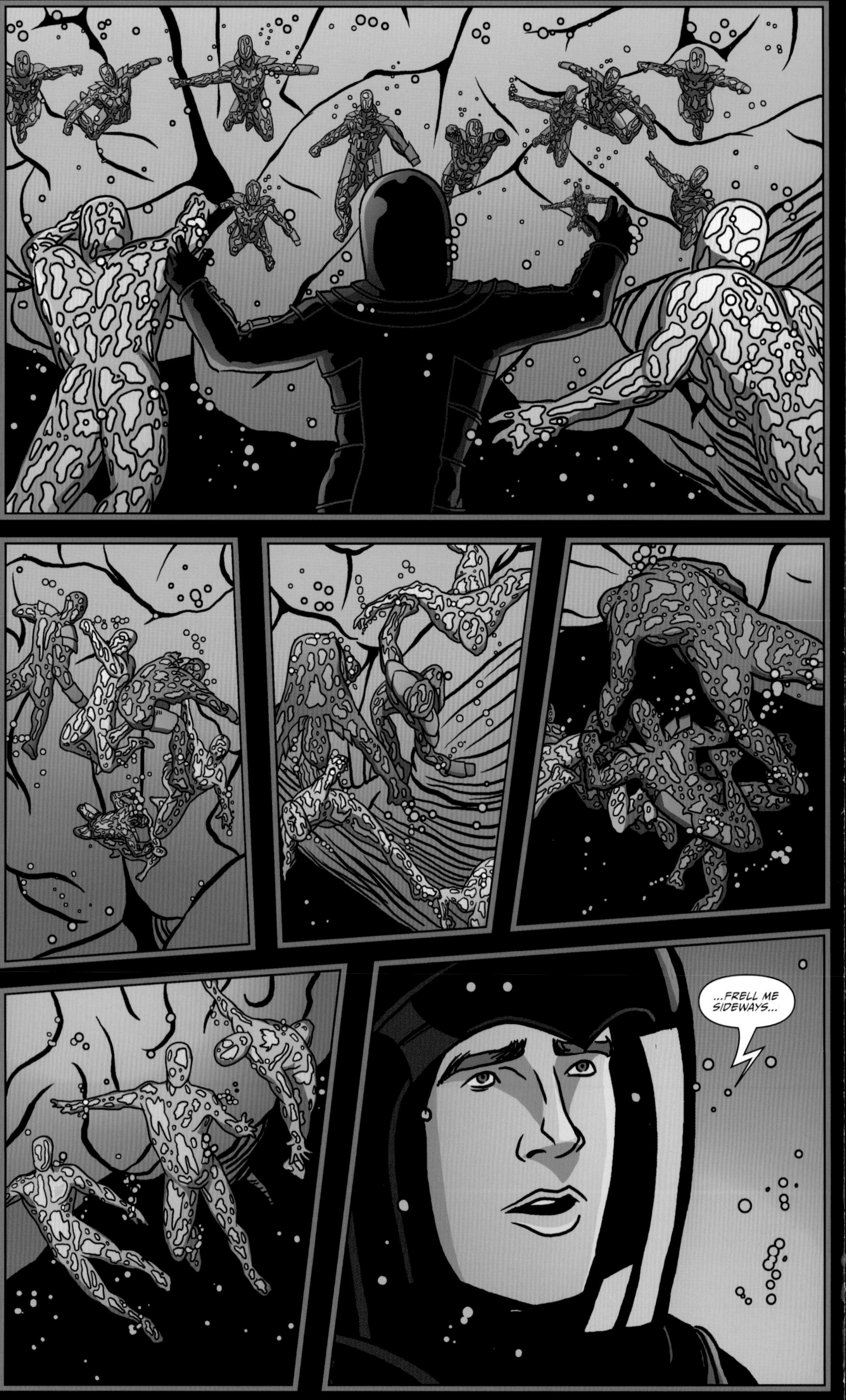
...FRELL ME SIDEWAYS...

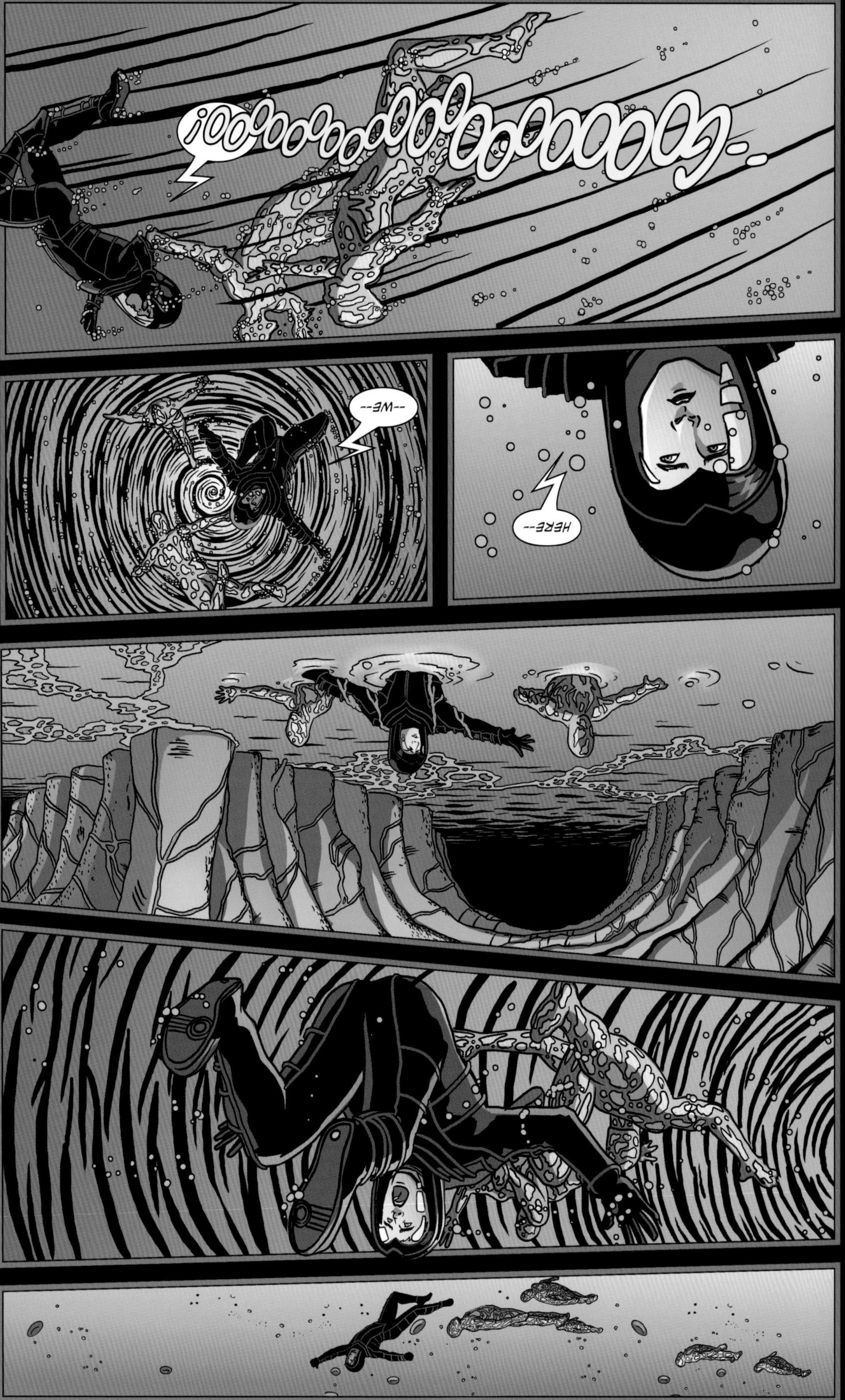

¡OOOOOOOOOOOOOOOOOOg--
--WE--
HERE--

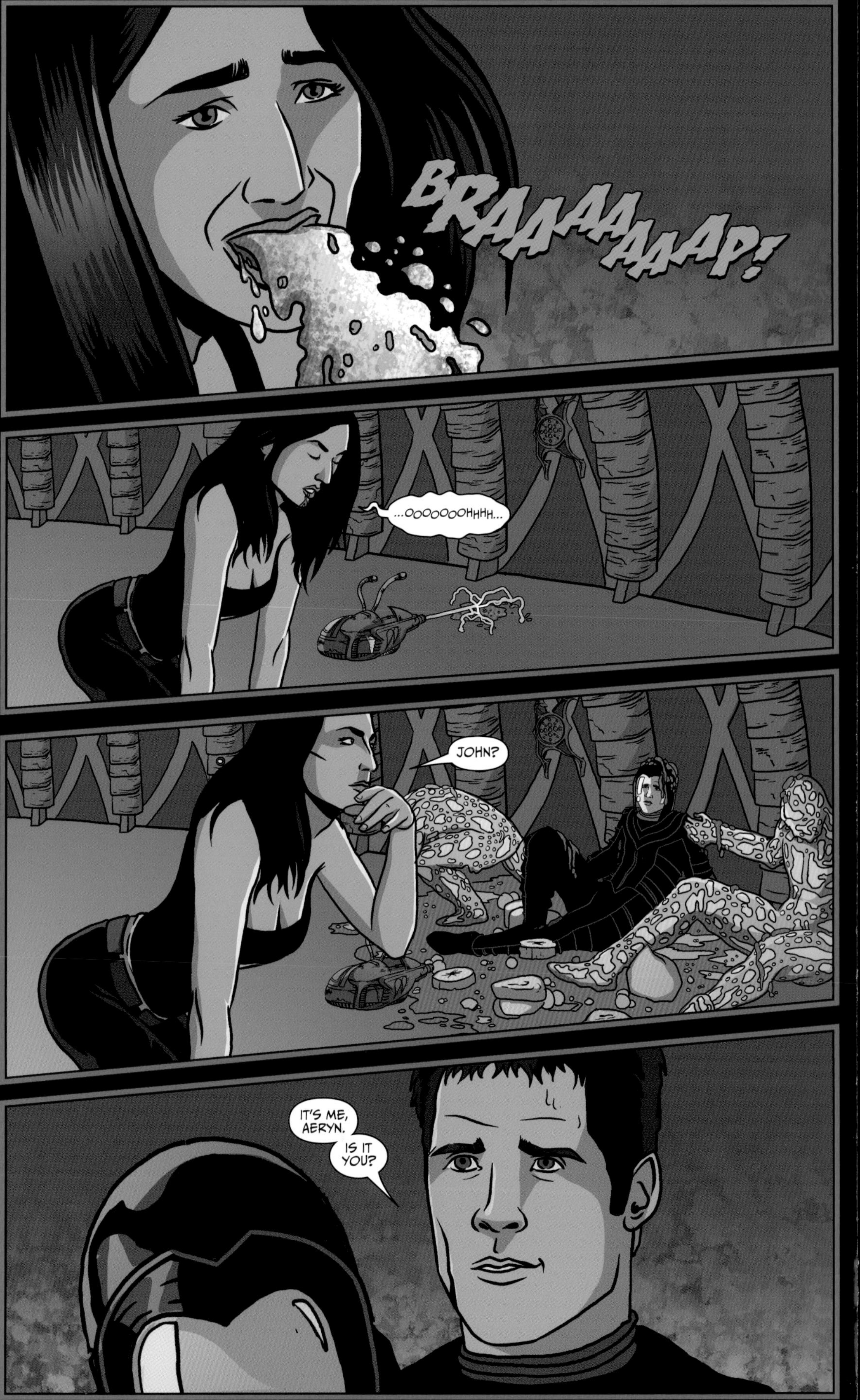
BRAAAAAAAAP!
...OOOOOOOHHHH...
JOHN?
IT'S ME, AERYN.
IS IT YOU?

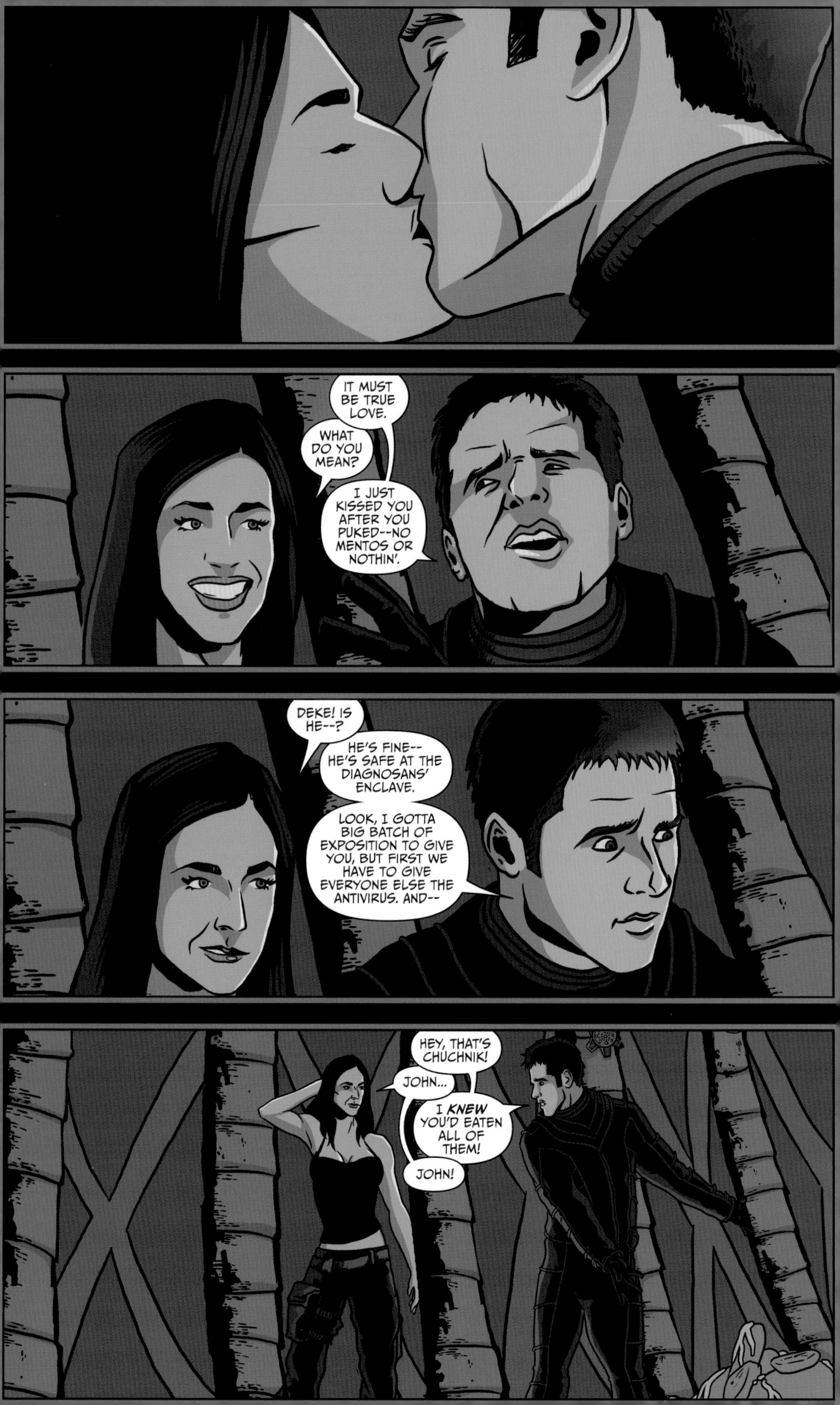
IT MUST BE TRUE LOVE.
WHAT DO YOU MEAN?
I JUST KISSED YOU AFTER YOU PUKED--NO MENTOS OR NOTHIN'.
DEKE! IS HE--?
HE'S FINE--HE'S SAFE AT THE DIAGNOSANS' ENCLAVE.
LOOK, I GOTTA BIG BATCH OF EXPOSITION TO GIVE YOU, BUT FIRST WE HAVE TO GIVE EVERYONE ELSE THE ANTIVIRUS. AND--
HEY, THAT'S CHUCHNIK!
JOHN...
I *KNEW* YOU'D EATEN ALL OF THEM!
JOHN!

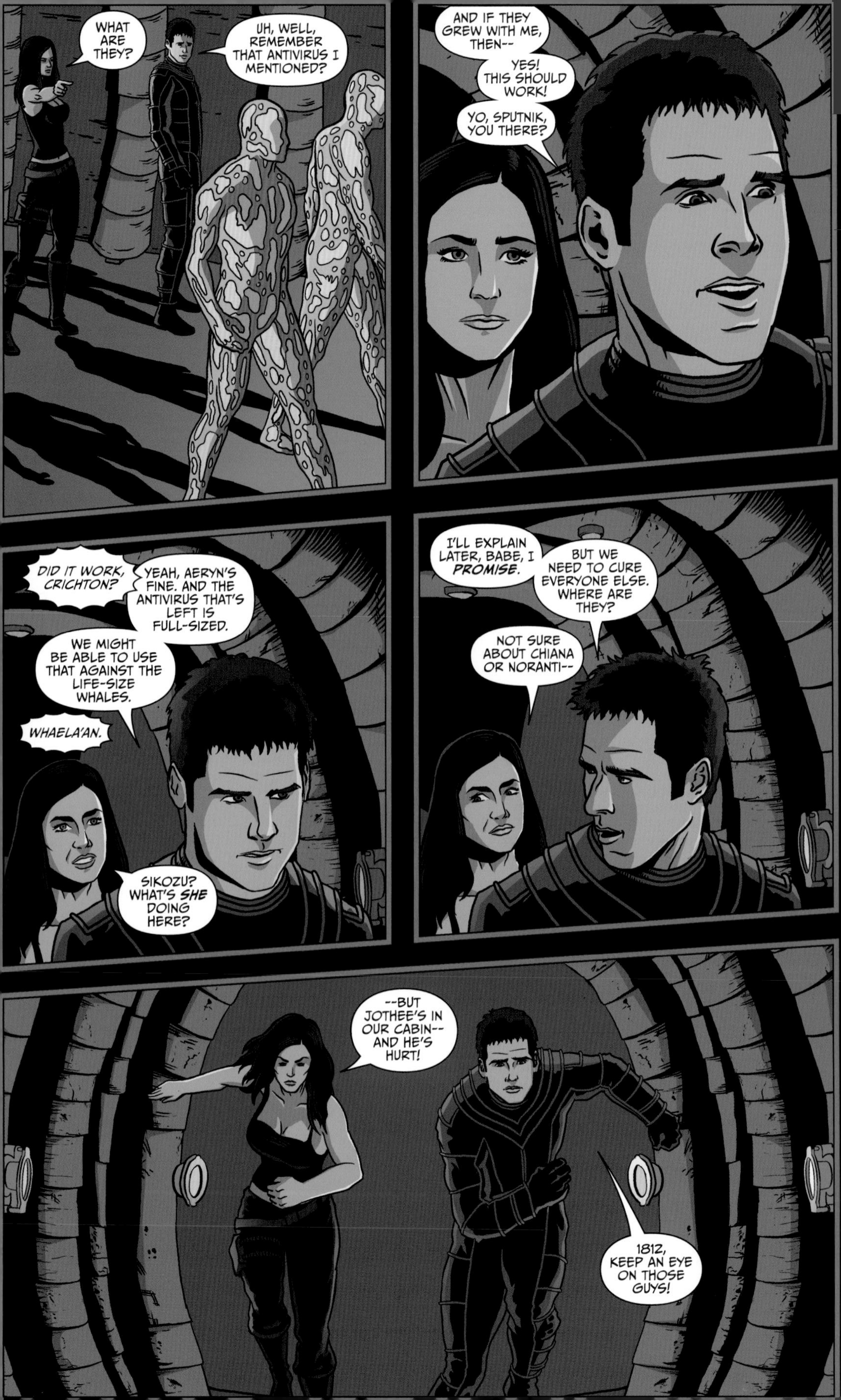
WHAT ARE THEY?
UH, WELL, REMEMBER THAT ANTIVIRUS I MENTIONED?
AND IF THEY GREW WITH ME, THEN--
YES! THIS SHOULD WORK!
YO, SPUTNIK, YOU THERE?
DID IT WORK, CRICHTON?
YEAH, AERYN'S FINE. AND THE ANTIVIRUS THAT'S LEFT IS FULL-SIZED.
WE MIGHT BE ABLE TO USE THAT AGAINST THE LIFE-SIZE WHALES.
WHAELA'AN.
SIKOZU? WHAT'S *SHE* DOING HERE?
I'LL EXPLAIN LATER, BABE, I ***PROMISE***.
BUT WE NEED TO CURE EVERYONE ELSE. WHERE ARE THEY?
NOT SURE ABOUT CHIANA OR NORANTI--
--BUT JOTHEE'S IN OUR CABIN-- AND HE'S HURT!
1812, KEEP AN EYE ON THOSE GUYS!

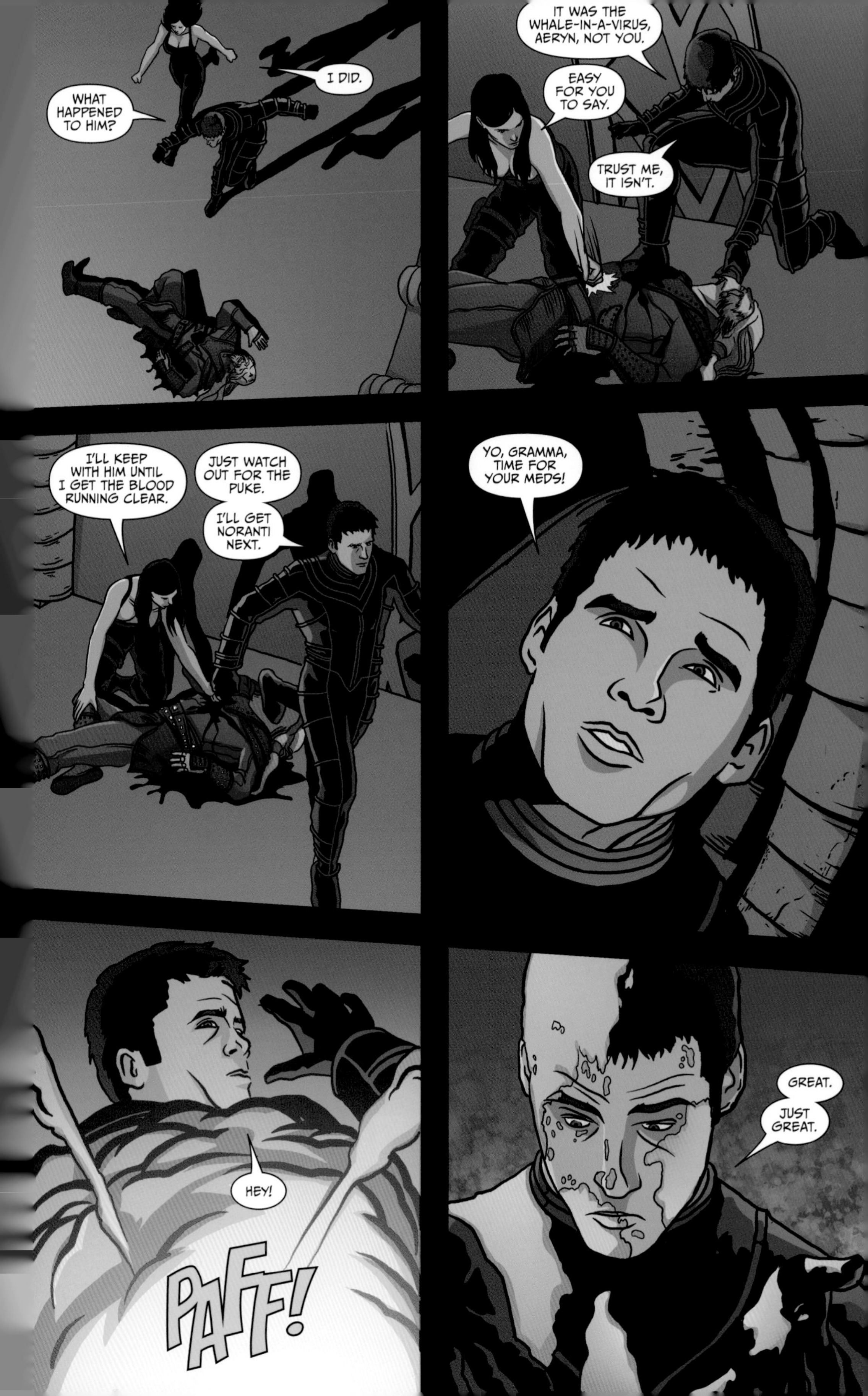
WHAT HAPPENED TO HIM?
I DID.
IT WAS THE WHALE-IN-A-VIRUS, AERYN, NOT YOU.
EASY FOR YOU TO SAY.
TRUST ME, IT ISN'T.
I'LL KEEP WITH HIM UNTIL I GET THE BLOOD RUNNING CLEAR.
JUST WATCH OUT FOR THE PUKE.
I'LL GET NORANTI NEXT.
YO, GRAMMA, TIME FOR YOUR MEDS!
HEY!
PAFF!
GREAT.
JUST GREAT.

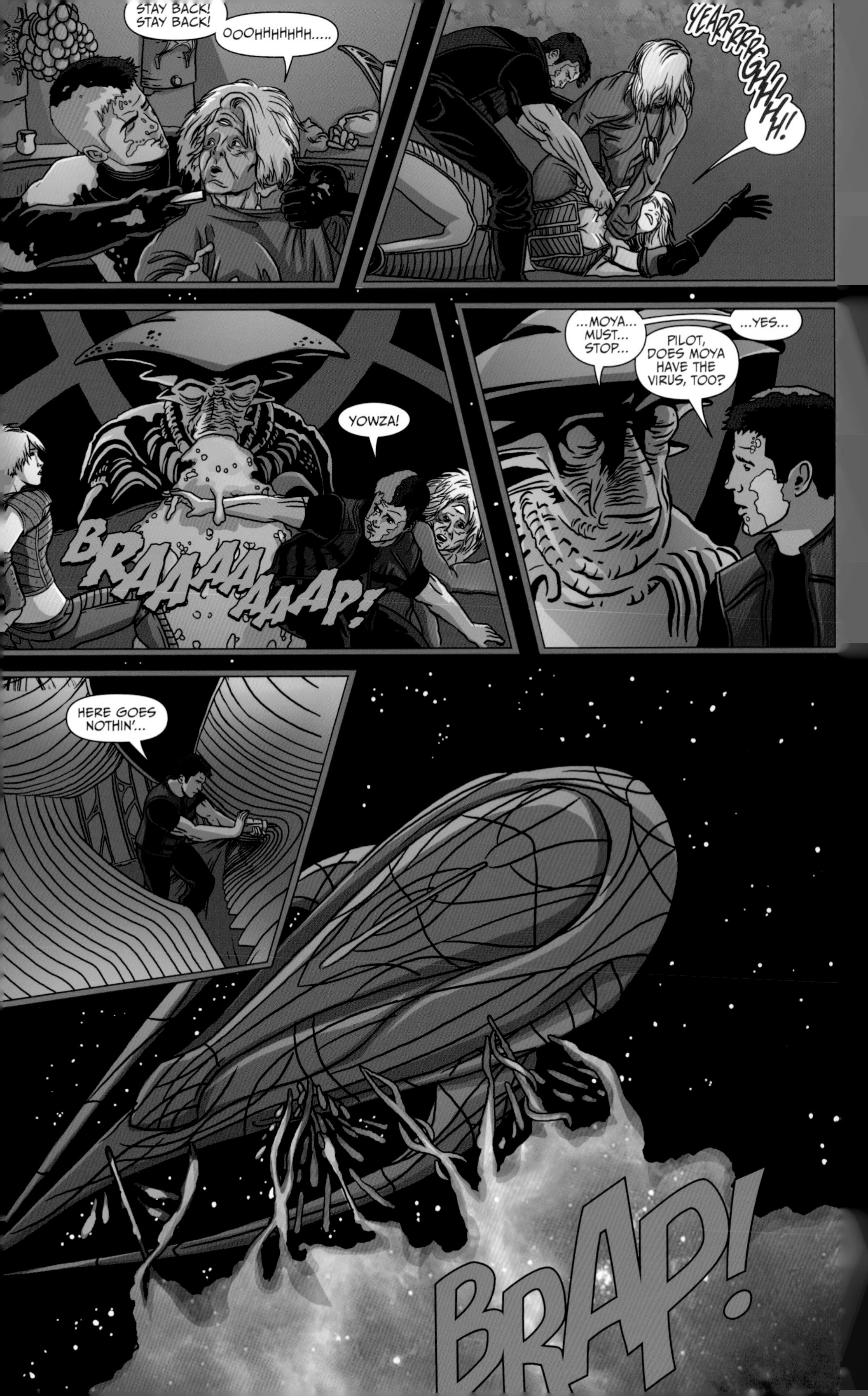
STAY BACK! STAY BACK!
OOOHHHHHHH.....
YEARRRGHHH!
YOWZA!
BRAAAAAAAAP!
...MOYA... MUST... STOP...
PILOT, DOES MOYA HAVE THE VIRUS, TOO?
...YES...
HERE GOES NOTHIN'...
BRAP!

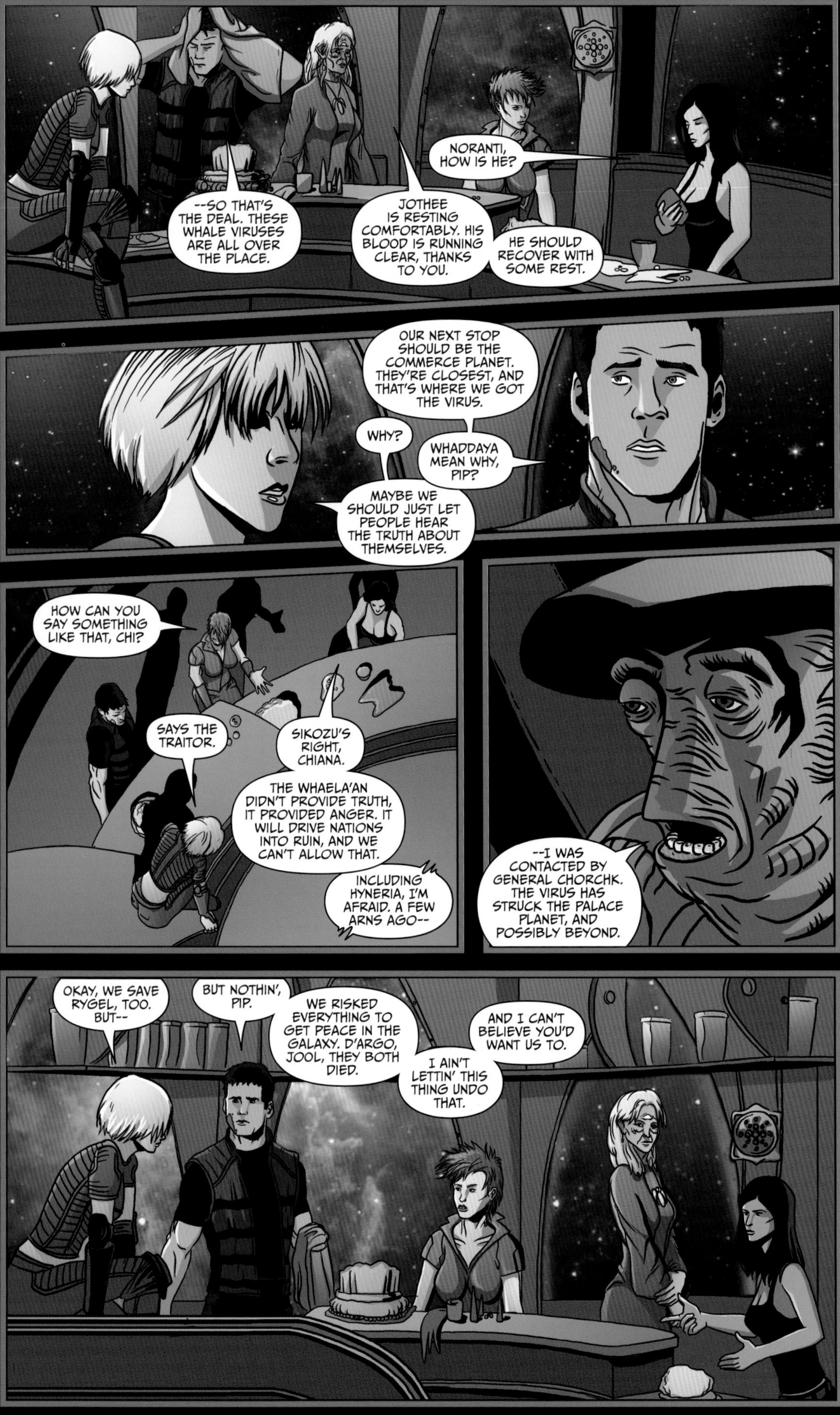
--SO THAT'S THE DEAL. THESE WHALE VIRUSES ARE ALL OVER THE PLACE.
NORANTI, HOW IS HE?
JOTHEE IS RESTING COMFORTABLY. HIS BLOOD IS RUNNING CLEAR, THANKS TO YOU.
HE SHOULD RECOVER WITH SOME REST.
OUR NEXT STOP SHOULD BE THE COMMERCE PLANET. THEY'RE CLOSEST, AND THAT'S WHERE WE GOT THE VIRUS.
WHY?
WHADDAYA MEAN WHY, PIP?
MAYBE WE SHOULD JUST LET PEOPLE HEAR THE TRUTH ABOUT THEMSELVES.
HOW CAN YOU SAY SOMETHING LIKE THAT, CHI?
SAYS THE TRAITOR.
SIKOZU'S RIGHT, CHIANA.
THE WHAELA'AN DIDN'T PROVIDE TRUTH, IT PROVIDED ANGER. IT WILL DRIVE NATIONS INTO RUIN, AND WE CAN'T ALLOW THAT.
INCLUDING HYNERIA, I'M AFRAID. A FEW ARNS AGO--
--I WAS CONTACTED BY GENERAL CHORCHK. THE VIRUS HAS STRUCK THE PALACE PLANET, AND POSSIBLY BEYOND.
OKAY, WE SAVE RYGEL, TOO. BUT--
BUT NOTHIN', PIP.
WE RISKED EVERYTHING TO GET PEACE IN THE GALAXY. D'ARGO, JOOL, THEY BOTH DIED.
I AIN'T LETTIN' THIS THING UNDO THAT.
AND I CAN'T BELIEVE YOU'D WANT US TO.

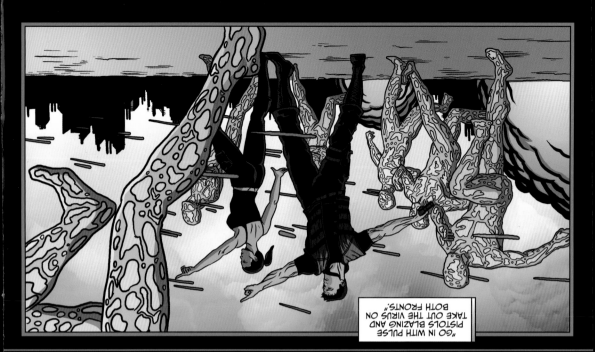

"GO IN WITH PULSE PISTOLS BLAZING AND TAKE OUT THE VIRUS ON BOTH FRONTS."

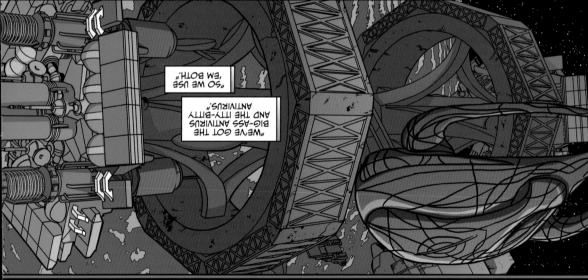

"WE'VE GOT THE BIG-ASS ANTIVIRUS AND THE ITTY-BITTY ANTIVIRUS."

"SO WE USE 'EM BOTH."

"DAMMIT."

"OKAY, HERE'S MY IDEA..."

"FINE. DO WHATEVER YOU WANT. I DON'T CARE."

"PIP! WHAT THE HELL'S WITH YOU?"

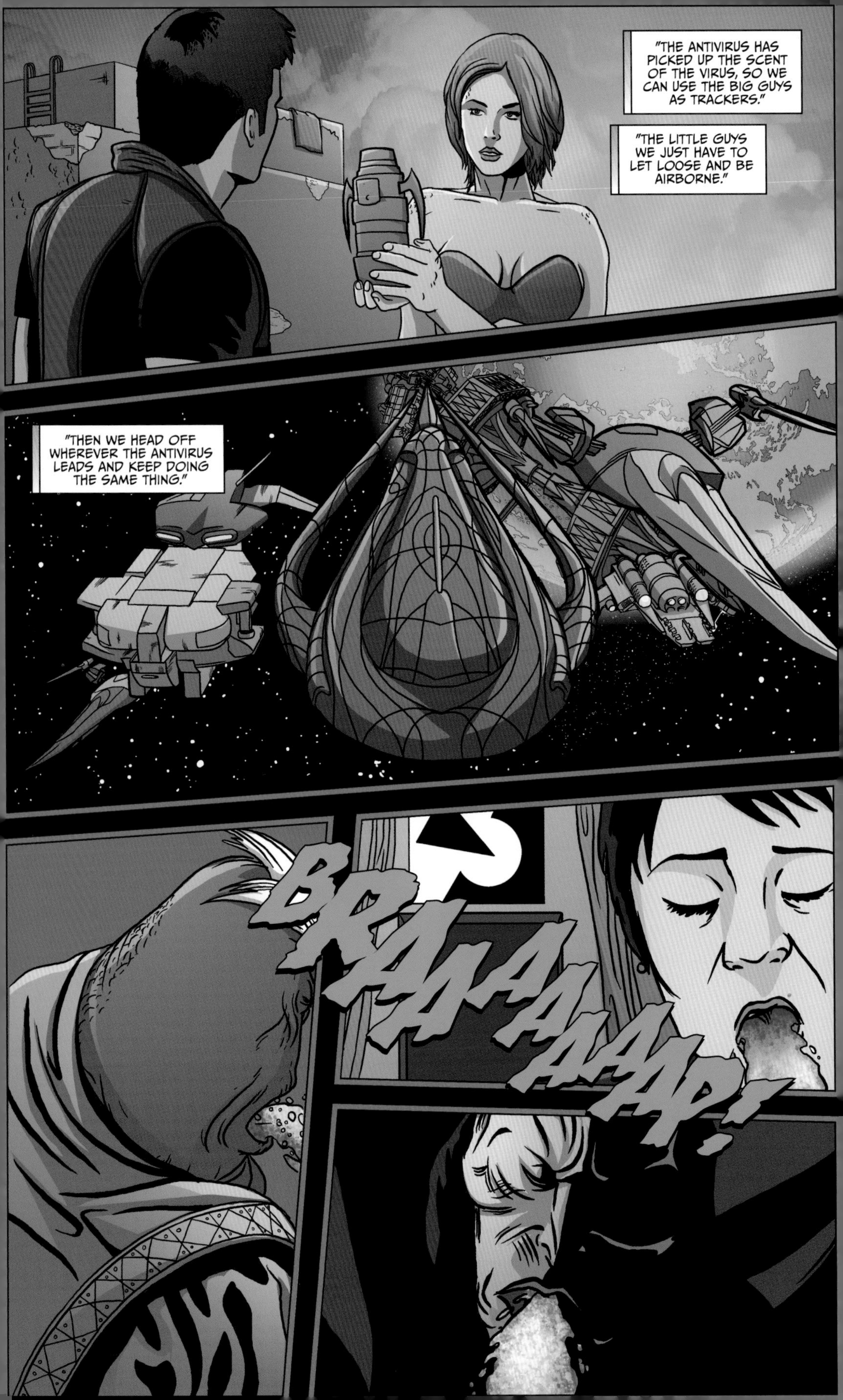
"THE ANTIVIRUS HAS PICKED UP THE SCENT OF THE VIRUS, SO WE CAN USE THE BIG GUYS AS TRACKERS."
"THE LITTLE GUYS WE JUST HAVE TO LET LOOSE AND BE AIRBORNE."
"THEN WE HEAD OFF WHEREVER THE ANTIVIRUS LEADS AND KEEP DOING THE SAME THING."
BRAAAAAAAP!

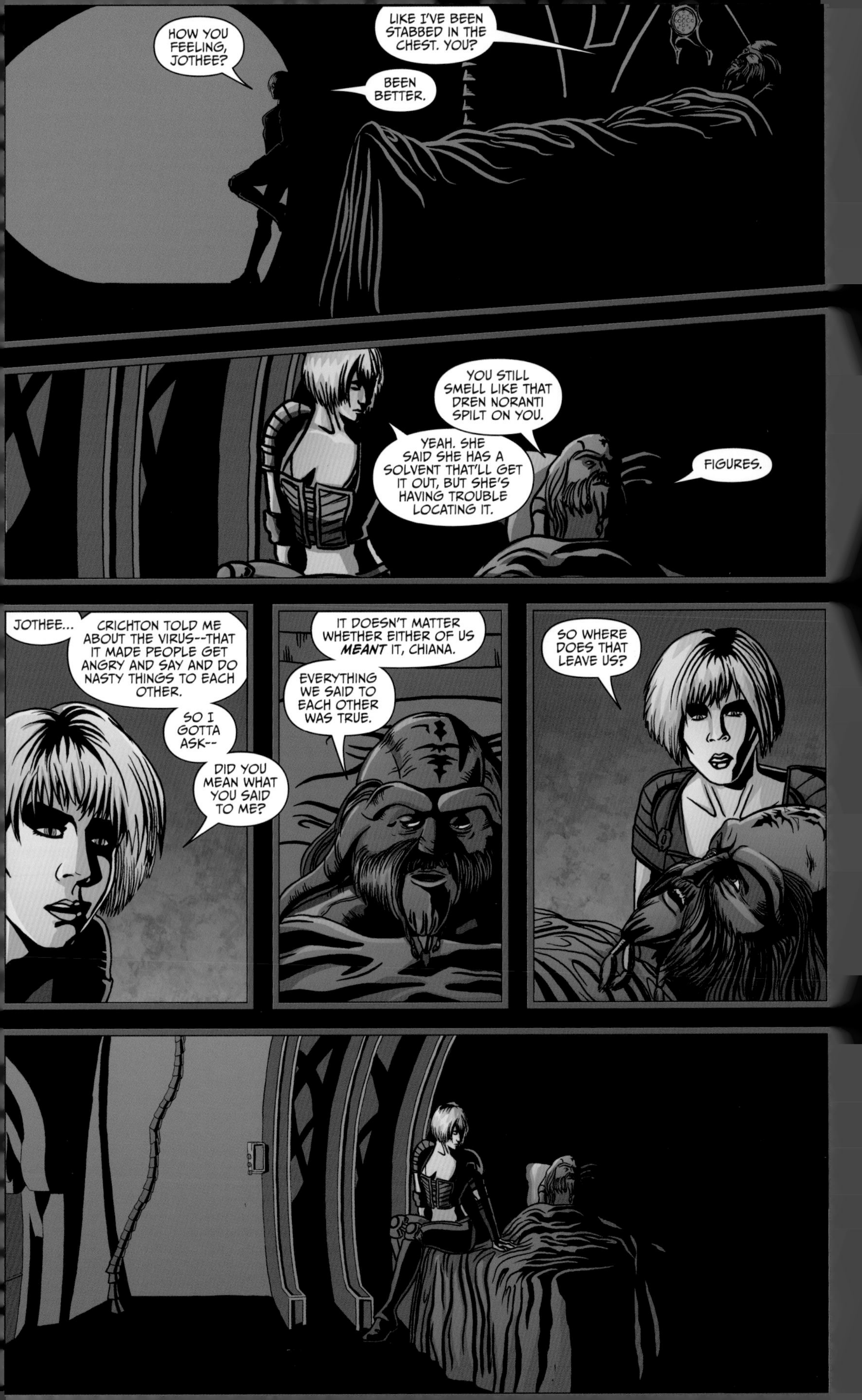
HOW YOU FEELING, JOTHEE?
LIKE I'VE BEEN STABBED IN THE CHEST. YOU?
BEEN BETTER.
YOU STILL SMELL LIKE THAT DREN NORANTI SPILT ON YOU.
YEAH. SHE SAID SHE HAS A SOLVENT THAT'LL GET IT OUT, BUT SHE'S HAVING TROUBLE LOCATING IT.
FIGURES.
JOTHEE...
CRICHTON TOLD ME ABOUT THE VIRUS--THAT IT MADE PEOPLE GET ANGRY AND SAY AND DO NASTY THINGS TO EACH OTHER.
SO I GOTTA ASK--
DID YOU MEAN WHAT YOU SAID TO ME?
IT DOESN'T MATTER WHETHER EITHER OF US **MEANT** IT, CHIANA.
EVERYTHING WE SAID TO EACH OTHER WAS TRUE.
SO WHERE DOES THAT LEAVE US?

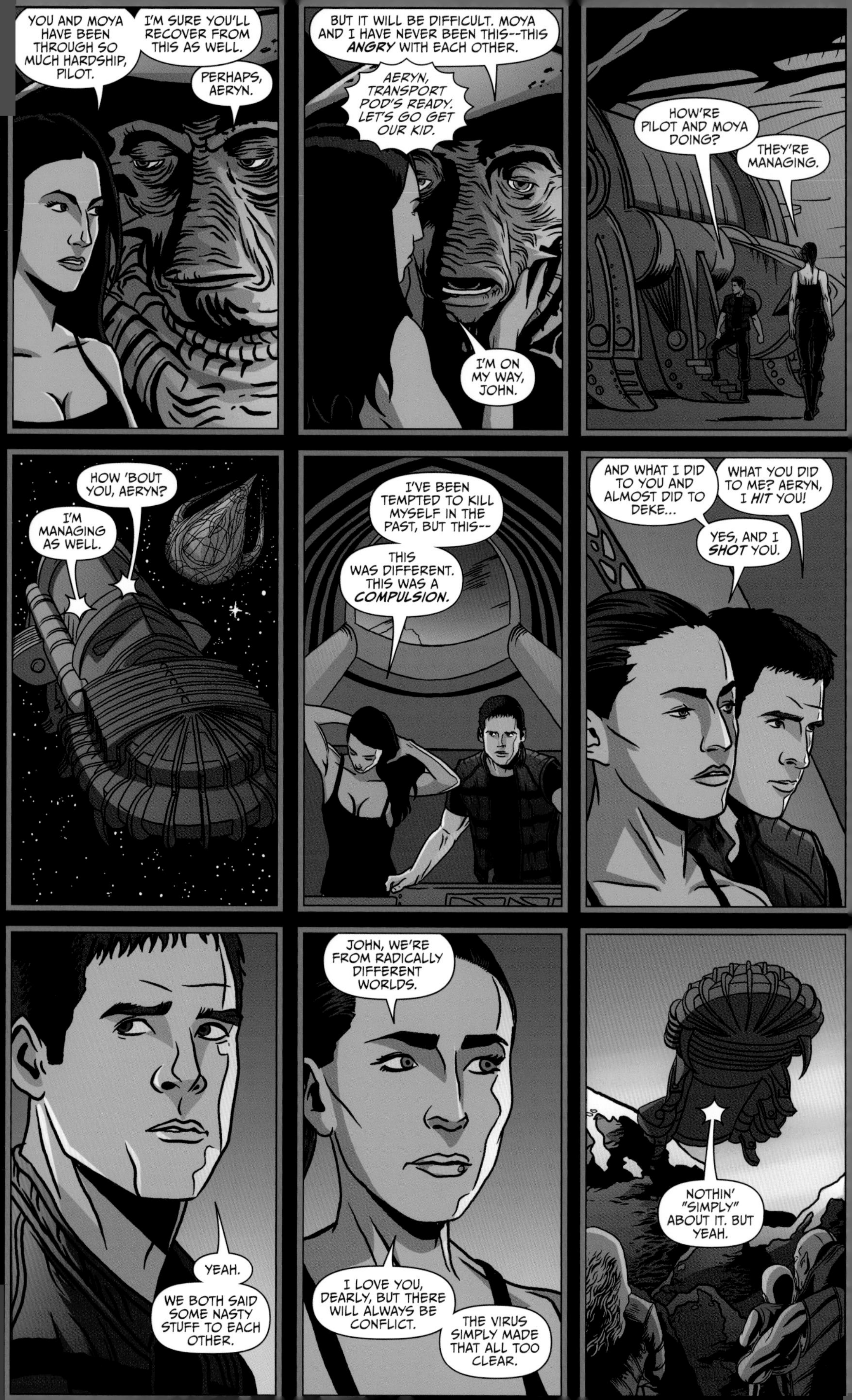
YOU AND MOYA HAVE BEEN THROUGH SO MUCH HARDSHIP, PILOT.
I'M SURE YOU'LL RECOVER FROM THIS AS WELL.
PERHAPS, AERYN.
BUT IT WILL BE DIFFICULT. MOYA AND I HAVE NEVER BEEN THIS--THIS *ANGRY* WITH EACH OTHER.
AERYN, TRANSPORT POD'S READY. LET'S GO GET OUR KID.
I'M ON MY WAY, JOHN.
HOW'RE PILOT AND MOYA DOING?
THEY'RE MANAGING.
HOW 'BOUT YOU, AERYN?
I'M MANAGING AS WELL.
I'VE BEEN TEMPTED TO KILL MYSELF IN THE PAST, BUT THIS--
THIS WAS DIFFERENT. THIS WAS A *COMPULSION.*
AND WHAT I DID TO YOU AND ALMOST DID TO DEKE...
WHAT YOU DID TO ME? AERYN, I *HIT* YOU!
YES, AND I *SHOT* YOU.
YEAH.
WE BOTH SAID SOME NASTY STUFF TO EACH OTHER.
JOHN, WE'RE FROM RADICALLY DIFFERENT WORLDS.
I LOVE YOU, DEARLY, BUT THERE WILL ALWAYS BE CONFLICT.
THE VIRUS SIMPLY MADE THAT ALL TOO CLEAR.
NOTHIN' "SIMPLY" ABOUT IT. BUT YEAH.

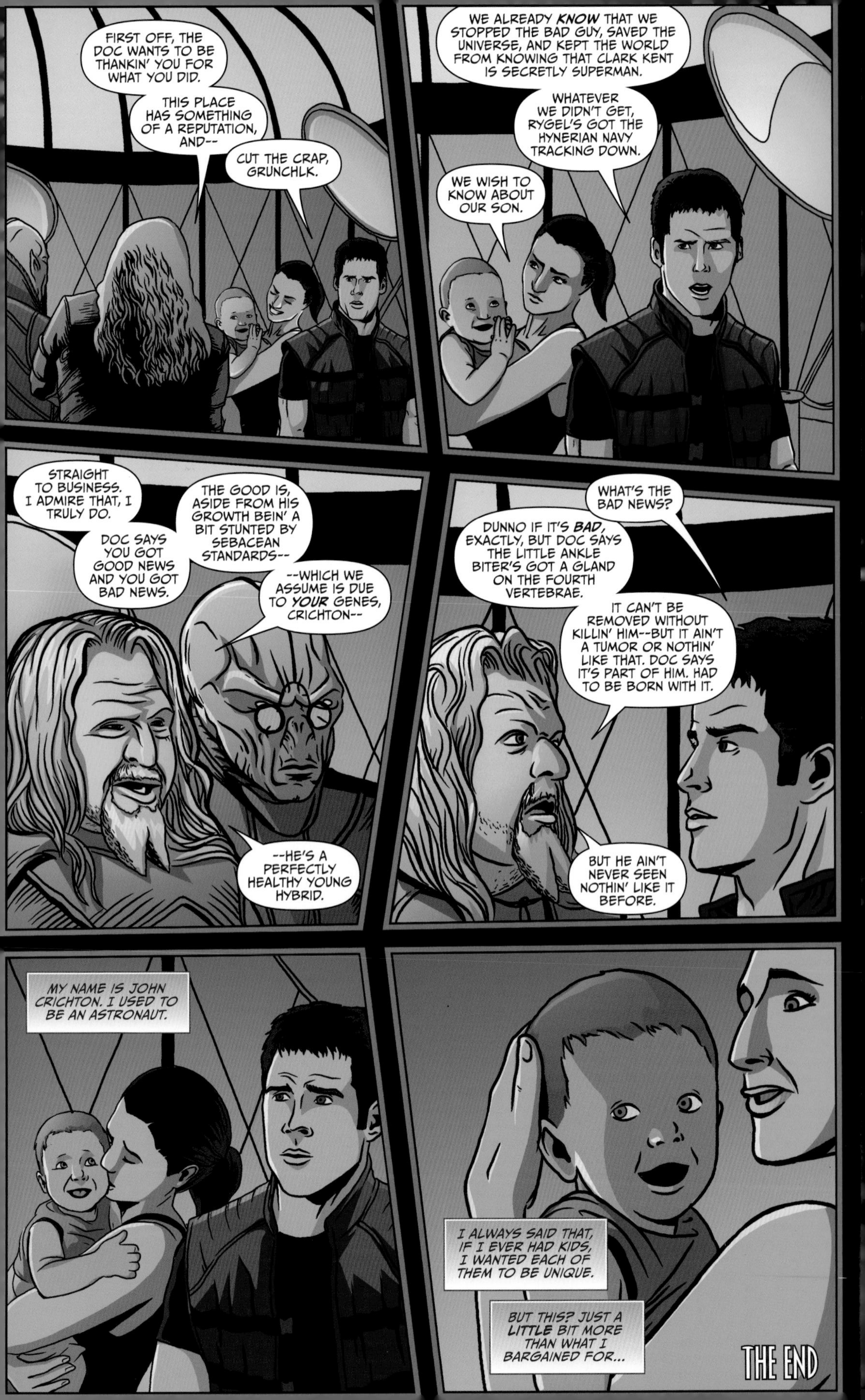
FIRST OFF, THE DOC WANTS TO BE THANKIN' YOU FOR WHAT YOU DID.
THIS PLACE HAS SOMETHING OF A REPUTATION, AND--
CUT THE CRAP, GRUNCHLK.
WE ALREADY KNOW THAT WE STOPPED THE BAD GUY, SAVED THE UNIVERSE, AND KEPT THE WORLD FROM KNOWING THAT CLARK KENT IS SECRETLY SUPERMAN.
WHATEVER WE DIDN'T GET, RYGEL'S GOT THE HYNERIAN NAVY TRACKING DOWN.
WE WISH TO KNOW ABOUT OUR SON.
STRAIGHT TO BUSINESS. I ADMIRE THAT, I TRULY DO.
DOC SAYS YOU GOT GOOD NEWS AND YOU GOT BAD NEWS.
THE GOOD IS, ASIDE FROM HIS GROWTH BEIN' A BIT STUNTED BY SEBACEAN STANDARDS--
--WHICH WE ASSUME IS DUE TO YOUR GENES, CRICHTON--
--HE'S A PERFECTLY HEALTHY YOUNG HYBRID.
WHAT'S THE BAD NEWS?
DUNNO IF IT'S BAD, EXACTLY, BUT DOC SAYS THE LITTLE ANKLE BITER'S GOT A GLAND ON THE FOURTH VERTEBRAE.
IT CAN'T BE REMOVED WITHOUT KILLIN' HIM--BUT IT AIN'T A TUMOR OR NOTHIN' LIKE THAT. DOC SAYS IT'S PART OF HIM. HAD TO BE BORN WITH IT.
BUT HE AIN'T NEVER SEEN NOTHIN' LIKE IT BEFORE.
MY NAME IS JOHN CRICHTON. I USED TO BE AN ASTRONAUT.
I ALWAYS SAID THAT, IF I EVER HAD KIDS, I WANTED EACH OF THEM TO BE UNIQUE.
BUT THIS? JUST A LITTLE BIT MORE THAN WHAT I BARGAINED FOR...
THE END

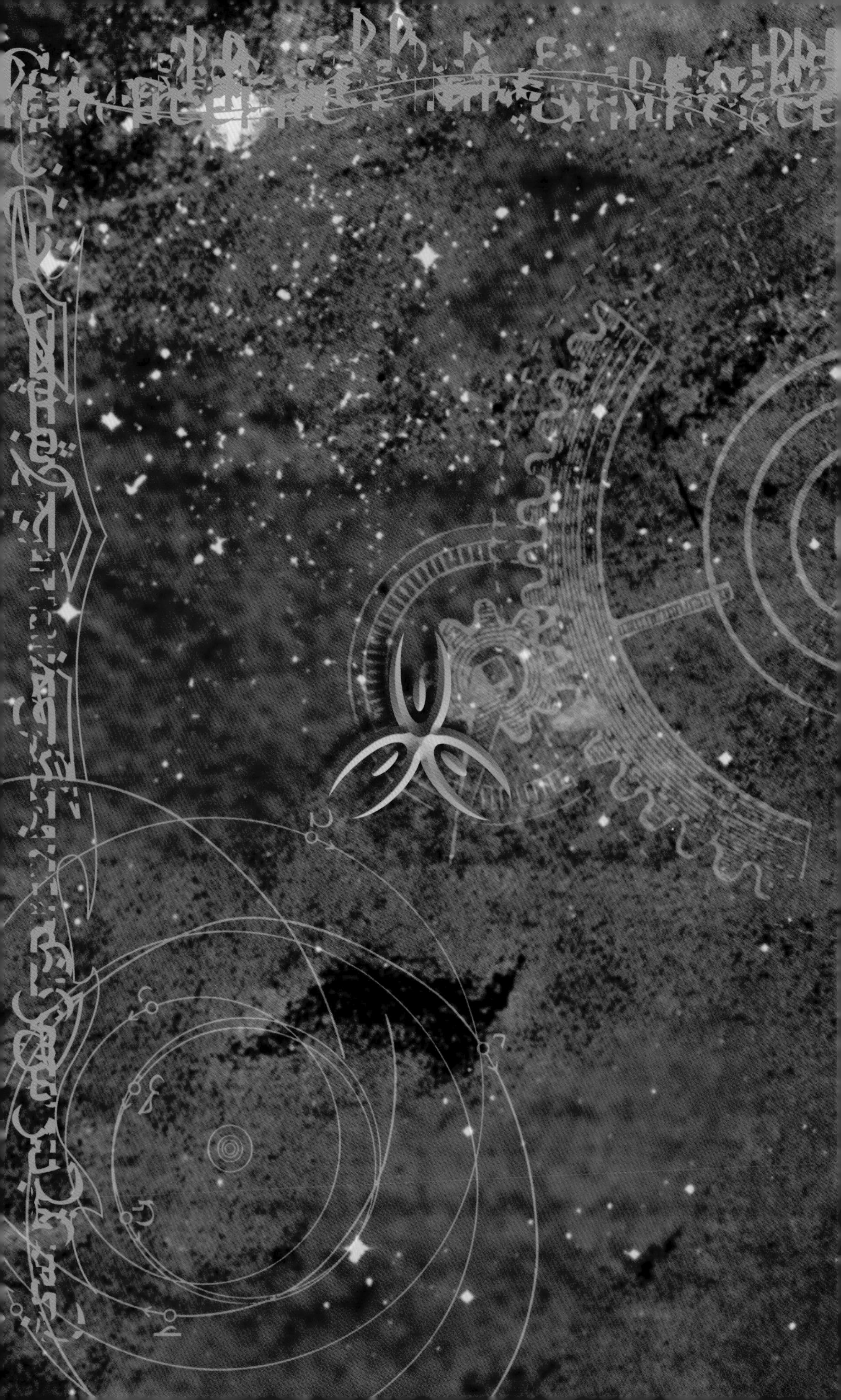

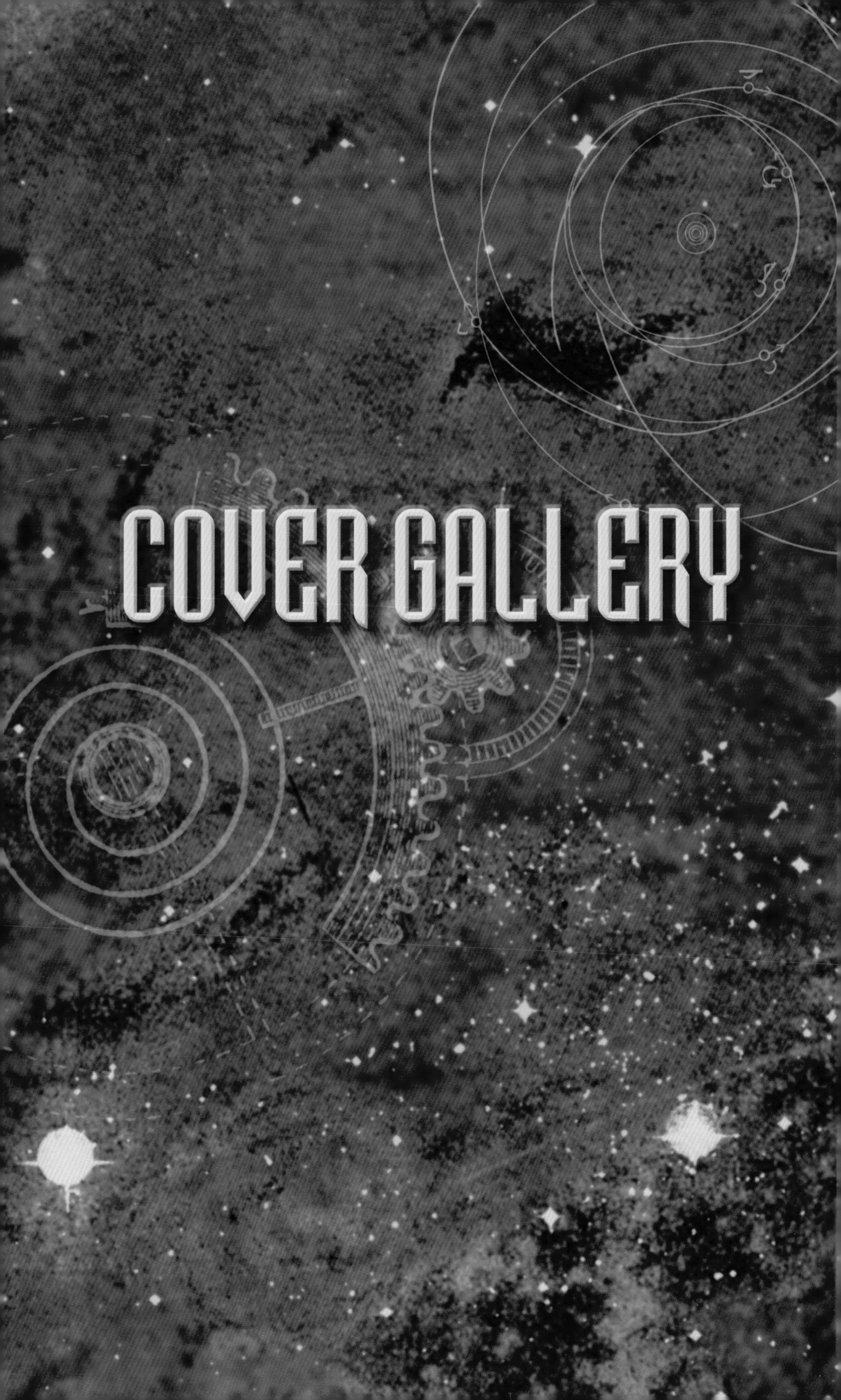
COVER GALLERY

ISSUE ONE

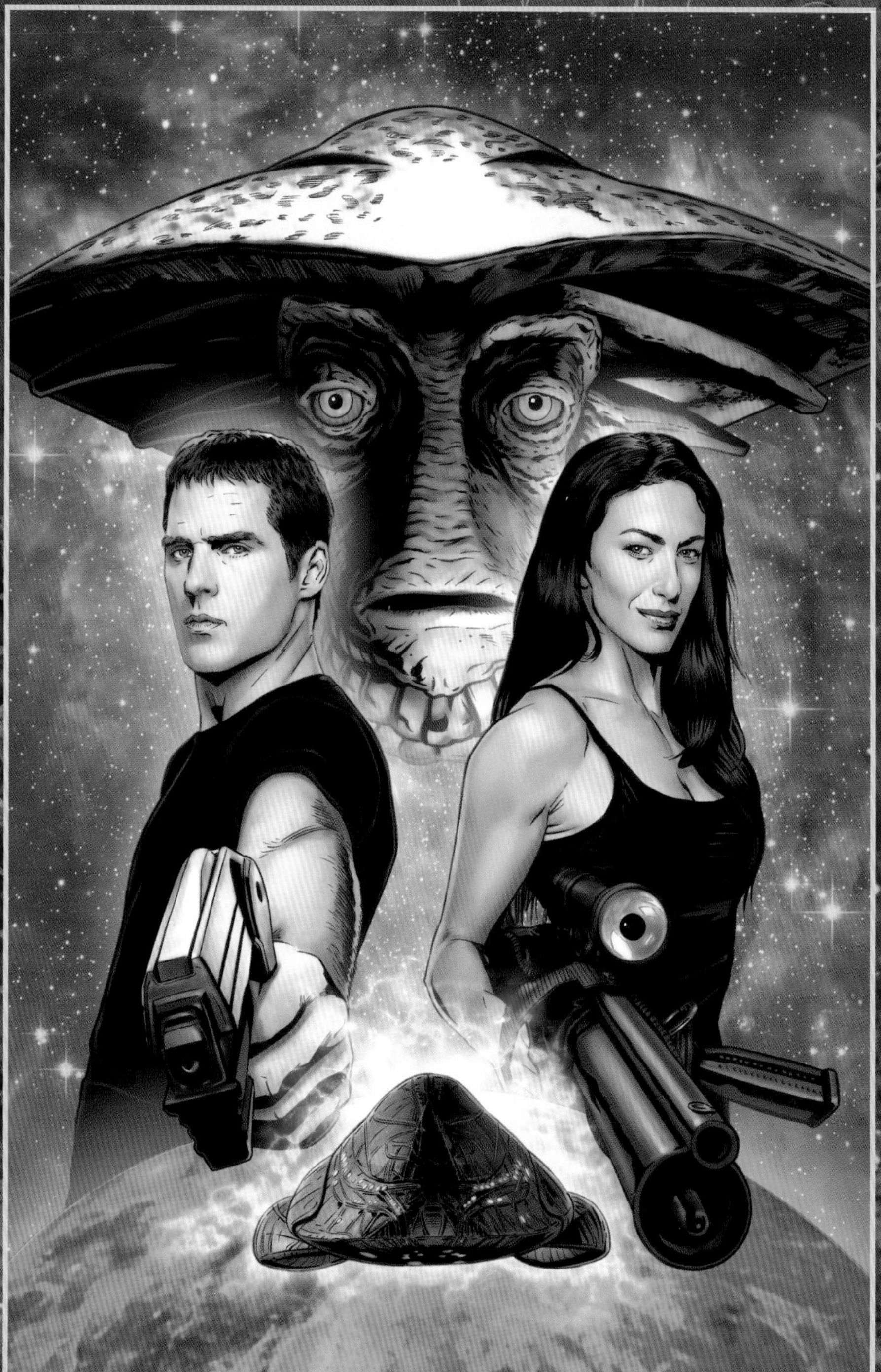

COVER A: JOE CORRONEY

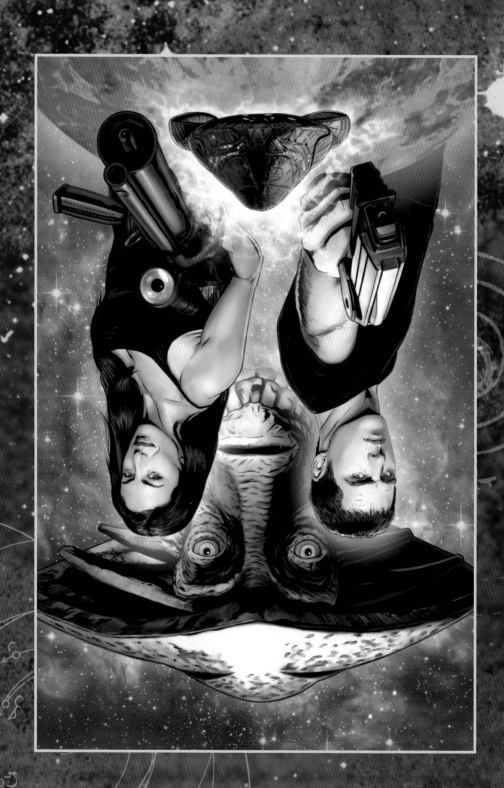

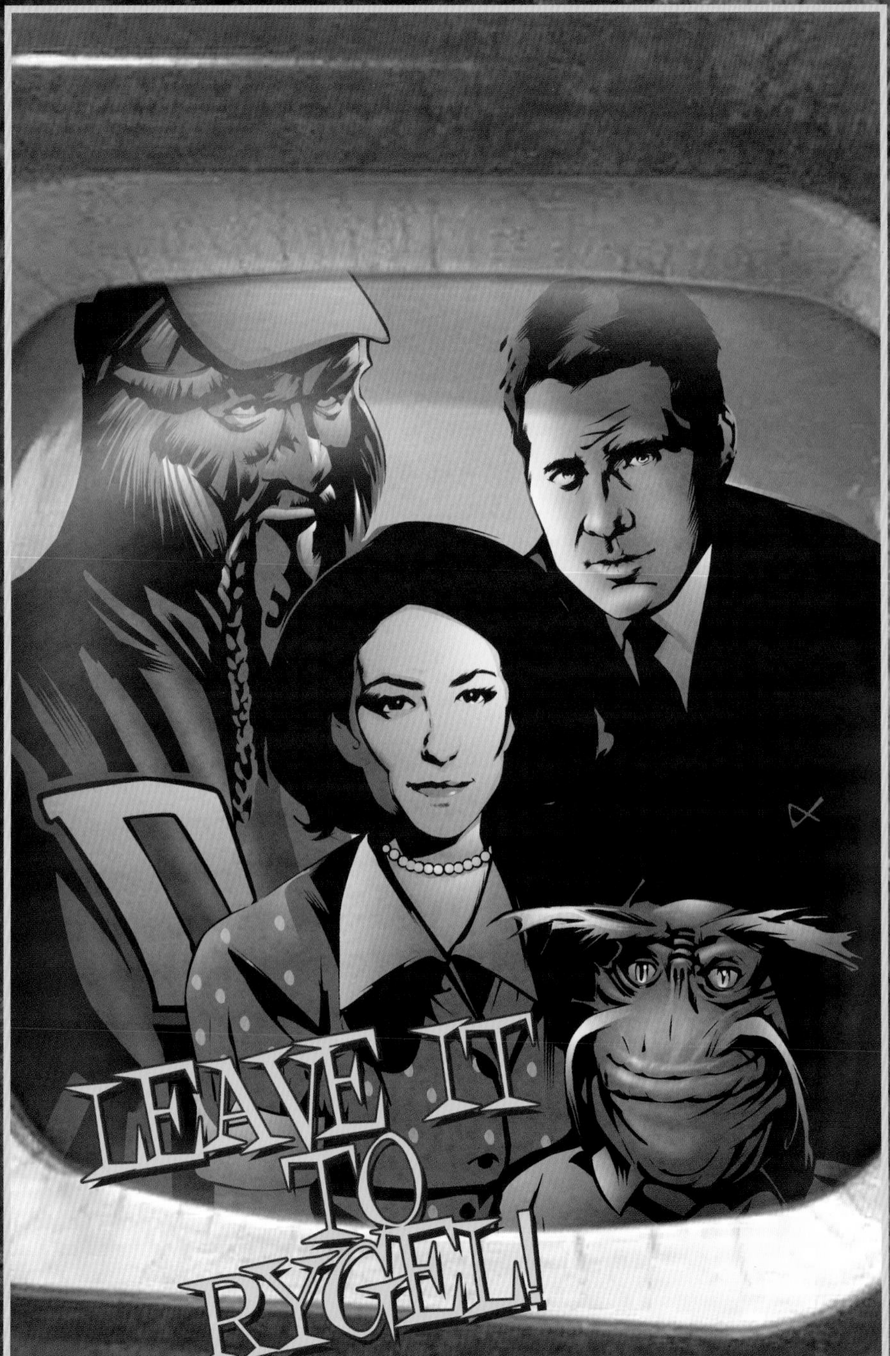
LEAVE IT TO RYGEL!

COVER B: DENNIS CALERO

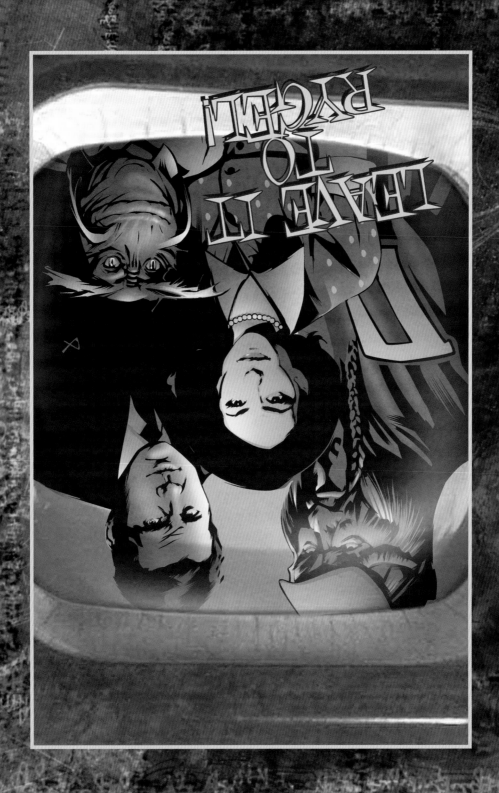

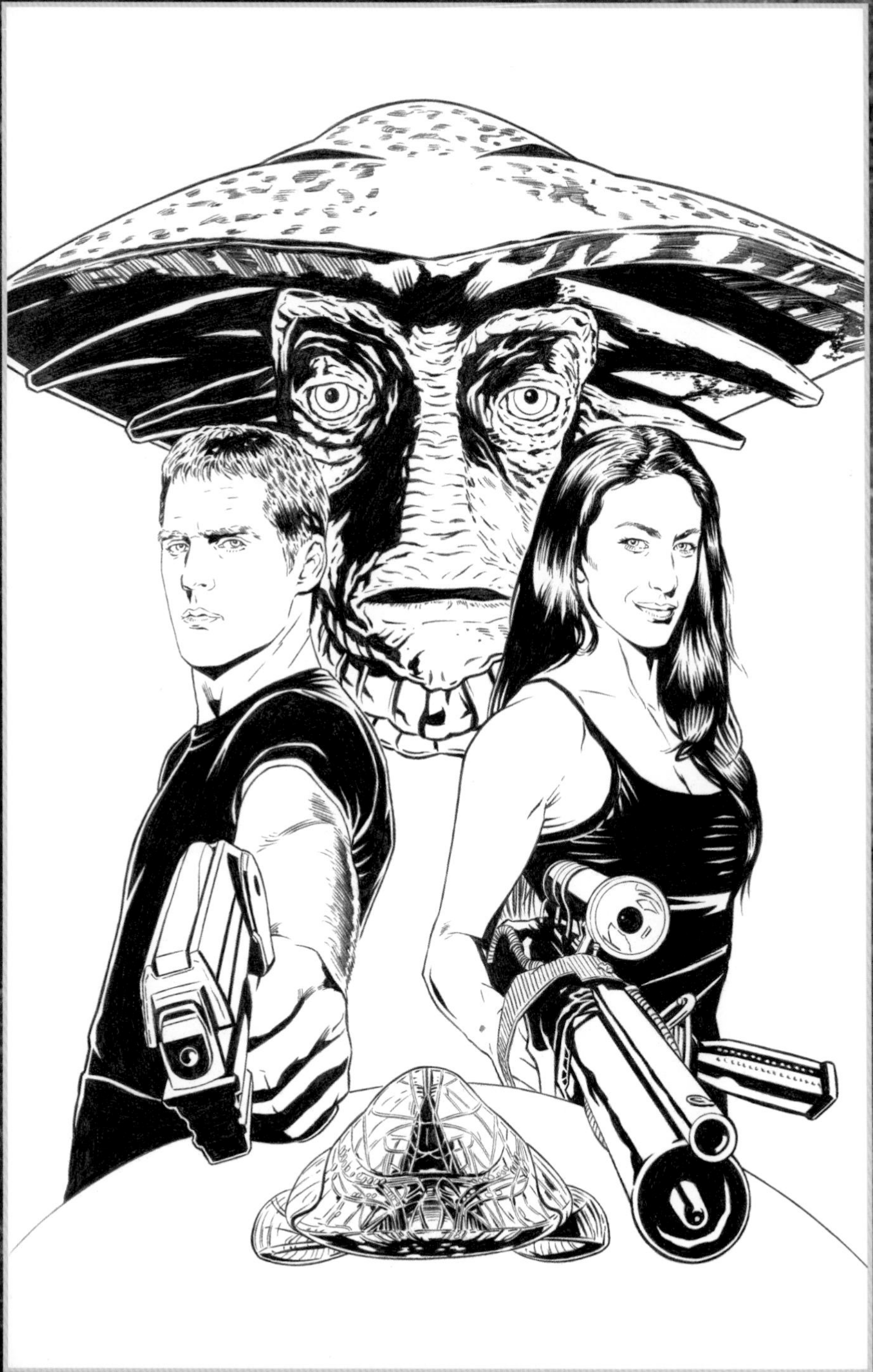

SKETCH COVER: JOE CORRONEY

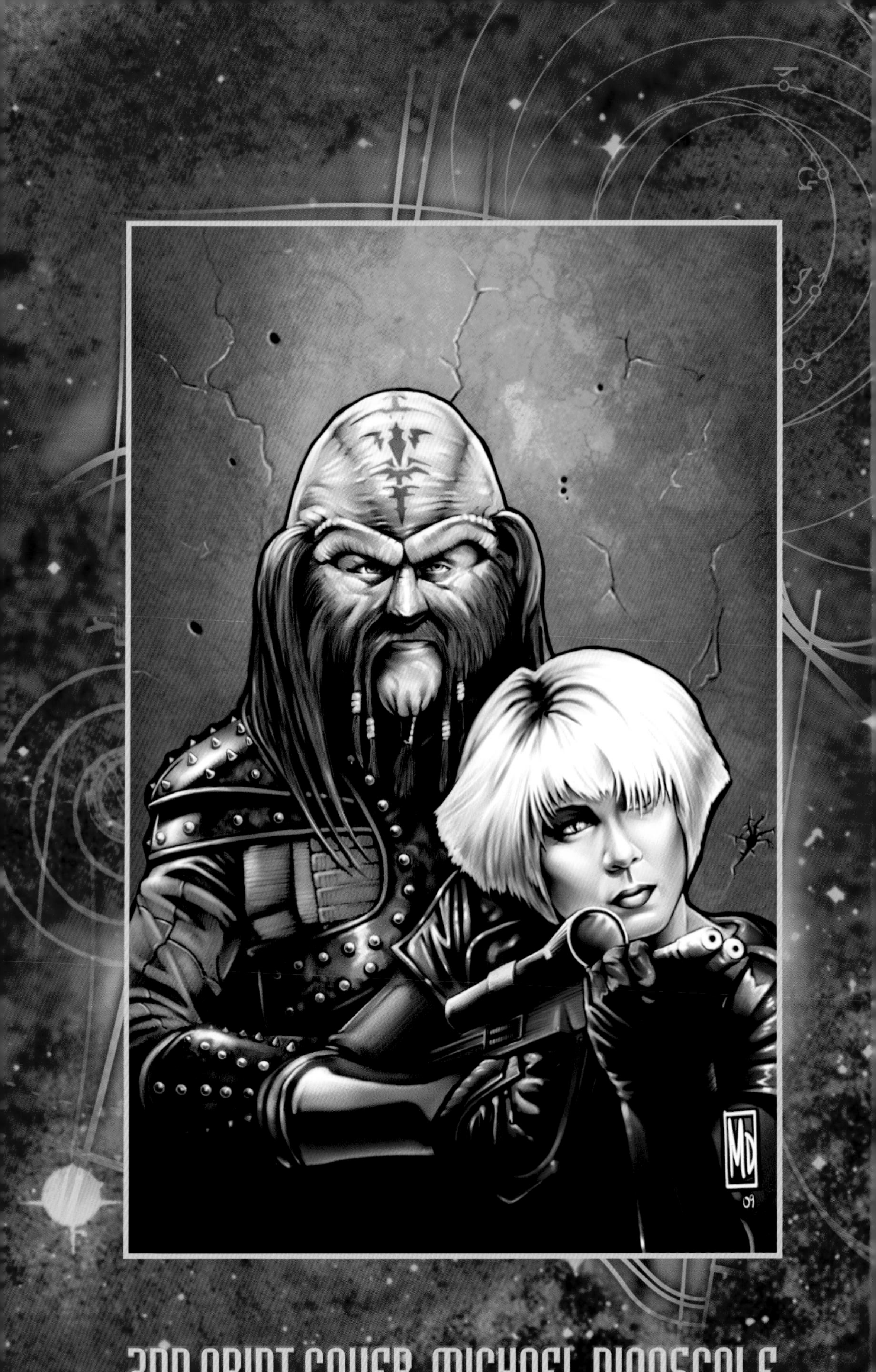

2ND PRINT COVER: MICHAEL DIPASCALE

ISSUE TWO

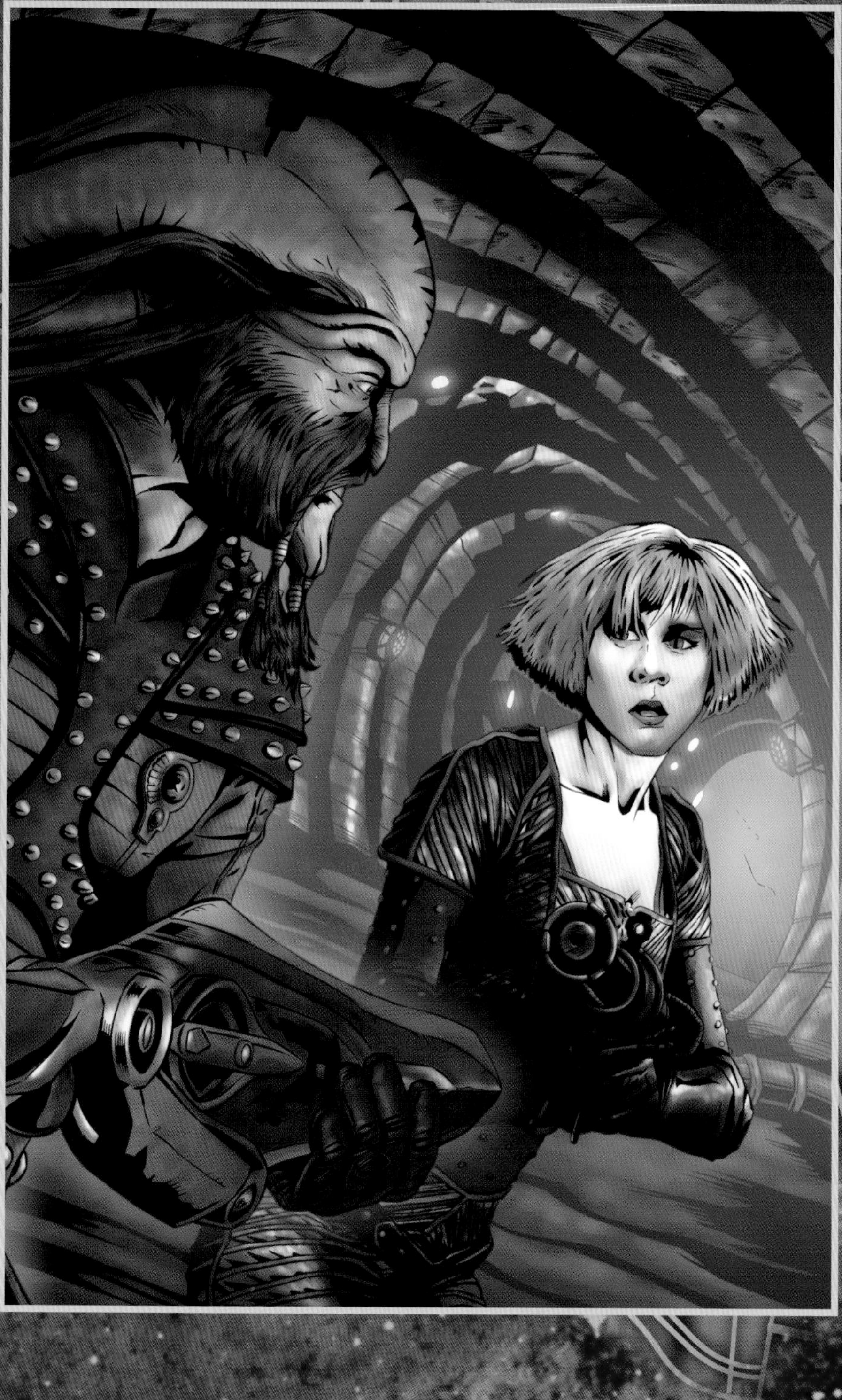

COVER A: JOE CORRONEY

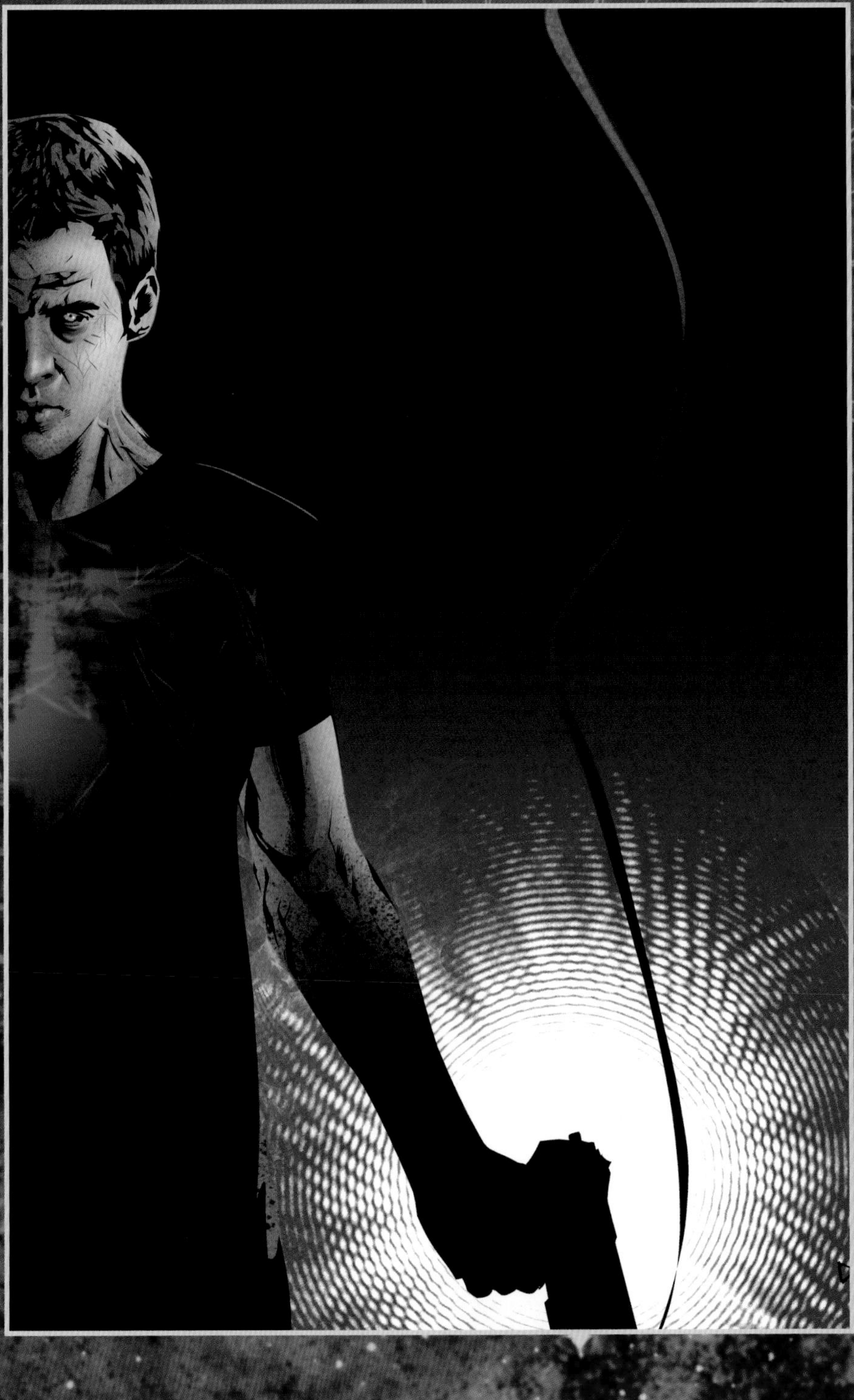

COVER B: DENNIS CALERO

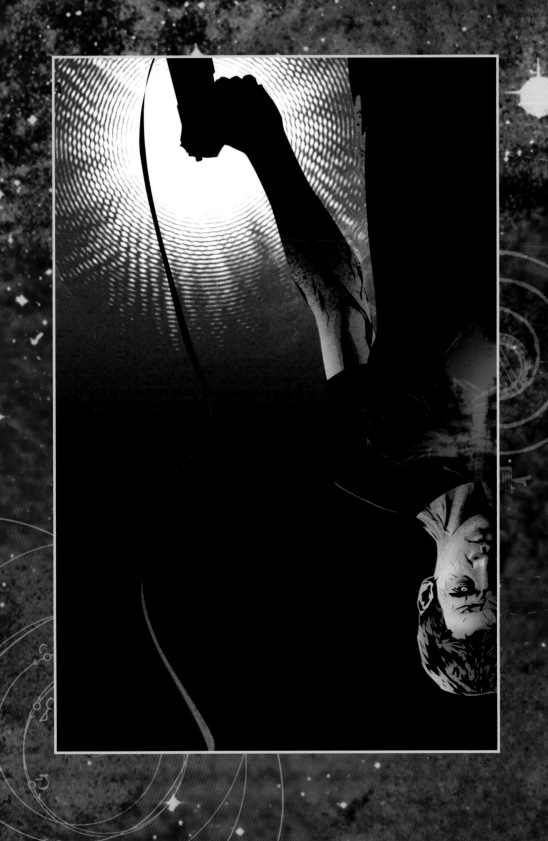

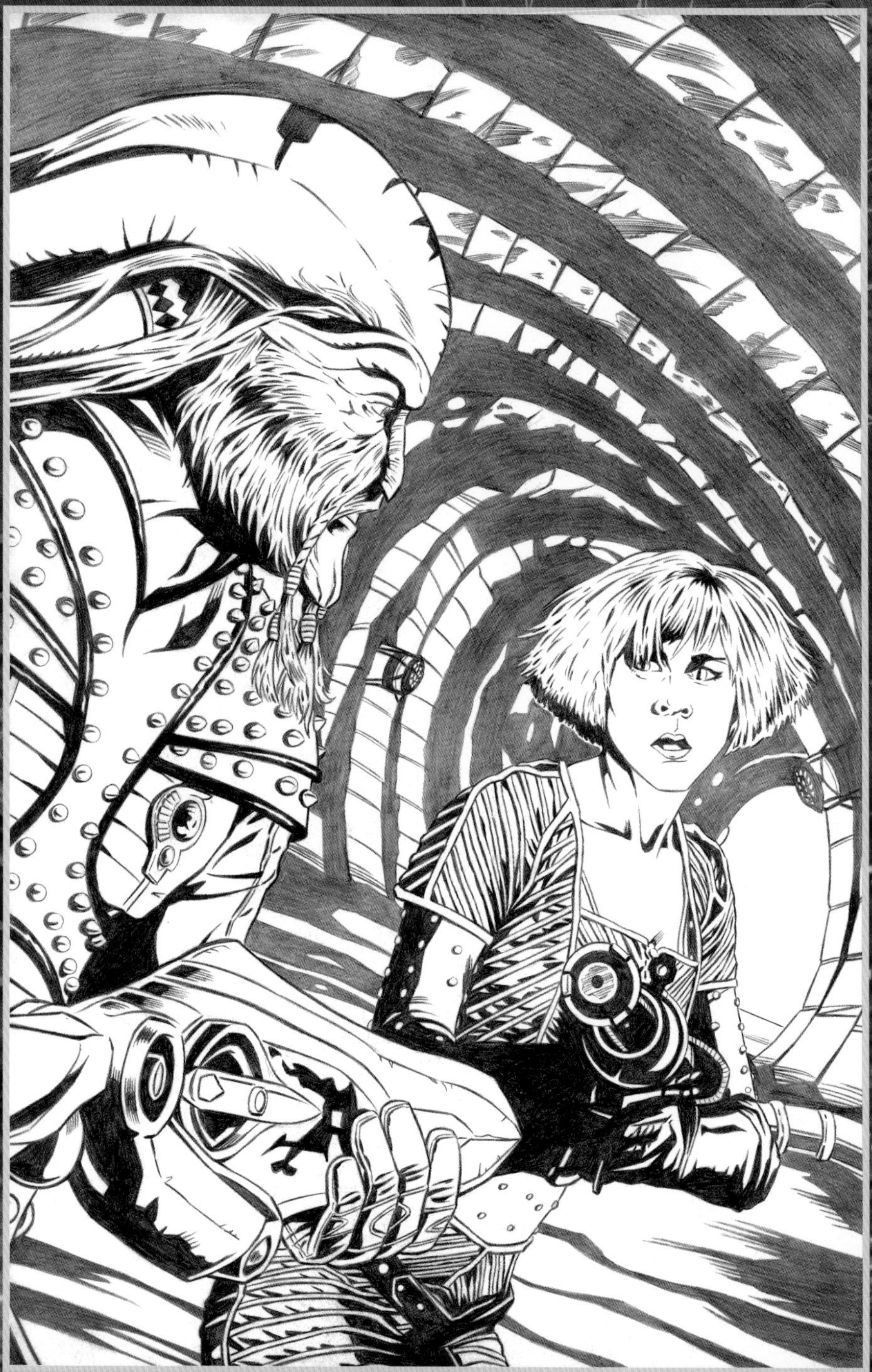

SKETCH COVER: JOE CORRONEY

ISSUE THREE

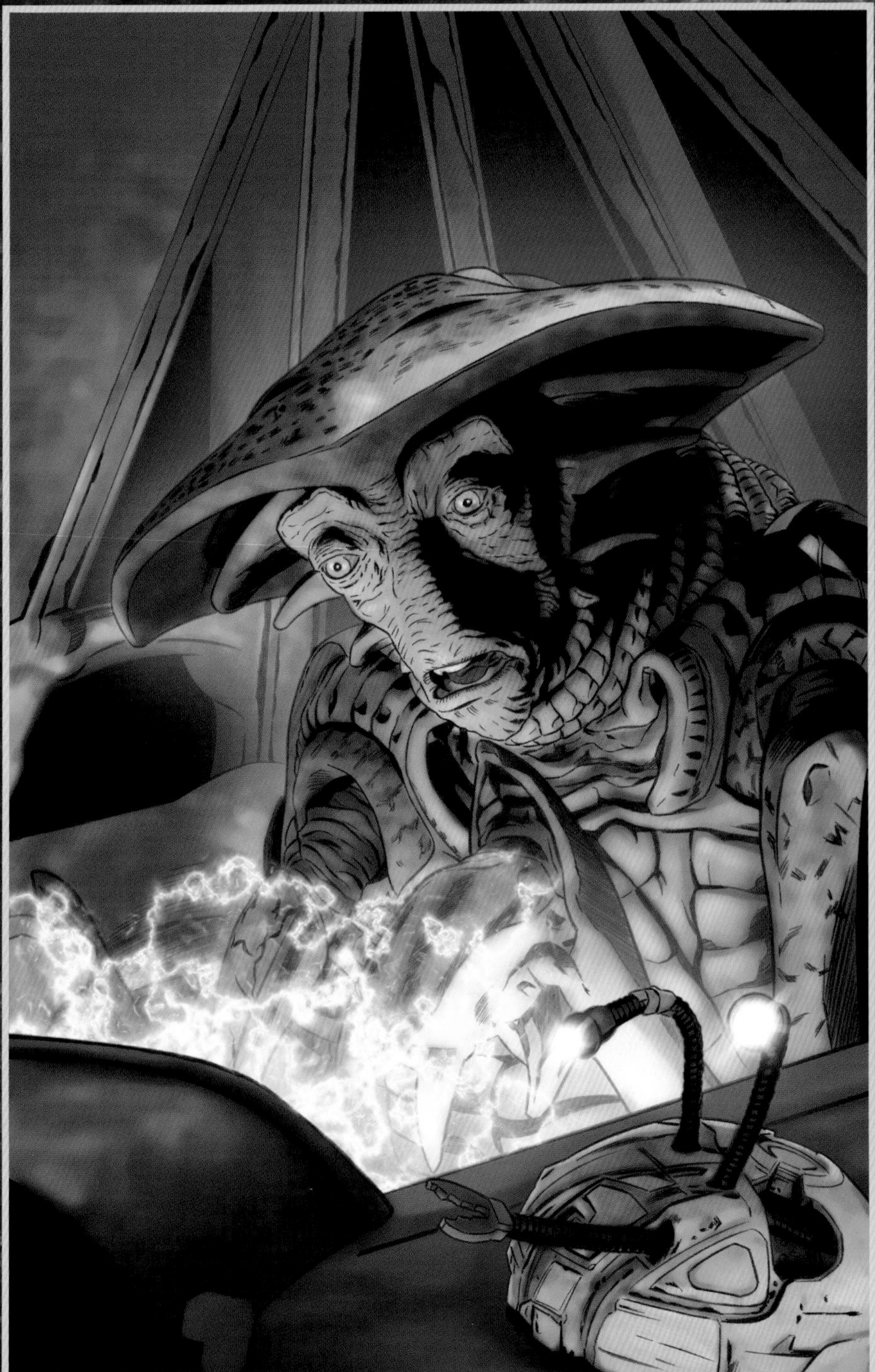

COVER A: JOE CORRONEY

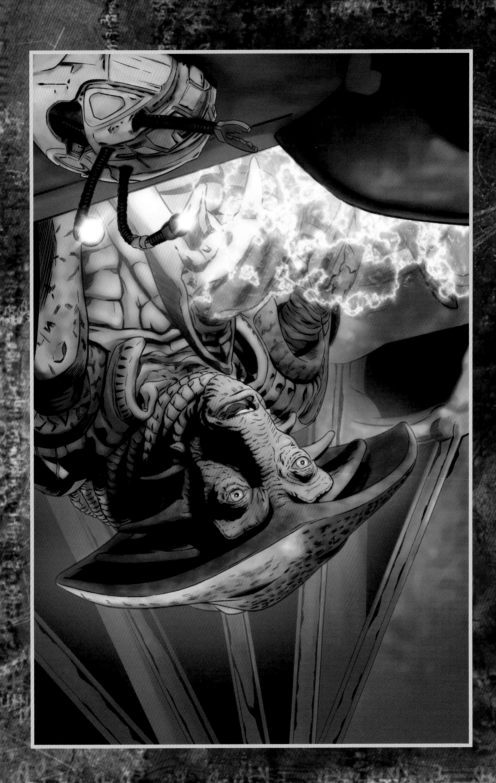

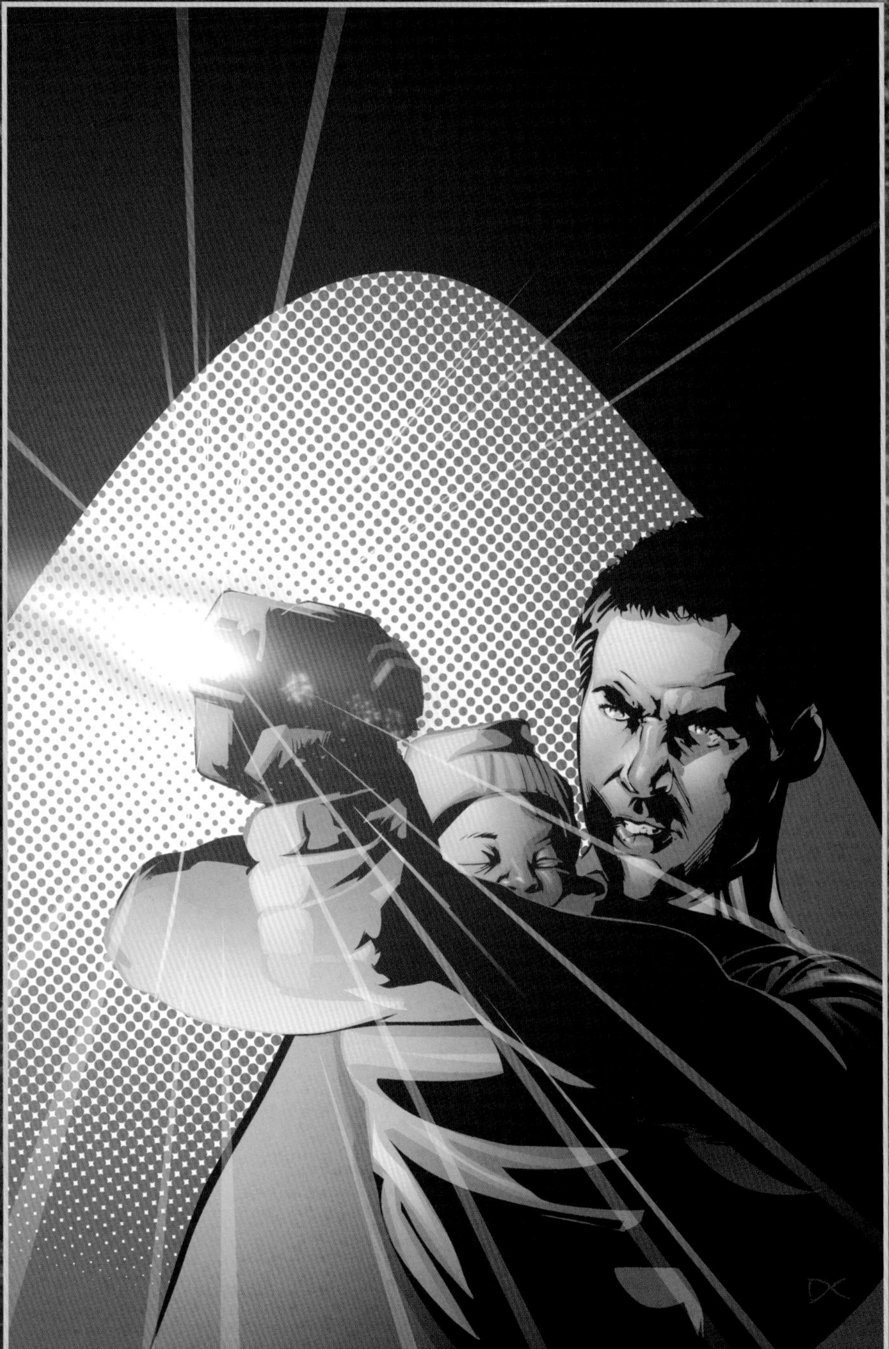

COVER B: DENNIS CALERO

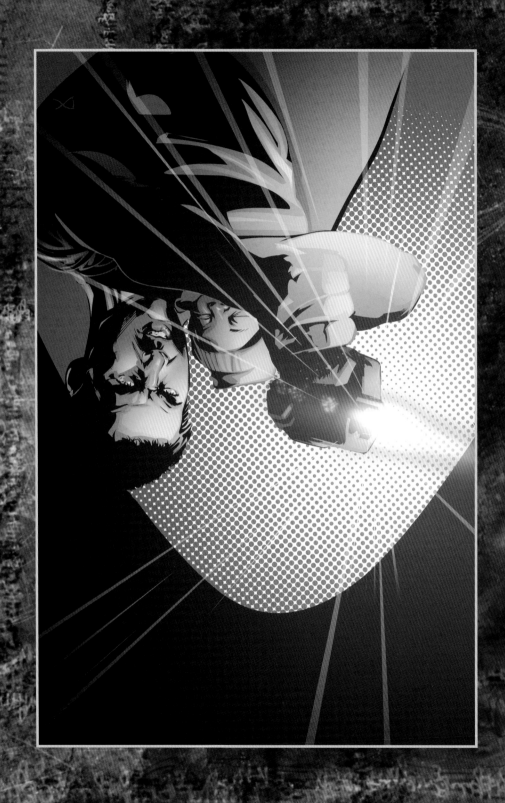

ISSUE FOUR

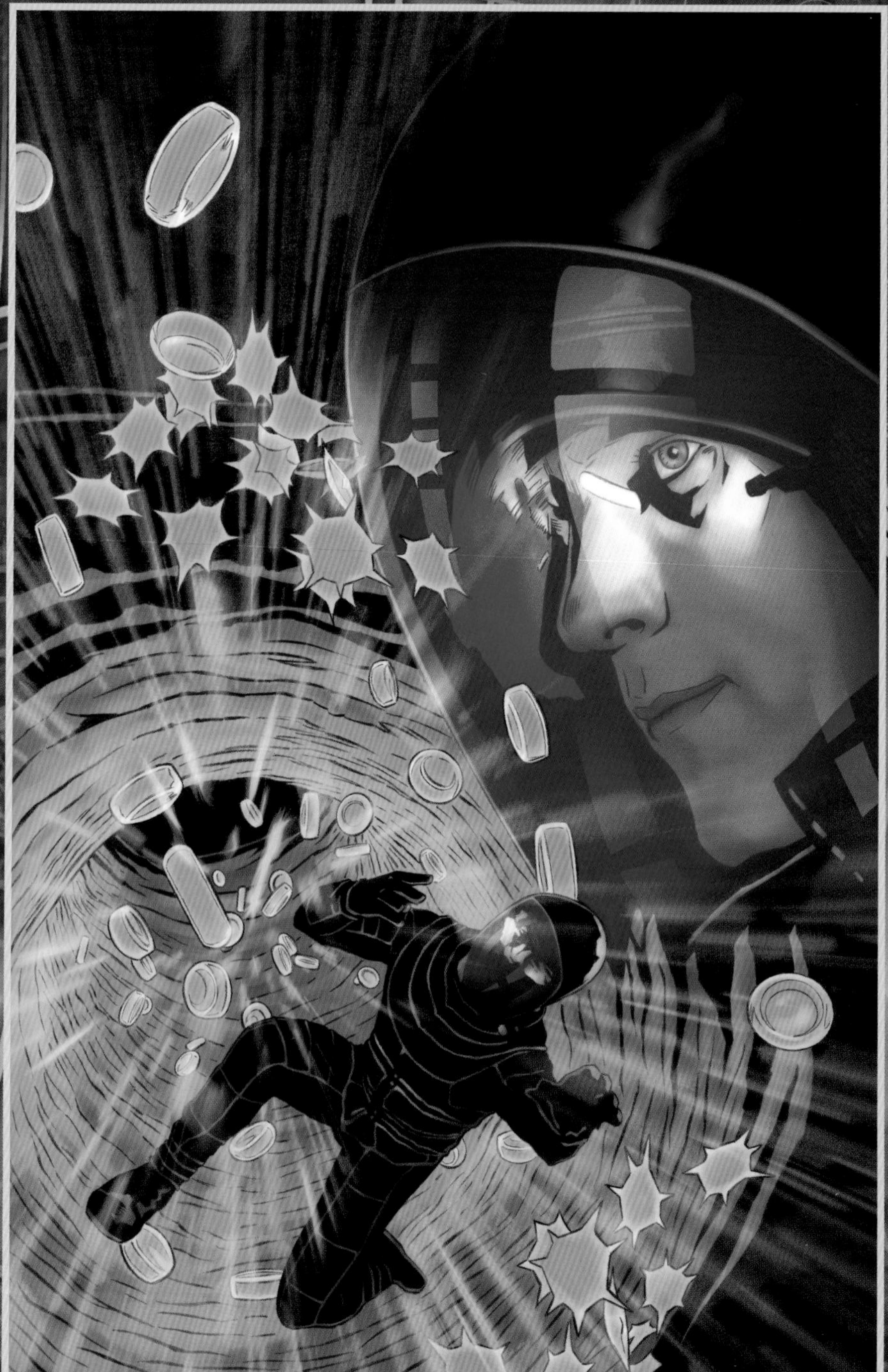

COVER A: JOE CORRONEY

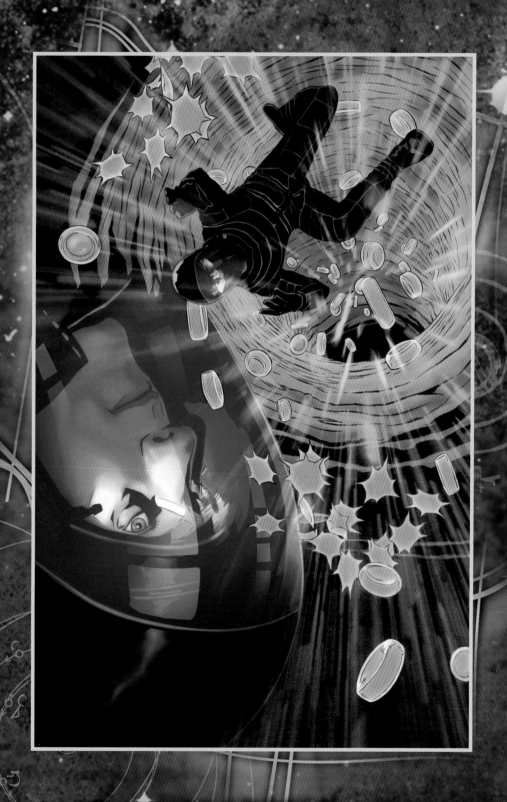

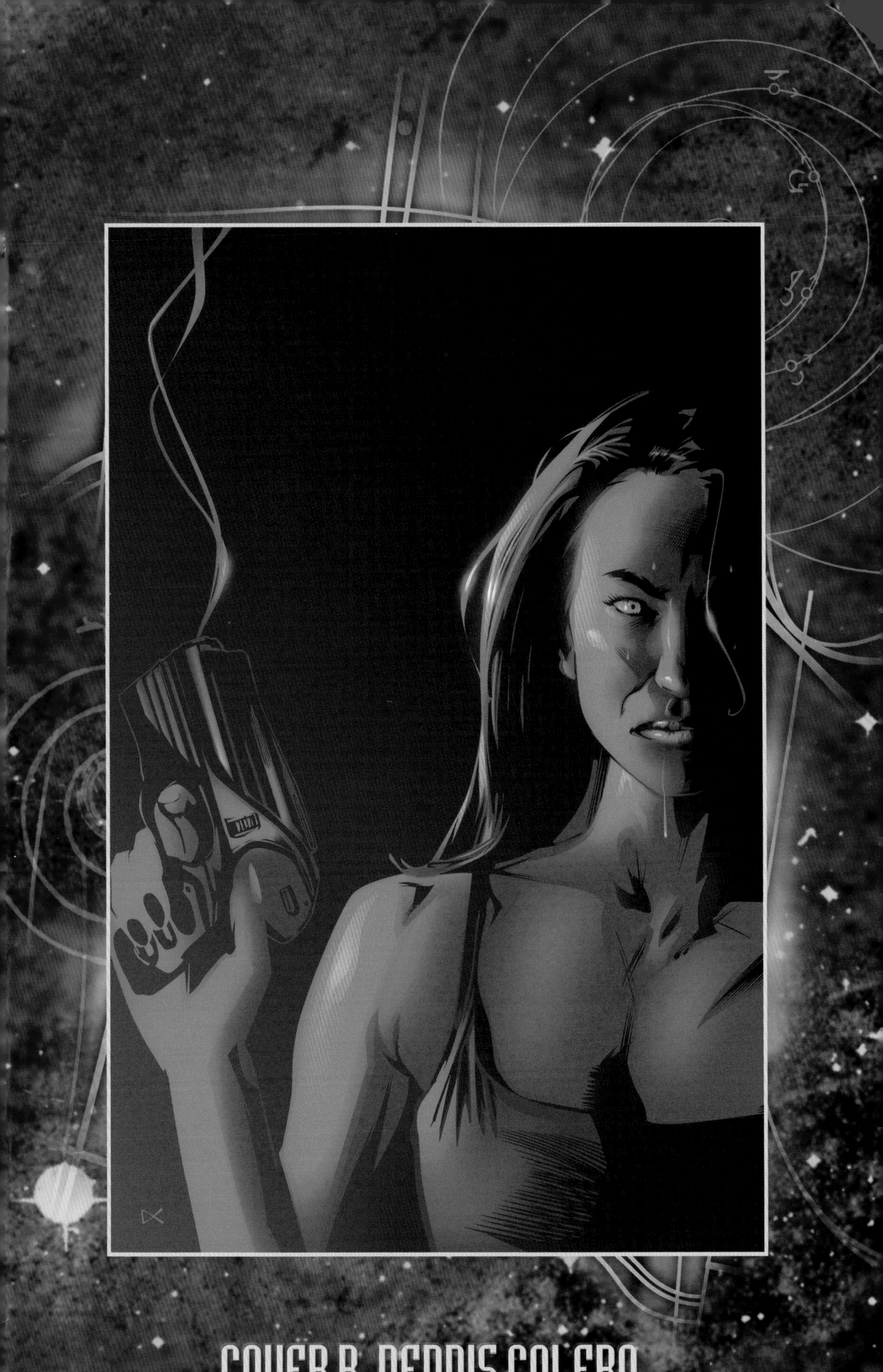

COVER B: DENNIS CALERO

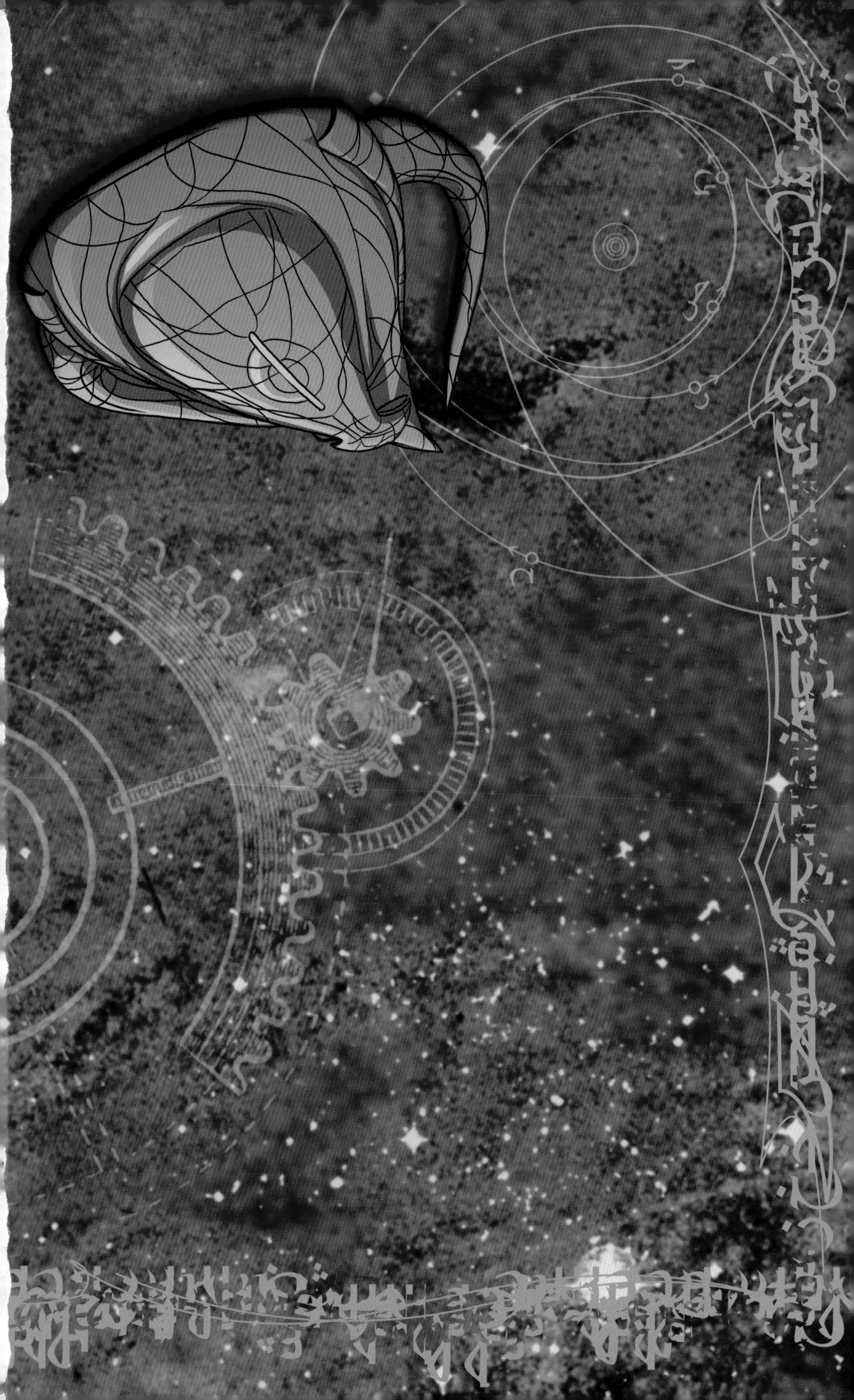